GW00367318

Stephen Spender
knew that, like Blake's fiery Orc, each generation
must create anew its own images of freedom
— internal and external — or else perish.
To his memory this anthology is dedicated.

INDEX ON CENSORSHIP 6 1996

Volume 25 No 6 November/December 1996 Issue 173

Index on Censorship (ISSN 0306-4220) is published bi-monthly by a non-profit-making company: Writers & Scholars International Ltd, Lancaster House, 33 Islington High Street, London N1 9LH

Tel: 0171-278 2313
Fax: 0171-278 1878
E-mail:
indexoncenso@gn.apc.org
http://www.oneworld.org/index_oc/

Index *on Censorship* is associated with Writers & Scholars Educational Trust, registered charity number 325003

Periodicals postage (US subscribers only) paid at Newark, New Jersey. Postmaster: send US address changes to *Index on Censorship* c/o Mercury Arifreight Int/ Ltd Inc, 2323 Randolph Avenue, Avenel, NJ 07001, USA

Subscriptions 1996
(6 issues p.a.)
Individuals: UK £36, US $50, rest of world £42
Institutions: UK £40, US $70, rest of world £46
Students: UK £25, US $35, rest of world £31

© This selection Writers & Scholars International Ltd, London 1996
© Contributors to this issue, except where otherwise indicated

Printed by Martins, Berwick upon Tweed, UK

Cover design: Senate
Back cover illustrations: Jeff Fisher

Former Editors: Michael Scammell (1972-81); Hugh Lunghi (1981-83); George Theiner (1983-88); Sally Laird (1988-89); Andrew Graham-Yooll (1989-93)

EDITORIAL

Word power

'ONE result of the present fragmentation through which we are living seems to be the disappearance of the literature which previously attained a kind of notoriety through its being banned, or smuggled out of the countries where it was banned.' Stephen Spender's foreword to the relaunched *Index* in May 1994 reflected the entirely different world from the one in which he founded *Index* in 1972. Then, censorship had, at least to the West, a monolithic look: the Soviet Union and Eastern Europe under Communism became synonymous with our notions of lack of freedom. And in *Index*'s earlier issues there was much of the *samizdat* literature which the West had heard so much about and was so eager to read.

Censorship is still with us, in spades, though in a post-Communist and post-modern world of nationalisms, fundamentalisms, monopoly ownerships and unmediated market economies, it has become more complex and more subtle. Nevertheless, writers continue to be silenced, in the old tried and tested ways as well as the new, for exploring subjects which threaten the status quo, break the rules, ask difficult questions.

Yet since the fall of Communism there has been less public space for banned writers in the West, less public protest about their condition, less reading of their work — in other words, less interest — perhaps because many of them come from 'far off countries of which we know little'.

Whatever the reasons, to honour these writers, *Index*, for the first time in its history is devoting an entire issue to fiction by censored writers (and some fiction about censoring). We intend banned writing — fiction, poetry and prose — to be an annual *Index* publication, and with it a public reading (see inside back cover). In this way we hope to perpetuate the vision of our founder, who believed that failing to help a banned writer to get published was colluding with the censorship.

These are new times, bringing new ambiguities in relations between censor and censored, more elaborate ways of creating a climate of silencing. But some things don't change. Censors, as the introduction suggests, still bear witness to the transforming power of the word, and, as the collection demonstrates, in the long run fail in their task. ❏

Funded by
**THE
ARTS
COUNCIL**
OF ENGLAND

Index on Censorship **and
Writers and Scholars Educational Trust**
would like to thank

The Arts Council of England
and
The John S Cohen Foundation
for their grants towards this issue of the magazine
and
Virgin Communications
for their support for the New York launch of the issue

LOST WORDS

Edited by Alberto Manguel & Craig Stephenson

Illustrations by Jeff Fisher

contents

ALBERTO MANGUEL & CRAIG STEPHENSON

Dangerous subjects

SOMETIME in the early sixties, in the Argentinian comic book *El Tony,* there appeared a new and startling series, *El Eternauta*, signed by a certain Héctor G. Oesterheld. In the first instalment, El Eternauta — a wonderful word that combined 'cosmonaut' with 'eternity' and conjured up the image of a time traveller through the infinity of ages — arrived one day in a vaguely mythical Buenos Aires during a freak snowstorm. The reason for his quest was vague; more important than the plot were El Eternauta's melancholic reflections on Argentina and its people, and on the human race in general. 'Look at the beauty of this single object,' he said in one of his early adventures, picking up a common coffee-pot left on someone's kitchen table. 'Centuries to achieve this exquisite form to which we no longer pay attention. Beauty which a single explosion can destroy in less than a second.' In El Eternauta's future (these were the days of the Cuban missile crisis) loomed the threat of a third world war.

A decade and a half later, on 27 April 1977, the 50-year old Oesterheld was abducted by the Argentinian military. The psychologist Eduardo Arias, imprisoned without trial a few months later, reported having seen Oesterheld in very bad physical condition at one of the clandestine detention centres. 'One of the most unforgettable memories I have of Héctor,' said Arias, 'was on Christmas Eve 1977. The guards gave us permission to take off our hoods and smoke a cigarette. They also allowed us to talk to each other for five minutes. Then Héctor said that as he was the oldest he wanted to shake hands with all the prisoners present, one by one. I will never forget that handshake.' Oesterheld was not seen again, one of the 30,000 'disappeared' during the military dictatorship.

It isn't clear what threat Oesterheld represented to the military regime. Nothing in his comic strips — of which *El Eternauta* remained the most famous — overtly protests military abuses, denounces government corruption or encourages subversion in any obvious political sense. It is as if the military censors, with keener eyes than those of the common reader, discovered in Oesterheld's science-fiction romances and tales of adventure a hidden accusation, a reminder of the sanctity of individual freedom or a wordless call to arms.

Oesterheld's comic strips were never banned in Argentina; the military didn't find it necessary to ban a book officially in order to prevent its being read. During those years merely holding certain books was deemed sufficient proof of political activity, and it was equally dangerous not to carry identity papers as it was to be seen with a copy of Neruda's poems or Cortázar's stories. A book by any Russian author, from Dostoevsky to Yevtushenko, labelled the reader as Communist, and many writers whose work seemed to hint at hidden meanings (Pinter, Ionesco, Kafka) were considered criminally subversive. Ambiguity was judged a threat to established authority. Reading — that quiet, seemingly private pleasure— became in itself a political act.

The long history of literary censorship, probably as long as that of the art of writing itself, is a parallel and equally powerful history of literature in which banned books form strange alliances and banned writers find themselves in involuntary fellowships. Censors bear witness to the power of the word even more forcefully than writers and readers, because they acknowledge in their fear the possibility of social and individual transformation running through the weave of stories such as those collected here. Censors will no doubt argue against Auden's dictum that 'poetry makes nothing happen'. They, more than any poet, believe in literature as a force for change.

In our vertiginous century, it is obvious that, as in Oesterheld's case, censors don't work from tidy offices in which books seen as threatening are merely indexed, labelled 'banned!' and denied a '*nihil obstat*'. Imprisoning the writer, torturing the writer, killing the writer are extensions — exaggerated extensions, no doubt — of the censor's task. More effective, however, as the Argentinian military discovered, is to create either a climate of public censorship in which readers become fearful of searching out 'dangerous' books, or self-censorship which makes writers despondent of writing those books. As Arthur Miller so wisely noted, this censoring of oneself ultimately becomes unconscious since 'the next step after censoring yourself is to deny that you've done it.'

But there are other subtle and pervasive ways in which the censor has learned to work in these enlightened times: denying a writer paper to print a book (in countries where paper is a government monopoly, as in Egypt), refusing a writer state-held positions (in countries where all of a writer's bread-and-butter jobs such as teaching, publishing, etc. are in the hands of the state, as in Cuba), employing customs officials to act as censors with the excuse of disallowing the distribution of pornography or 'hate literature' (in countries that uphold a liberal regime, as in Canada). With these methods, governments can keep away — or attempt to keep away — from the social forum subjects whose discussion might threaten established conventions and official rules: the infallibility of religion, the role of women, the status of immigrants, notions of sexual fluidity, the exploitation of children. For the censor, the library of dangerous subjects is limitless.

And yet, in spite of its venerable antiquity, the history of censorship has apparently not served censors well. Its lesson, repeated over and over again across all ages and across all countries — that when all is said and done, censorship never succeeds in censoring — is lost on its tireless executors. From the remote afternoon when the Emperor Augustus banned the works of Ovid and banished the poet to a desolate coast, to our irascible age in which Salman Rushdie has become the reluctant symbol of basic intellectual freedom under threat, censors haven't learned that writing cannot be eliminated by eliminating a particular writer or a particular book. A line, a poem, a novel, an entire library can be burnt to the ground, as many have, and a writer can be thrown into jail and murdered, as many are, but whatever has been written becomes enmeshed in that vast construction we call literature, and which Shelley, in somewhat purple words, called 'the immortal soul of the world'. A murdered poet and the poet's banned writings will echo through other writers not yet born — writers who will have forgotten that dead poet's name — and in other writings still to come — writings that will bear no resemblance to the page now in ashes. Censorship and censorship's fears only confirm that modest immortality.

The strategies of the censor are answered by the strategies of the reader and the writer. In Nazi Germany, many of the persecuted victims carried in their memories the libraries that Goebbels condemned to the bonfire. Under Chinese occupation, Tibetan monks sewed pages of their sacred texts to the inside of their robes, to save them from destruction. In Communist Russia, readers and writers developed a system of underground literature that gave the word *samizdat* to the world.

And the recent technology that has, on the one hand, sharpened the censor's tools has also, on the other, provided readers with new and effective counter-devices. In January 1996, shortly after the death of President Mitterrand, the French doctors Claude Gubier and Michel Gonod revealed intimate details of their illustrious patient's decline and made public the official efforts to conceal the gravity of his illness in a book called *Le Grand Secret*. Outraged at what it saw as an act of *lèse-majesté*, the French government promptly banned the book. On 23 January 1996 Pascal Barbraud, owner of a cybercafé in Besançon — where customers could, for a fee, use the café's Internet service — decided to scan *Le Grand Secret* on to the Internet. Since Internet was beyond any one government's jurisdiction, and since no one person is responsible for an Internet text, *Le Grand Secret* became the first banned book to escape openly the power of the censors, becoming the biblical *verba*, the spirit on the screen.

And yet, neither the role of the censor nor the role of the freedom-seeking writer is neatly divided into saints and sinners. While censors seek order as an end that is famously supposed to justify the means, and artists consciously embrace the creative chaos, writers and censors both find themselves at times straying into one another's territories. This means, in our post-Freudian age, that those same freedom-seeking artists have the potential of being (unconsciously) fascistic, and those same torch-wielding censors can be (equally unconsciously) drawn to that which they most fear.

Neither are we, the readers, exempt from this complex stranglehold of contradictions. A defence of free speech in the West will lead the western bite-driven media to be quick to label a writer as 'banned' on the flimsiest circumstantial evidence. A repressive government such as the Chinese (who deny their own colonialist policy in Tibet) will attack the Universal

Declaration of Human Rights for being 'colonialist' and 'idiosyncratic' —
and in response be granted a preferred trading status. The flow of western
tourists to China increased in 1996 by as much as 35 per cent. During that
same year, the writers Bai Hua and Bei Cun were arrested for 'unorthodox
behaviour' (a criminal offence in China which ranges from soliciting
prostitutes to participating in a 'demonic' [sic] Catholic sect), and the
Anhui novelist Dai Houying was brutally murdered in her Shanghai home.
In the meantime, the dissident Wei Jingsheng, carrier of our collective
conscience, continues to languish in prison.

The writers whose stories are collected here grapple with these
contradictions, and insist on their right to ponder and probe and accuse
and defend, using the kinds of creative ambiguities that censors abhor. For
upholding this right, Haroldo Conti and Ken Saro-Wiwa are now dead.
Ma Thida has been in prison since 1993. Pramoedya Ananta Toer remains
under city arrest in Djakarta. Duong Thu Huong's works are banned in
her own country. Nedim Gürsel and M.T. Sharif spend their days in exile.

At the height of Stalin's dictatorship, Boris Pasternak was invited to an
official writers' conference in Moscow. Pasternak knew that if he attended
and spoke, he would be arrested for what he would say; if he attended and
didn't speak, he would be arrested for contempt; if he didn't attend, he'd
be arrested for disobeying the Dictator's invitation. Pasternak attended.
The conference lasted three days. During the first day Pasternak said
nothing. His friends begged him to speak, since he would be arrested
anyway, and urged him to profit at least from the presence of an audience.
Pasternak remained silent. He also remained silent on the second day. On
the third day, however, he rose to his feet. The audience held its breath.
At last, Pasternak opened his mouth and said 'Thirty-two'. And the
audience, recognising that he meant Shakespeare's thirty-second sonnet
which Pasternak had brilliantly translated, roared out the words they knew
by heart, and which across three centuries Pasternak had transformed into
a promise of hope addressed to the reader, far beyond the will of Stalin:

'If thou survive my well-contented day,
When that churl Death my bones with dust shall cover.' ❏

© *Alberto Manguel & Craig Stephenson 1996*

ITALO CALVINO

A general in the library

ONE DAY, in the illustrious nation of Panduria, a suspicion crept into
the minds of top officials: that books contained opinions hostile to
military prestige. In fact trials and enquiries had revealed that the
tendency, now so widespread, of thinking of generals as people actually
capable of making mistakes and causing catastrophes, and of wars as
things that did not always amount to splendid cavalry charges towards a
glorious destiny, was shared by a large number of books, ancient and
modern, foreign and Pandurese.

Panduria's General Staff met together to assess the situation. But they
didn't know where to begin, because none of them was particularly
well-versed in matters bibliographical. A commission of enquiry was set
up under General Fedina, a severe and scrupulous official. The
commission was to examine all the books in the biggest library in
Panduria.

The library was in an old building full of columns and staircases, the
walls peeling and even crumbling here and there. Its cold rooms were
crammed to bursting with books, and in parts inaccessible, with some
corners only mice could explore. Weighed down by huge military
expenditures, Panduria's state budget was unable to offer any assistance.

The military took over the library one rainy morning in November.
The general climbed off his horse, squat, stiff, his thick neck shaven, his
eyebrows frowning over pince-nez; four lanky lieutenants, chins held
high and eyelids towered, got out of a car, each with a briefcase in his
hand. Then came a squadron of soldiers who set up camp in the old
courtyard, with mules, bales of hay, tents, cooking equipment, camp
radio, and signalling flags.

Sentries were placed at the doors, together with a notice forbidding entry, 'for the duration of large-scale manoeuvres now under way'. This was an expedient which would allow the enquiry to be carried out in great secret. The scholars who used to go to the library every morning wearing heavy coats and scarves and balaclavas so as not to freeze, had to go back home again. Puzzled, they asked each other: 'What's this about large-scale manoeuvres in the library? Won't they make a mess of the place? And the cavalry? And are they going to be shooting too?'

Of the library staff, only one little old man, Signor Crispino, was kept so that he could explain to the officers how the books were arranged. He was a shortish fellow, with a bald, eggish pate and eyes like pinheads behind his spectacles.

First and foremost General Fedina was concerned with the logistics of the operation, since his orders were that the commission was not to leave the library before having completed their enquiry; it was a job that required concentration, and they must not allow themselves to be distracted. Thus a supply of provisions was procured, likewise some barrack stoves and a store of firewood together with some collections of old and it was generally thought uninteresting magazines. Never had the library been so warm in the winter season. Pallet beds for the general and his officers were set up in safe areas surrounded by mousetraps.

Then duties were assigned. Each lieutenant was allotted a particular branch of knowledge, a particular century of history. The general was to oversee the sorting of the volumes and the application of an appropriate rubber stamp depending on whether a book had been judged suitable for officers, NCOs, common soldiers, or should be reported to the Military Court.

And the commission began its appointed task. Every evening the camp radio transmitted General Fedina's report to HQ. 'So many books examined. So many seized as suspect. So many declared suitable for officers and soldiers.' Only rarely were these cold figures accompanied by something out of the ordinary: a request for a pair of glasses to correct short-sightedness for an officer who had broken his, the news that a mule had eaten a rare manuscript edition of Cicero left unattended.

But developments of far greater import were under way, about which the camp radio transmitted no news at all. Rather than thinning out, the forest of books seemed to grow ever more tangled and insidious. The officers would have lost their way had it not been for the help of Signor Crispino. Lieutenant Abrogati, for example, would jump to his feet and

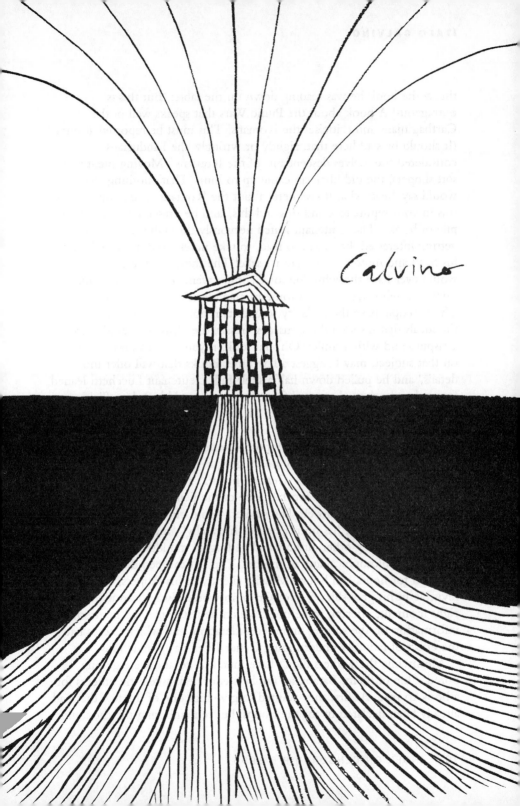

throw the book he was reading down on the table: 'But this is outrageous! A book about the Punic Wars that speaks well of the Carthaginians and criticises the Romans! This must be reported at once!' (It should be said here that, rightly or wrongly, the Pandurians considered themselves descendants of the Romans.) Moving silently in soft slippers, the old librarian came up to him. 'That's nothing,' he would say, 'read what it says here, about the Romans again, you can put this in your report too, and this and this,' and he presented him with a pile of books. The lieutenant leafed nervously through them, then, getting interested, he began to read, to take notes. And he would scratch his head and mutter: 'For heaven's sake! The things you learn! Who would ever have thought!' Signor Crispino went over to Lieutenant Lucchetti who was closing a tome in rage, declaring: 'Nice stuff this is! These people have the audacity to entertain doubts as to the purity of the ideals that inspired the Crusades! Yessir, the Crusades!' And Signor Crispino said with a smile: 'Oh, but look, if you have to make a report on that subject, may I suggest a few other books that will offer more details,' and he pulled down half a shelf-full. Lieutenant Lucchetti leaned forward and got stuck in, and for a week you could hear him flicking through the pages and muttering: 'These Crusades though, very nice I must say!'

In the commission's evening report, the number of books examined got bigger and bigger, but they no longer provided figures relative to positive and negative verdicts. General Fedina's rubber stamps lay idle. If, trying to check up on the work of one of the lieutenants, he asked, 'But why did you pass this novel? The soldiers come off better than the officers! This author has no respect for hierarchy!', the lieutenant would answer by quoting other authors and getting all muddled up in matters historical, philosophical and economic. This led to open discussions that went on for hours and hours. Moving silently in his slippers, almost invisible in his grey shirt, Signor Crispino would always join in at the right moment, offering some book which he felt contained interesting information on the subject under consideration, and which always had the effect of radically undermining General Fedina's convictions.

Meanwhile the soldiers didn't have much to do and were getting bored. One of them, Barabasso, the best educated, asked the officers for a book to read. At first they wanted to give him one of the few that had already been declared fit for the troops; but remembering the thousands

of volumes still to be examined, the general was loth to think of Private
Barabasso's reading hours being lost to the cause of duty; and he gave
him a book yet to be examined, a novel that looked easy enough,
suggested by Signor Crispino. Having read the book, Barabasso was to
report to the general. Other soldiers likewise requested and were granted
the same duty. Private Tommasone read aloud to a fellow soldier who
couldn't read, and the man would give him his opinions. During open
discussions, the soldiers began to take part along with the officers.

Not much is known about the progress of the commission's work:
what happened in the library through the long winter weeks was not
reported. All we know is that General Fedina's radio reports to General
Staff headquarters became ever more infrequent, until finally they
stopped altogether. The Chief of Staff was alarmed; he transmitted the
order to wind up the enquiry as quickly as possible and present a full
and detailed report.

In the library, the order found the minds of Fedina and his men prey
to conflicting sentiments: on the one hand they were constantly
discovering new interests to satisfy and were enjoying their reading and
studies more than they would ever have imagined; on the other hand
they couldn't wait to be back in the world again, to take up life again, a
world and a life that seemed so much more complex now, as though
renewed before their very eyes; and on yet another hand, the fact that
the day was fast approaching when they would have to leave the library
filled them with apprehension, for they would have to give an account
of their mission, and with all the ideas that were bubbling up in their
heads they had no idea how to get out of what had become a very tight
corner indeed.

In the evening they would look out of the windows at the first buds
on the branches glowing in the sunset, at the lights going on in the
town, while one of them read some poetry out loud. Fedina wasn't with
them: he had given the order that he was to be left alone at his desk to
draft the final report. But every now and then the bell would ring and
the others would hear him calling: 'Crispino! Crispino!' He couldn't get
anywhere without the help of the old librarian, and they ended up
sitting at the same desk writing the report together.

One bright morning the commission finally left the library and went
to report to the Chief of Staff; and Fedina illustrated the results of the
enquiry before an assembly of the General Staff. His speech was a kind

of compendium of human history from its origins down to the present day, a compendium in which all those ideas considered beyond discussion by the right–minded folk of Panduria were attacked, in which the ruling classes were declared responsible for the nation's misfortunes, and the people exalted as the heroic victims of mistaken policies and unnecessary wars. It was a somewhat confused presentation including, as can happen with those who have only recently embraced new ideas, declarations that were often simplistic and contradictory. But as to the overall meaning there could be no doubt. The assembly of generals was stunned, their eyes opened wide, then they found their voices and began to shout. General Fedina was not even allowed to finish. There was talk of a court martial, of his being reduced to the ranks. Then, afraid there might be a more serious scandal, the general and the four lieutenants were each pensioned off for health reasons, as a result of 'a serious nervous breakdown suffered in the course of duty'. Dressed in civilian clothes, with heavy coats and thick sweaters so as not to freeze, they were often to be seen going into the old library where Signor Crispino would be waiting for them with his books. ❏

© *Italo Calvino, reprinted from* Numbers in the Dark, *Jonathan Cape, 1995*
© *Translation Tim Parks 1995*

REINALDO ARENAS

Traitor

I AM GOING to speak fast, just as it comes. So don't expect much from
your little gadget. Don't think you're going to get a lot from what I
tell you, and that you are going to patch it up, add this and that, make it
into a big opus, or whatever, and become famous on my account...
Though I don't know, maybe if I speak just out of my head, it might
work out better for you. It might go over better. You could exploit it
more. Because you are the devil. But since you're already here, and with
all that paraphernalia, I'll talk. A little. Not much. Only to show you
that without us you are nothing. The ashtray is over there, on top of the
sink, use it if you want... What a show, impeccable shirt and all — is it
silk? Can you get silk now? — but you'll have to stand there, or sit on
that chair with the ruined cane seat — yes, I know it could be repaired
now — and you can start asking me.

And what do you know about him? What does anyone know? Now
that Fidel Castro has been ousted, well, overthrown, or he got tired,
everybody is talking, everybody can talk. The system has changed again.
Oh, now everybody is a hero. Now, everybody was against him. But
then, when on every corner, day and night, there was a Surveillance
Committee always watching every door, every window, every gate, every
light, and every one of our moves, and every word, and every silence,
and what we heard on the radio, and what we did not, and who were
our friends, and who were our enemies, and what kind of sex life we
had, and what kind of letters, and diseases, and dreams... All of these
were also being checked. Ah, I see you don't believe me. I'm an old
woman. Think whatever you want to. I am old, and out of my mind.
Keep thinking that way. It's better. Now it's possible to think — oh, you
don't understand me. Do you not understand that then one could not
think? But now you can, right? Yes. And that in itself should make me
worry, if there were still something that could make me worry. If you
can think out loud, you have nothing left to say. But, listen to me, they

are still around. They have poisoned everything, and they are still around. And now anything that is done will be because of them, either for them or against them — not now, though — but because of them... I'm sorry, what am I saying? Is it true I can say whatever I please? Is it true? Tell me. At first I couldn't believe it. And I still can't believe it. Times change. I hear talk about freedom again. Screams. That is bad. Shouts of 'Freedom' usually mean just the opposite. I know. I saw... There must be a reason why you came, looked me up, and you're here now with your little machine.

It works, doesn't it? Remember that I'm not going to repeat anything. There will be plenty of people to spin their tales. Now we'll have the testimonials, of course, everybody has a story to tell, everybody makes a big fuss, everybody screams, and everybody was — isn't that nice? — against the tyranny. And I don't doubt it. Oh, but then! Who didn't have a political badge, awarded, of course, by the regime? Make sure you find out, didn't your father belong to the militia, didn't he do voluntary work? *Voluntary*, that was the word. Even I, when Castro was thrown out of power, almost got executed as a *castrista*. How awful! What saved me were the letters I had written to my sister, who was living in exile. What if I didn't have them anymore? She had to send them back to me fast, or else I would be dead and gone. And that's why I haven't dared go out of the house, because some, a lot, of that still exists. And I don't want to get any closer to it. I...so you are asking me to speak, to contribute, to cooperate — I'm sorry, that's not the way you say it now — with whatever I know, because you intend to write a book or something, with one of the victims. A double victim, you will have to say. Or triple. Or better, a victimised victim. Or better still, a victim victimised by the victims. Well, you'll have to fix that. Write whatever you want. You don't need to give it to me for approval. I don't want to see anything. I'm taking advantage, however, of this freedom of 'expression' to tell you that you are a vulture. Turkey vultures we called them. Have they all been eliminated? No longer needed? What wonderful birds! They used to feed on carrion, on corpses, and then, they soared into the skies. And what was the reason for their extermination? Didn't they clean up the Island under every regime? And how they gorged themselves... Perhaps they got poisoned by eating the bodies of those executed by justice — is that still how you say it? — that is, by you... Listen, will you bring that machine closer to me? Quickly,

20   INDEX ON CENSORSHIP 6 1996

because I'm in a rush, and I'm old and tired. And to tell you the truth, I've been poisoned too. This machine — is it working? — was very popular, though people usually never knew when it was being used... Today you tell me what you're going to do and why you have come to see me. We talk. And nobody is watching at the corner, right? And nobody will come and search my house after you're gone, right? Anyway, I have nothing else to hide. And is it true I can say whether I'm for something or against it? Right now I can, if I want to, speak against the government, and nothing would happen? Maybe. Is it so, really? Yes, everything is like that now. Right there on the corner, they were selling beer today. There was a lot of noise. Music, they call it. People don't look so scraggly, or so angry anymore. There are no more slogans on the trees. People are going out, I see it, and you can get genuinely sad, with your own brand of sadness, I mean. People have food, aspirations, dreams (do they have dreams?), and they dress in bright colours. But I still don't believe this, as I already told you. I've been poisoned. I have seen...but, oh well, we should go straight to the point, which is what you want. We cannot waste any more time. Now we have to work, right? Before, the main thing was to pretend you were working. Now we have aspirations... It's a simple story. Yes; of course. But anyway, you won't understand these things. Practically nobody can anymore. These things can't be understood unless you have experienced them, like almost everything... He wrote some books that should be around somewhere. Or maybe not. Maybe they were burned during the early dismantling of the regime. Then, at the very beginning, of course, those things happened. Inherited bad habits. I really know it's been difficult to overcome all these 'tendencies' — can you still call them that? All those books, as you know, spoke well of the deposed regime. However, it's all a lie. You had to go to the fields, and he went. Nobody really knew that when he was working like a maniac, he was not doing it out of loyalty to the regime, but out of pure hate. You really had to see the fury with which he broke the lumps of earth, how he sowed the seeds, weeded, dug. Those earned the big bonus points then. Oh, God! there was

such hate in him while he was doing everything and contributing to everything. How much he hated the whole thing... They made him — he made himself — 'a model youth', 'a front-line worker', and they awarded him 'the pennant'. If an extra shift of guard duty was needed, he would volunteer. If one more hand was needed at the sugarcane harvest, there he went. During his military service, was there anything he could say no to, when everything was official, patriotic, revolutionary, that is, inexcusable? And even out of the service, everything was compulsory. But by then it was worse, because he was not a youth anymore. He was a man, and he had to survive; that is, he needed a room, and also, for instance, a pressure cooker; and, for instance, a pair of pants. Would you believe me if I told you that the authorisation for buying a shirt, and being able to pick it up, involved political privilege? I see you don't believe me. So be it. But I hope you always can do that... Since he hated the system so much, he spoke little; and since he didn't speak much, he didn't contradict himself, while others did, and what they said one day, they had to retract or deny the next — a problem of dialectics, people called it. And then, since he didn't contradict himself, he became a well-trusted man, a respected man. He would never interrupt the weekly meetings. You had to see his attitude of approval while in reality he was dreaming of sailing, travelling, or being somewhere else, in 'the land of the enemy' (as it was called), from which he would fly back carrying a bomb; and right there at the meeting — just like so many that he, ominously, had attended and applauded — in a plaza full of slaves, he would drop the bomb... And so, for his 'exemplary discipline and dutifulness in the Circles of Study' (that was the name given to the compulsory sessions on political indoctrination), he received another diploma. He would be the first one, when the time came, to read from *Granma* — I still remember the name [of the official newspaper] — not because he was really interested, but because his hatred for that publication was such that in order to get it over with quickly (as you would with anything you abhor), he would read it right away. When he raised his hand to donate this or that — we donated everything in public — how he secretly laughed at himself; how, inwardly, he exploded... He would always do volunteer work for four or five extra hours — and pity thee if you didn't! He did his compulsory guard duty with a rifle on his shoulder, and the building he was protecting had been built by the former regime — he was protecting his own hell. How many times had he thought of blowing his head off while shouting 'Down with Castro,' or something like that...

But life is something else. People change. Do you know what fear is? Do you know what hatred is? Do you know what hope is? Do you know what total helplessness is?... Take care of yourself, and do not take anything for granted, don't trust anything. Not even now. Even less now. Now that everything seems trustworthy, this is precisely the time to mistrust. Later it will be too late. Then you will have to obey orders. You are young, you don't know anything. But your father, no doubt, was in the militia. Your father, no doubt,... Don't take part in anything. Leave! — can one leave the country now? It's incredible. To leave... 'If I could leave,' he would tell me, he would whisper in my ear after coming home from one of those everlasting events, after three hours of beating his palms. 'If I could leave, if I could escape by swimming away, since any other way is impossible now, or soar above this hell and get away from it all...' And I: *Calm down, calm down, you know very well that is impossible, fragments of fingernails is what the fishermen are bringing back. Out there, they have orders to shoot point-blank, even if you surrender. Look at those searchlights...* And he himself at times had to take care of those same searchlights, and clean and shine the guns, that is, to watch over the tools of his own subjugation. And how disciplined he was, how much passion he put into it, you might say he was trying to create a cover-up through his actions, so that they would not reveal his authentic being. And he would come home exhausted, dirty, full of slaps on his back, and badges of honour. 'Oh, if I had a bomb,' he would then tell me, or rather whisper into my ear, 'I would have blown myself up with it all. A bomb so powerful that there would be nothing left. Nothing. Not even me.' And I: *Calm down, for goodness sake, wait, don't say anything else, they can hear you, don't spoil everything with your rage...* Disciplined, polite, hard-working, discreet, unpretentious, normal, easy-going, extremely easy-going, well adapted to the system precisely for being its complete opposite — how could they not make him a member of the Party?

Was there any job he didn't do? And he was fast. What criticism didn't he accept with humility?... And that immense hatred inside, that feeling of being humiliated, annihilated, buried, unable to say anything and having to submit in silence. And how silently!, how enthusiastically!, in order not to be even more humiliated, more annihilated, totally wiped out. So that, someday perhaps, he could be himself, take revenge:

speak out, take action, live... Ah, how often he wept at night, very quietly in his room, in there, the next one on this side. He wept out of rage and hatred. I shall never be able to recount — it would take more than a lifetime — all the vituperations he used to rattle out against the system. 'I can't go on, I can't go on,' he would tell me. And it was true. Embracing me, embracing me — remember that I was also young, we were both young, just like you; though I don't know, maybe you're not so young: now everybody is so well fed... Embracing me, he would say: 'I can't take it any longer, I can't take it any longer. I'm going to cry out all my hatred. I'm going to cry out the truth,' he whispered, choking. And me?, what did I do? I used to calm him down. I would tell him: *Are you insane?* — and I would rearrange his badges. *If you do it, they are going to shoot you. Keep on pretending, like everybody else. Pretend even more than the others, make fun of him that way. Calm down, don't talk nonsense.* He never stopped performing his tasks dutifully, only being himself for a while at night, when he came to me to unburden his soul. Never, not even now when there is official approval, and even encouragement, did I ever hear anybody reject the regime so strongly. Since he was in the inner circle, he knew the whole operation, its most minute atrocities. Come morning, he would return, enraged but silenced, to his post, to the meeting, to the fields, to the raising of hands to volunteer. He accumulated a lot of 'merits'. It was then that the Party 'oriented' him — and you don't know what that word meant then — to write a series of biographies of high officials. 'Do it,' I would say to him, 'or you will lose all you have accomplished until now. It would be the end.' And so he became famous — they made him famous. He moved away and was assigned a large house. He married the woman they oriented him to... I had a sister in exile. She used to come, though, and visit me. Very cautiously, she would bring his books under her arm. And she told me the truth: they were all monsters... Were they? Or were we? What do you think? Have you found out anything about your father? Have you learned anything else? Why did you choose precisely this tainted character for your job? Who are you? Why are you looking at me that way? Who was your father? Your father... 'At the first opportunity, I'll leave,' he used to tell me, 'I know there is strict surveillance, that it's practically impossible to defect, that there are many spies, many criminals on the loose; and that even if I manage to, someone shall murder me in exile. But before that I shall speak out. Before that, I will say what I feel,

I will speak the truth...' *Calm down, don't talk,* I would tell him — and we were not that young anymore — *don't do anything crazy.* And he: 'Do you think that I can spend my whole life pretending? Don't you realise that going so much against myself I won't be me anymore? Don't you see that I'm already but a shadow, a marionette, an actor who is never off the stage, where he only plays a shady character?' And I: Wait, wait. And I, understanding, weeping with him, and harbouring as much, or even more, hatred in me — after all, I am, or was, a woman — pretending just like everybody else, conspiring secretly in my thoughts, in my soul, and begging him to wait, to wait. And he managed to wait. Until the moment came.

It happened when the regime was overthrown. He was tried and sentenced as an agent of the Castro dictatorship (all the proofs were against him) and condemned to the maximum punishment, death by shooting. Then, standing in front of the liberating firing squad, he shouted: 'Down with Castro! Down with tyranny! Long live Freedom!' Until the full discharge silenced him, he kept on shouting. Shouts that the press and the world defined as 'cowardly cynicism'. But that I — and please write this down, just in case your machine is not working — I can assure you that this was the only authentic thing your father had ever said out loud in his whole life. ❑

Havana, 1974

PRAMOEDYA ANANTA TOER

Encounter with the devils

*More than three hundred years ago the
nutmeg groves of Buru Island were burnt by
the soldiers of the Dutch East Indies Trading
Company. Fruit dissolved to ash; seeds, carried
away by the wind, landed on barren earth. A savanna formed and the island's
nutmeg trade was wiped out forever. Forced to leave their coastal settlements, the
island's inhabitants were gradually absorbed in the embrace of the forest. They
became hunters and gatherers; their only farming implement, a kind of spear used
to poke holes in the soil. Arab traders who visited the island called these people
'Alfuru,' 'the people of the interior.'*

*Over the course of three and a half centuries little changed on this island. It
was a stagnant world of malaria, filariasis, tiling ringworm, parasites and
tuberculosis, a continuum of intertribal warfare and intervillage disputes. And
then there came a most historic time, August 1969, when Buru Island became a
prison camp for more than 10 thousand political prisoners.*

IN THE *SOA* (a small Alfuru settlement) in the Way Apo Valley, a group
of young boys was playing in the shade of a grove of towering *laban*
trees. They were honing their hunting skills with a game of *coko*. The
game's referee bowled a pomelo across the clearing and shouted the
command: 'Coko!' His cry was immediately followed by the whizzing of
bamboo spears in pursuit of the green fruit. One spear hit the mark and
abruptly stopped the fruit's rapid roll.

Three young girls, stooped beneath the large bundles of faggots on their heads, emerged from the forest. Showing little sign of interest in the boys or their hunting game, the girls proceeded toward the *soa*. They wore lengths of Javanese batik around their waists and strips of cloth around their small chests. The boys were dressed in dirty loincloths. There was not a clean one among them and their skin was rough from ringworm scars — concentric overlapping circles of raised flesh, which the Alfuru believed was a sign of affection shown by the ancestors to all Buru inhabitants: elders, parents and children.

'Hunt!' The cry erupted again and bamboo spears flew through the air once more. This time none hit the mark.

A man in ragtag trousers stepped out from the forest. A singlet covered his torso; a batik headcloth, whose free end rested on the man's shoulders, covered his head. The man carried two new spears across his shoulders. Ignoring the boys, he headed directly for his *soa*. His skin, like that of the other inhabitants of the *soa*, was blackened by ringworm.

The boys paused momentarily in their game when a young couple, husband and wife, exited their hut. Since custom forbade sexual intercourse inside the house, the couple were going to the forest to find a place in the bushes to make love. Outside the entrance to their nest, the man will plant two spears in the shape of a diagonal cross, a sign that no-one might enter. Inside, the woman will kneel and bend forward; the man, holding another spear in one hand, enters her from behind...

One of the boys whistled in delight and, in raucous unison, the other boys followed suit. Their game of coko was dispersed by fantasy. But soon, as the sun began to set, fantasies, too, began to lose their hue. An Alfuru dugout was suddenly spotted coming down the Way Apo. It slowed, then stopped. Men with machetes and spears jumped from the boat to the shore and made their way up the river bank.

'Go home! Now!' the men shouted to the boys, who immediately scampered away towards the *soa*. Their path was soon traced by the men, who had just returned from upriver.

THE *SOA* was made up of eight houses, plus an open-sided meeting house and a storehouse on stilts where sacred objects were stored. In the open air outside the entrance to the meeting house, an ancestral wooden totem stood guard.

Inside the meeting house, all the members of the *soa*, as well as members of other, nearby settlements, had gathered together. Even the young newlyweds, who not long before had been making love in the forest, were present. All of the elders of the settlements' government wore red waistbands — the red was reserved for their use alone, a sign of authority — and long trousers. They had just returned from a meeting with the Chief of Kayeli and had brought back with them important news; on this day, the government elders were to bring a yellow-cloth army to the island. We must be careful, the government elders warned the villagers, for the yellow army is made up of criminals — killers, rapists and thieves. They are different from the green-cloth army elders. They are coming here to live and plant rice. Be careful! If you meet them, run away. The yellow army is made up of evil-spirited men. They are devils in human form.

Manarote, the head of this *soa* and the guardian-of-tradition, raised a hand, his five fingers splayed. 'For three times five fingers, you do not leave the *soa!*' he told the assembly. Then he gave the sign that the meeting was at an end.

One by one the torches dimmed and the settlement was drowned in the darkness of night and a new fear: that of the devils, they of the yellow army.

THE 15 days of taboo passed and the people still had no idea what the yellow army might look like. But as hunger was a force more powerful than fear, on the sixteenth morning all the members of the settlement left the *soa* together. No-one dared to go out alone. They headed warily to a swampy area not too far distant to seine fish, fell trees and prepare *sago*. By sunset they had caught a week's supply of fish and prepared 20 *tomang* (seven-kilogram bundles) of *sago* flour.

On the journey back to the *soa*, this laden parade of villagers in mud-caked clothing came to a sudden halt. Manarote ordered everyone to fall back. Up ahead, and not too far from their settlement, was a group of devils, dressed in their distinctive and ragged faded-yellow uniforms and armed with hoes and machetes. They were carving a road through the brush, two or three arm lengths wide, and had almost reached the grounds of the *soa*'s meeting house. They were, in fact, but a few arm lengths from the ancestral totem.

The villagers retreated in haste to the bush. Manarote, his spear ready in hand, shadowed the devils from behind the blind of *laban* trees. The yellow army — these devils, this troupe of evil spirits — look like normal human beings after all, he observed. And with their dull machetes, their axes and hoes, they could be no more dangerous than other enemies — the foreign Papuan invaders, the fierce mountain tribes, or vengeful neighbouring *soa*. But even more evident to him was that this crew of criminal workers was simply carrying out the orders of the green army.

As the sun set, the ragged, yellow-uniformed devils ceased their work and gathered their tools. With their implements resting on their shoulders, they left by way of the straight path that had just been carved through the forest. All eyes of the villagers followed their retreat until they disappeared in the night's consuming darkness.

Manarote clucked his tongue in amazement, for never in all his life had he ever seen such a straight path cut through the jungle. But then his amazement turned to anger. 'Taboo!' the *soa*'s guardian-of-tradition mumbled. In the murky light, he unsheathed his machete and pointed it toward the spot where the troupe of devils had vanished. 'Taboo!' he roared.

Each and every member of the *soa* understood the guardian's anxiety: their hunting area was now cleft by a road. The welfare of their settlement, and that of other *soa* located in the low plain of the Way Apo Valley, was threatened.

SIX MONTHS later, the yellow army of devils was no longer dressed in ragged uniforms. Some wore only loincloths. Others had donned multicolored patchwork pants. Still others had covered themselves in plastic bags. The hunting areas had been carved up by roads, irrigation canals and rice fields. Stretches of the elephant-grass plain were now fields. Where once wild boar wallowed, there were now water-filled squares.

It was useless for the Alfuru to try to frighten the devils with machetes or spears; the devil band was only carrying out the orders of the government elders. Besides, with the green army keeping constant watch, the devils hadn't the power to do anything for themselves or in their own names. For that reason, perhaps, they exhibited no sign of the criminal behaviour for which they were being punished. They didn't even possess spears or knives.

Still, in time, an encounter with the devils became unavoidable.

PR

OE DAY a conflict arose between two *soa*. Mana, a young man, had
been caught sleeping illicitly with Muka, the wife of a man from
another settlement. Whenever her husband went downriver to Namlea
to trade his harvest of *sago* for salt, Mana would call on Muka and take
her to the forest. Soon, their meetings were no longer a secret. Muka,
finally confronted by her husband, had confessed. He decided to bring it
up before the elders at the next *soa* meeting. A second meeting was then
arranged between representatives of both settlements, and a fine was
subsequently levied on the transgressor.

But Mana had failed to fulfil his obligation. Men from Muka's *soa*
came to Mana's *soa* armed with fighting spears and short knives. Screams
of attack and cries of defence filled the mist morning air, and everyone
unable to run away or defend himself, dogs and chickens included, was
killed by flying spears. Only the sudden appearance of a green army
patrol, firing shots into the air, halted the battle. Both the attackers and
the attacked fled. Only the dead and the wounded were left on the
battleground. Under supervision of the green army, a group of devils
came forth and was ordered to carry the wounded to its lair.

Up close, the devils proved not to be frightening creatures at all. They
laid out the victims and attended to their wounds, cleansing them with
strange-smelling ointments, applying salves with nose-burning odours,
sticking needles into flesh and filling veins with strange liquids.

The wounded cringed at the feel of the devils' skin. It was smooth,
like snakeskin, not rough like the skin of the Alfuru people. That
sensation alone was far more memorable than the intertribal battle that
had just taken place.

The devils gave them food and whatever else they needed. They had,
of course, eaten rice before, and many of the vegetables, too. But never
had they eaten them cooked in such a fashion. They asked each other,
what kind of spices did the devils use? The taste of the food was
incredible; they had never experienced such tastes before.

Since they were hungry, almost anything would have tasted good. But
the limit was reached when the devils offered them fermented cassava.
The smell alone caused them to shake their heads. 'No, no! It smells
rotten,' they said. Nonetheless, one curious young man decided to try a
little, and he nibbled on a piece of the fermented cassava. 'It's sweet, like
palm wine!' he shouted, jumping up.

Suddenly everyone began to fight over the rest of the cassava. Even the wounded joined in the fray.

The proud Alfuru men, who felt it not at all beneath them to take food from these newly arrived devils, were chagrined only by the fact that the children had been offered food first and not them. Their superior status came from guarding the welfare of the women, children, family and village with their spears, knives and physical strength. The devils had no understanding of the high value placed on males in the savanna. Through the natural selection process and intertribal warfare, the adult male had come to occupy the most important role in communal life.

Strange also to many of the Alfuru was the willingness of the devils' guardian-of-tradition to provide assistance without thought of recompense. This was so unlike their own guardian-of-tradition, who also served as the community's doctor. He was forever coming up with special demands: find this leaf or locate that root on this or that mountain and make an offering to the tree from which the leaf or root was taken. In centuries past, their people had offered to the trees coins of the East Indies Trading Company but, over the years, their coins had disappeared, swallowed by the soil beneath the trees. Now they offered the trees a fish or a slab or two of venison or boar meat. Another odd thing was that the devils' guardian-of-tradition and his assistants performed most of the work themselves.

Eventually those who were not seriously wounded were allowed to be taken home. The more seriously injured were made to stay in the devils' lair. Visits were permitted in the evenings only.

ONLY A few days after the intertribal skirmish, a band of mountain Alfuru came down from their hilltop home to the valley. Their long hair fell over their shoulders and was held in place by headcloths, which left the crown of their heads exposed. Only loincloths covered their bodies. They swooped down unexpectedly on the devils who were opening a field. Two of the devils fell beneath their spears. One was beheaded and his head taken away for ceremonial use.

After that incident, the people of the Way Apo Valley felt themselves as one with the devils against the mountain tribes. The devils had put up a defence. There was proof of that: even in death, the dead devil, his arm impaled by a spear, tightly clutched the steel machete that a government elder had given him. Beside his body was a bloodied headcloth that belonged to one from the mountain tribe. Silently, the valley people paid honour to the devils, who had so courageously faced the mountain warriors.

It was just too bad that these newcomers felled so many trees. The commotion caused by their felling of trees and sawing of logs into planks raised havoc in the Alfurus' hunting areas. Deer, wild boar and cuscus fled the areas the devils disturbed. Not only that, the devils had superior methods for catching fish from their swamps. And in hunting, it wasn't they who chased after the deer, but their dogs. All they did was release their dogs, and the dogs would drive the deer towards the closest slope. And there, with the deer unable to run farther, the dogs would attack. After the dogs returned to their owners, the devils would go out to collect the now-powerless deer. They didn't bother to hunt for wild boar and made no use of spears. They simply surrounded their gardens with a sharp wooden stakes, leaving only one way out. And there, they set a trap, a hole in the ground with sharpened bamboo stakes at the bottom.

In the long dry season, the heat that befell the low plain parched kilometre after kilometre of riverbed. Thousands of hawks circled the skies in search of floundering fish, which the devils harvested as food for their livestock. In the rainy season, the devils did the same. When the streams and rivers rose out of their banks, thousands of climbing perch could be found swimming atop the ground in search of the upstream course. For the devils, the fish were easy pickings.

Alfuru chickens were scraggly and thin, but the devils' chickens were fat and bred rapidly, every month producing thousands of eggs, which proved to be a much better bartering chip at the port town of Namlea than the Alfuru's bundles of *sago*. When butchering a chicken, an Alfuru always said, 'The meat for me, the bones for the dog and the blood for the land.' But the devils never recited such a mantra. Perhaps they were unafraid of threats — or they had no ancestors.

The Alfuru believed that their own ancestors had come to the island from the kingdom of Majapahit. Was this only a tall tale? Possibly so, but they offered proof of their ancestors' origins: a box made of *sago* leaves that contained copperplate inscriptions in a script no-one could understand.

The Alfuru hadn't thought that the devils would be on their side against the mountain tribes; and these newcomers were superior in many

other ways. While the Alfuru used a long, pointed spear to plant crops, the devils used hoes. They also employed buffalo and cattle to turn over the soil and to transport the harvest in wheeled carts. The devil doctor and his assistants proved to be much wiser than their own guardian-of-tradition.

What else was there about them? At the meeting house, an assembly concluded that the key to the devils' superiority was education: the devils had gone to school. Beginning then, school education became a myth whose power rivalled that of the ancestors.

A NEW chapter began in the life of the Alfuru. The people of the Way Apo Valley began to befriend the devils. The green army elders had warned them: 'Watch out for yellow army devils entering the village. Report them to us. And if they resist, kill them!' But they began to ignore this command. Even the elders, whose authority among the younger members of the *soa* had begun to wane, did nothing to obstruct this intercourse. The devils brought with them new things. The ones who visited the village gave them antidotes against influenza and other illnesses, a boon to ridding the interior of contagious diseases. They brought acupuncture needles and pills to guard against ringworm. Ringworm, they said, was not a sign of love from the ancestors. It was a skin disease. The children gathered around the devils and asked to be taught to read and write, to learn their names for edible leaves and fruit, even for the wild jackfruit and breadfruit.

For their part, the Alfuru people secretly visited the devils' lairs. These homes — or barracks as they were called — were 10 times larger than their own huts and were made not from plaited *sago* palm fronds but from hewn wood. The favourable reputation of the devils began to spread among the Alfuru women. The devils were 'very delicious', they said. 'And it's nice to be able to see their faces.' They began to contemplate taking devils for husbands. They liked the idea of being able to look at their husbands and not having to kneel, face down, when making love.

During periods when the devils were unable to visit, the people spoke fondly of them, especially of those who could speak in the Buru language and who had been adopted as *soa* members and been given family names. These periods of absence always followed momentous events in the life of the devils' village. Twice their visits had stopped because of a slaughter of the devils by the green army men and once because a large group of devils had run off to the interior.

Notwithstanding all these times and others, too, there was one event above all others that caused amazement in all the *soa* of the Way Apo Valley.

Years had passed since the little boys had ceased playing *coko*. They were now young adults. A few had even accumulated a dowry large enough to acquire a woman from another settlement. Traditionally, the Alfuru marry outside their own tribe, and the dowry a man must obtain prior to marriage is fixed by consensus. It might, for example, be 16 spears and a few dozen plates.

Thus Manalele, having attained the requisite dowry, obtained the hand of Mukarowa, a thin, black-skinned girl from a settlement 15 kilometres distant from his own village. After he brought her back to his *soa*, the young couple proceeded to build their own hut. But it was made with joists and nails, as the devils' homes were. When Manalele and Mukarowa made love, they did not build a nest in the jungle undergrowth. And in time, even though this young couple had violated ancestral law, Mukarowa became pregnant.

One morning, following the dictates of the ancestors, Manalele accompanied his heavily pregnant wife into the jungle, to a site where a few days earlier he had erected a small hut on stilts. It was there that she was to give birth.

For seven consecutive days Mukarowa remained in the hut, alone. With the exception of Manalele, who brought her food each day, no-one else was allowed to visit. Still their child had not descended. On the eighth day, however, Manalele discovered Mukarowa prone on the floor of the hut, her eyes closed tightly. He threw down the cooked *sago* and fish he had brought for her and ran back to the *soa*. He screamed and called for his childhood friends, begging them to help him carry Mukarowa back to the *soa*.

Even before Manalele's friends had gathered, the guardian-of-tradition had tried to stop him. 'That woman may only return to the *soa* with a child in her hands or as a corpse,' he had declared.

But Manalele was adamant. 'This is no business of yours! The devil doctor will cure her.'

Without waiting for another burst of anger from the guardian, Manalele and three of his friends hurried away from the *soa* and into the jungle. They carried bamboo poles and a sarong, a stretcher on which to carry Mukarowa. When the men returned to the *soa* with her, she was unconscious. The guardian offered them no greeting at all; he knew that his authority over the younger members of the *soa* had been broken.

After a brief rest, the young men continued their journey, onward to the devils' lair and to the house in which the devils' guardian-elder cured the ill. Other members of the *soa* followed closely behind.

The devil-doctor ordered Manalele and his companions to place Mukarowa on a wooden, mat-covered platform, then told the group to leave the room, although he did allow them and the other villagers to look in through the window.

A quick check of the woman's blood produced in the devil-doctor a mournful cry. 'Dear God, her haemoglobin is only four and a half.'

Mukarowa moaned continuously, whispering ever so slowly, 'Mother, oh, Mother...'

In the middle of the savanna, there could be no sterile room. And because Mukarowa's haemoglobin was so low, the devil-doctor dared not administer an anaesthetic, either general or local. Even if he had wanted to, he had neither the tools nor the expertise to do it. But he had to make a quick decision and could only hope that it would be the right one. The doctor's assistants, well aware of the seriousness of the situation, bowed their heads beneath the intent stares of the *soa* members. Something had to be done, and soon. Other devils, ones who had been working near the clinic, also gathered outside to witness the event. All eyes were on the devil-doctor as he paced to the opposite window of the room. Looking upward at the sky, he took a deep breath, then suddenly turned and walked back to Mukarowa, whose weak cries continued. The doctor nodded to his assistants. They immediately fetched him his instrument box.

The doctor whispered, 'Caesarean!'

The eyes of each and every witness were wide with the sight of Mukarowa, the thin child-woman with black skin and reddened hair, whose thighs were no larger than a man's forearm. Her moaning droned endlessly, 'Mother, oh, Mother...', each 'oh' stretching into an eerie screech. The devil-doctor had his assistants swab her abdomen with antiseptic. Her belly was a peakless mountain sprouting on top of flat land. All eyes were fixed on the gleaming knife the doctor held in his hand.

The doctor slowly lowered the blade — then made a long incision in the woman's stomach.

'Oh, Mother!' Momentarily, the woman's screams intensified.

Blood began to pour from the woman's belly. 'Aiieee!' the Alfuru people screamed in unison. One man tore away from the crowd and ran off towards the *soa*, screaming crazily: 'He's cut her stomach! The devil has cut open Mukarowa's stomach!' The villager's voice was taken by the arid flatland wind and carried across the savanna, where it was finally and mercifully muffled by the forest and mountains that encircled the plain.

Within two hours, inhabitants of other *soa* had also gathered at the clinic. No fewer than 70 people of all ages were there as witnesses.

The doctor had removed a tiny child from the woman's womb. A girl child. Dead. Finally, he ordered someone to take the corpse home.

'Oh, Mother...,' Mukarowa still moaned, now deliriously.

'Go home! Everyone go home!' the devil-doctor demanded. 'Only her husband and parents may stay.'

The clinic grew hushed once more. The young woman's husband and parents squatted beside her, tears pouring from their eyes. Mukarowa was unable to witness this outpouring of emotion: after the operation, she slept for 35 hours.

On the following day, inhabitants of Manalele's *soa* gathered at the clinic once more. This time they brought with them baskets of betel nut, a sign of thanks. Not knowing what to do with so much betel, the devils refused to accept the gift. None of them ate betel or knew how the nuts could be used to tan hides.

Eventually, Mukarowa was allowed to be taken home. She was carried home not in the sarong-and-bamboo stretcher but on the clinic's litter. And in place of the betel nuts, the Alfuru people brought the devils the best of their hunt: a deer and a wild boar.

What happened to Mukarowa was a turning point for the island. With her return to health, the authority of the guardians-of-tradition was ended. And the relationship between the Alfuru and the devils was not just closer; it was now one of greater respect.

NINE MORE years passed. The Alfuru men no longer stole food from the mouths of children. They had even begun to help care for the children themselves. The incidence of elephantiasis had diminished and,

regardless of whether or not it was a gift from the ancestors, tiling
ringworm had all but disappeared. Fathers no longer sold their female
children to buy new wives. As for the young women themselves, they
now were willing to accept a marriage proposal from a devil even
without hope of a dowry. And now in times of changing seasons and
epidemics of flu, children were no longer marched off to the grave.

Some of the guardians and elders tried to reinstitute their former
influence through threats and dire predictions. 'A large flood is coming.
Prepare rafts and place them near your homes,' they would say, but the
devils ignored such warnings and the floods never came.

Nonetheless, warnings were issued time and again. Then one day a
prophecy was heard that struck the devils at their most vulnerable point:
'You will return to Java. A ship with a red and white flag will come, and
you will return to Java.'

For more than a decade, the devils had filled the jails of Java and the
prison that was Buru Island. And because the devils on Buru had dreamt
so long that one day they would return to Java as free men, this
prediction, when it was heard, seemed to catch them unawares. In very
little time, the foretelling had spread by word of mouth throughout the
entire island.

Some of the devils continued to maintain a more cynical view: 'Sure a
white ship will come, but it will be flying a skull and crossbones!' In
Namlea, ships came and went, embarked and disembarked. Gradually,
the prediction lost some of its force.

But then, one day, the foretold time did come. And it was not a white
ship with a red flag or a flag with a skull an crossbones that came, but a
real ship, the *Tanjung Pandan*. Five hundred devils, those who could no
longer endure forced labour — the aged, those crippled by accidents,
people suffering from cancer or mental illness — were put on board and
transported back to Java. Almost all the local inhabitants came out in
force to escort these men to the river that ran to the port.

In 1978 the *Tanjung Pandan* made three trips to Java, each time taking
with it another 500 devils. So, too, the next year and the following year.
By the end of 1979, the devils had forsaken Buru, and the low plain of
the Way Apo Valley reverberated with an ancient quiet.

The devils had left behind for the local people, without thought of
recompense, no fewer than 220 houses they themselves had constructed,
in part or in entirety, with no fanfare. They had also left roads: the 175

kilometres of roads the devils bequeathed the Alfurus made travel for them much faster and safer. And thousands of hectares of irrigated and dry fields; these, too, they left behind. They gave the Alfuru people greater stability. Now the Alfuru had their own small field of rice and other crops and the option of release from their semi-nomadic life. But the number of Alfuru people was so small that new settlers were brought in from Java. They were not devils this time, but the poor.

The yellow army of devils had gone. But they had left behind new customs. They had come to the island, not like Dutch merchants to burn the nutmeg groves, not like the Papuans to raid villages and to kill with bows and arrows, and not like the tribes of the other islands to occupy the coasts. But now, to Java, the devils had returned. ❑

© *Pramoedya Ananta Toer, reprinted from* Manoa, *Spring 1991*
© *Translation Willem Samuels 1991*

MA THIDA

The secret of successful transfusion

'IT'S LIKE this, you see...your little baby, he's got too much of this thing called bilirubin in his blood, that's what's making him yellow. He's still so little isn't he? Only four days old. At his age, it could hurt his brain. He could be permanently retarded. We could try and cure him by performing a blood transfusion. But we'll need your consent. If you don't want to give your consent, we could try other methods, but there's no doubt that a transfusion would be the best. So that's what we'd like to do — providing you agree of course...'

That was the best I could do. I couldn't make it any clearer to her. If I'd introduced any more medical terminology, she'd only have got more confused. She was already in tears.

'There there, sshhh, don't cry. Your son was born here at this hospital wasn't he?'

'Y...y...yes.'

'There, there. So? What do you think? Do you want to discuss it with your husband?'

'He's..he's...he's off travelling.'

'Not on business, though?' I wanted to check if he was a friend.

'Yes — he's gone away with his work.'

'Oh...I see.'

I could see he was not our friend.[1]

'Well, in that case, it's down to you. I've explained to you what we think would be the best treatment for your son, but you'll have to decide.'

I didn't want to force her into agreeing.

'Well in that case Doctor, I'll give you my consent.'

'OK, good. In that case, could you sign here please?'

She did not take my proffered ball-pen. Instead, she quickly rolled her thumb on the ink-pad and put a thumb-print on the spot I was pointing at. She was clearly used to doing it. My ball-pen was left dangling in mid-air.

'HMMM, it's a bit over 22 per cent. We haven't got time to give him a fluid injection and check it again. It's already 10pm and we need to order the blood.'

They were right. The way things were going, I could see I wasn't going to get any sleep that night. Ordering the blood could take at least an hour. Then we'd have to prep him before he was ready for transfusion which would take us to at least 11.30pm. The exchange transfusion could take at least two hours, so it would be one or 2am by the time that was over. Then at 6am I was going to have to take some blood samples from about 10 other children with jaundice. That didn't leave me much time for a nap.

I was meant to be on duty though, not asleep. And if the bilirubin ended up getting deposited in this baby's brain so he got kernicterus, he'd be permanently disabled. Sure it could ruin my night. But it could ruin the rest of his life. I knew I should feel more concerned about him. After all, what was one night without sleep? Still, it would have been easier if he was one of my own family, or the child of one of our

---

[1] *Readers would understand 'travelling without business' as a euphemism for being a political prisoner. 'Away on business' in this instance signifies that the man is a soldier at the frontier.*

friends.

His father, on the other hand, was most definitely no friend of mine. Enemy, more like. But he was my own compatriot — surely I shouldn't look on him as an enemy? Perhaps no — but he was no friend to my friends. He had sworn at them, abused them, tortured them and persecuted them. He had thrown them out of their jobs and ruined their lives. I was upset for them and angry too. I didn't see why I should lose a night's sleep on account of the child of one of my friends' oppressors. Let him suffer too.

No — that's wrong. I'd never even met the father of this baby. He might not be a friend, but that didn't make him an enemy. I couldn't be sure that he was one of the ones who had been cruel to my friends. He might even be one of our own people. And even if he had mistreated my friends, why should his baby son suffer as a result? I was a professional, not a mercenary, even if you couldn't say the same of other people. And anyway, 'revenge' isn't a word in my vocabulary or that of my friends.

Revenge might not be, but what about retaliation? Why shouldn't I retaliate? These people have ruined the lives, the health, the sanity of my friends. And after all, the mother hadn't been too keen to give consent for her baby to have the transfusion even though she knew it was for the best. Maybe we could just give the baby lots of fluid, and see if that got the percentage of bilirubin down to 17 by morning. Then there would be no need for a transfusion. And I could get a good night's sleep. I knew my colleagues would understand. At worst, the child's brain could be affected. Maybe he wouldn't be able to write his own name — but in that, he'd be no worse off than his mother, whose brain wasn't affected. He could follow his father's footsteps into the army — you didn't need a brain that worked to be a soldier. Even if you did have a brain in that job, they stopped you using it.

No, no, I shouldn't think like this. What was I turning into? This poor baby was only four days old. So little. If I left him overnight at 22 per cent without doing anything, tomorrow morning the bilirubin could well have shot up to 29 or 30 per cent. It surely wasn't right that people like me, the so-called best brains, should leave it until the toxins were too high before deciding to perform a transfusion. Could I honestly condemn this baby of four days to grow up with a body which would develop but a brain which wouldn't, that would leave him reliant on others for the rest of his life? He might not even live as long as his father. And anyway, who could say that he would not use his brains for our benefit? No matter who his father and mother were. He was just a blameless four-day-old baby. He hadn't ruined anyone's life — why should I ruin his?

I ran through the arguments in my mind, acting as prosecutor, defence lawyer, witness and judge for this four-day-old baby against whom I was filing a suit. I judged that I should carry out the transfusion. To be honest, though, my colleagues had already decided that for me, and these deliberations were only in my mind.

So I requested blood from the blood bank. After about 40 minutes, we still hadn't received a reply so I went myself to check what the matter was. It turned out that they were out of blood. They suggested I try Rangoon General, although they said in the same breath that RGH probably wouldn't have any either as it was a rare type. Never mind. I was determined to sort this out so I made the arrangements myself to get the blood from RGH. I got busy around midnight and my colleagues weren't happy with me for not helping out. But I kept on, and didn't take a break until the car sped off to collect the blood from RGH.

I went into the common room and revived myself with a drink of water and a biscuit. Then I took a look at myself in the mirror and gave myself a thumbs-up sign, pleased with my achievements. I noted that my left thumb appeared in the mirror as a right thumb.

THE two thumbs brought back memories of the recent past, and memories of a friend of mine.[2] Someone who I thought more of than any other friend. I saw our two thumbs in the mirror.

The last time I saw him was the first time we had met for a long time, although at one time I saw him almost daily. I had been missing him badly. Our last meeting was an occasion of great sadness. He was the patient. I was the doctor. But sadly he was not my patient. All I could

---

[2]*Author's note: A writer who had gone to jail. Translator's note: Ma Thida is almost certainly referring to Maung Thawka, the writer who was jailed in 1989 for 20 years and died in RGH in June 1991, having been transferred there from Insein Jail. Ma Thida met him briefly when he was transferred to RGH*

do was give him a quick examination and offer him a few brief words of encouragement. I saw how he was suffering, but all I could say was 'Are you OK?' The pain in my chest on seeing him felt like the pain in his own heart as he lay there.

I had taken his pulse holding his wrist in my hand. His thumb pressed hard against mine. I stared at it. Then I placed my hand on his upper arm and raised my head to look him in the eye. We looked at one another, our eyes full of recognition and understanding. We said everything through our hands and our eyes. And that was it. I never saw him again. I was meant to be measuring his pulse. Instead, I ended up measuring the force of his commitment and the depth of his suffering.

IT WAS almost 1am by the time the car brought the blood back from RGH. One of my colleagues would perform the transfusion. My job was to check and record progress on the transfusions, the baby's pulse rate, respiration and other vital signs. At 1.15am I let him know we were ready to get started.

The baby had been strapped down to a special X-shaped bed. His legs and arms were spread out and tied down with strips of white cloth wrapped around his wrists to stop him from wriggling and kicking. Even before we got started, he was bawling and screaming his head off. His mother was in tears. Looking at the two of them reminded me that someone had one said: 'Undeservedly you will atone for the sins of your fathers.'

His umbilical cord was slightly infected so it would have caused problems to inject a local anaesthetic through there, particularly with the wound healing. So we performed the operation without anaesthetic and the child bawled his eyes out. He couldn't move though, or kick. I wondered if this was the ultimate in suffering for the sins of the past.

I wondered what I could do to try and calm him down. Should I try to explain to him that it wouldn't be long, it would all be over soon. Would he understand? Would he believe me, even if he understood? 'Soon' for me would seem like a lifetime to someone as young as him. Nor could I say 'Now be brave and this won't hurt a bit' which is what we would say to an older child before giving him an injection in the buttock. I knew that this would hurt this baby a lot. I couldn't lie to him even if others might. So what could I do?

I reached beneath the sterilised cloths and stroked his forehead. It didn't do much good. He kept on crying, his little face red with anger and pain. I stroked his cheeks, his ears. I tried to give him some water. But he refused the drink and wouldn't stop crying.

My colleague was putting the finishing touches to the stitches. The little one kept on crying, even though he was exhausted. In fact, he probably didn't even realise how tired he must be, because he just cried and cried without taking the time to stop and think. The pain was so great it made him forget his exhaustion and just made him cry and cry. Hang on in there, little one. It'll be all over soon.

I stroked his ear again. He suddenly reacted to it, in astonishment and surprise, and tried to wriggle towards me, but the bandages were too tight. Then, with amazing strength, despite the ties around his wrist, he made a grab for my hand. He grasped my thumb tightly in his fist and wouldn't let go. There was no point in my trying to extricate myself. My thumb had done the trick. His sobbing died down. It seemed that my thumb was what he had been waiting for all this time.

Thanks to my colleagues' skill, the baby's bilirubin-poisoned blood — the blood of his parents — was successfully exchanged for clean blood free of contamination. I wish you well little one. I hope that you will put your cleansed brain to useful work. I hope that your newly cleansed heart will stay pure. I hope that the strength you have derived from my thumb, and the truth which passed to you from me and the thumbs of my friends will continue to flow in your veins.

And I hope and believe that one day we will become friends, you and I. How can it be otherwise, now that our thumbs have touched? ❏

© *Ma Thida 1991*
© *Translation Ohnmar Khin*

DUONG THU HUONG

The labyrinth

HUNGER tortured me. My knees trembled; my back was drenched in sweat. For two days, I had walked in circles in a valley covered with red colocassias. It was as if I had wandered into a haunted labyrinth. I had been walking since dawn. Now I realised I had come full circle to my point of departure: a colocassia bush wedged between three large boulders. I rested for half an hour and then struck out in another direction. Two hours later, at noon, I found myself back in front of the same bush. There was no longer any doubt; this wild, chilly grey valley was spirit-haunted...

I put my knapsack down on one of the boulders and began to search the brush. Both sides of the path were choked with the violet flowers and silvery leaves of creeper vines. The vines twined around one another chaotically, tougher than any man-made rope, weaving through the dwarf brambles and ferns. I got out my knife and started slashing the brambles that hung overhead. Green snakes might jump out of them in a flash; their venom was always fatal. For a long time all I had seen were brambles and creeper vines. By early afternoon, the north wind had started to howl. It seemed as if I could hear strains of a bamboo flute. My skin contracted, my hair bristled. Sweat trickled down my back in slow, chilly rivulets.

I pulled myself together. I examined the surrounding vegetation, a dense mass of greenness and silence. I headed north. A hundred paces on, I found myself again in a forest of giant colocassias almost two yards high. Their trunks glinted a strange, iridescent green. At their base, they entwined into one gnarled root the size of a banana-tree trunk. Dwarfed by these plants, anxiety seized me. The wind swelled with their dark, clammy shadows. I slashed with all my strength. The colocassias crashed down. A few paces on, I saw a carefully arranged cluster of large gray stones. I hacked away the colocassias along a rock wall. A house appeared, or more like a room without a roof, sealed off by four rock walls, meticulously layered like a box without a lid, bottomless. In the middle, in a hammock strung between two trees, lay a human skeleton. It looked as if it was sleeping there. The bones, intact, shone an immaculate white.

So it was you, companion, who held me back here, I murmured to myself in prayer. The dead man's face was frozen in a toothy grin; his teeth were shiny, straight. These were the teeth of a young man. Like me, he must have wandered for days and days in this surreal valley shrouded in fog, choked with vegetation.

His strength waning, his hope fading, he must have made one final effort to preserve his body from the animals, to leave it intact, if only in the shape of some distant memory, in the form his parents had given him. He must have been handsome, a stronger, more determined man than I. Otherwise, dying of hunger like that, he would never have been able to build such a tomb. A blade of ice ran down my spine: *Companion, I know how desolate this region is, how horrible it is to moulder in this wretched place. We've been condemned to the same gallows. On the day of our departure, who knows what destiny awaits us.*

The fog rolled across the ground, seeped into my armpits, crawled up my neck. I heard, as if in a dream, the strains of a flute. It was a song from the countryside, an evening song:

The moon has risen over the hillside
River water glistens, eternal
Slowly, the water buffaloes return from the fields

Never had this old music sounded so beautiful to me. The dead man still laughed. The arm and leg bones were well aligned. I remembered the plaster skeleton at our high school. The supervisor in his white jacket used to shoot us threatening looks through his round glasses and say: 'Watch it — it is forbidden to touch it. Look carefully and remember the placement of the bones. The skull bone, the hands, the

feet. Quan, stop fidgeting! The sixth form already broke one of the
femurs like that last year.'

That was the first time I had ever seen a human skeleton. This was
the second. The plaster skeleton had been fragile; this one looked more
resilient. Our parents had given birth to quality products. I gazed at the
skeleton stretched out on the hammock, tried to imagine a young man
slowly losing consciousness. How he must have felt his blood thicken
like glue, fading from red to grey, then mouldering, stinking of death,
his breath going chill. Surely, in that instant of fevered agony, he had
seen his life file past him like the images of a dream. Dreams of peace, of
hatred, of childhood, of love... This had been his last supper, his last
solace on this earth. Then the bloodied pus clogged his arteries and the
dreams had flickered out.

And then the feast for the animals. First, vultures, then crows. Next
ants, insects, worms. Finally, the rain. It would dissolve the corpse into a
liquid fertiliser. The colocassia flowers would grow more lushly,
nourished by this flesh that had been the pride and masterpiece of
creation. The immaculate skeleton looked at me, laughing, as if to say,
'So, I'm still whole. Magnificent, isn't it, companion?' The nylon
hammock was still in perfect shape. Our civilisation of plastics has
worked miracles for this century.

*Brother, in any case, solitude is your lot. I still have things to do. A young
man is waiting for me. They say he's crazy. If they put him in a psychiatric
camp, he's finished. I still have a father, a younger brother who's just been
mobilised. I don't know whether he's dead or alive. You lived as a man, may you
now die as one, and accept my prayer.*

I felt lighter. The deceased soul must have heard me. But my own
limbs remained paralysed, stiff with cold. I slapped them.

*No, there is still something more, some unfulfilled wish...a man who had
created such a dignified agony must surely have left behind a few relics.* I
squatted down and pulled back the grass. I cut away the vines. A small
tombstone appeared under the hammock, directly under the skull. I
tossed the stones to the side one by one. The knife sliced easily into the
earth. I dug a hole about a half a yard wide, imagining the dimensions of
a knapsack. About 25 inches deeper I cut into nylon. I widened the hole
and pulled out the knapsack. It had been tightly bound with nylon cord.
Impossible to unknot. I cut the cord and opened the sack. It only
appeared after three layers of nylon. Though intact, it exuded the odour

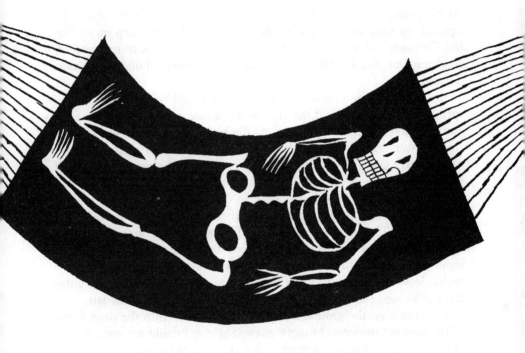

of musty cloth. A machine-gun, plus two and a half boxes of
ammunition. The cartridges weren't rusty. I opened the knapsack and
jumped back. A fine gray vapour. I heard the chant of bamboo:

The river water glistens eternally
The kite string has broken
Wind, O wind, go blow on the other side of the hill

As if a young man were playing the flute at sunset, out on the dykes. I
opened the knapsack and pulled out a card with handwriting on it: 'To
the Comrade Who Finds This Sack: Please bring it back to my mother,
Madame Dao Thi Lo, 68 years old, Em Mo Hamlet, Phung Commune.
Thanks.'

Inside were three uniforms, one for autumn and winter, two for
spring and summer. Amid the clothes was a rare, precious variety of
bamboo flute, with a silky patina. At the bottom, a diary. It was a
soldier's war journal, stained, dog-eared. Stuck to the first page, a photo
of a country girl, not so young, sort of pretty. On the next page, one of
a young man, barely 20 years old, clad in army uniform, laughing, his
face sparkling with optimism.

I had an almost identical photo. It was taken on the day of my
enlistment... The air vibrated with the frenetic beating of drums; the
space around us was resplendent with red flags. Drunk with hope, we
scoured the horizon for our own image, yearning for the moment we
would leave for the front. Over there, rising out of the smoke, were the
faces of heroes, proud happy, their uniforms dripping with medals.

I sat down on the ground and plunged my hands into the dank fabric
of the soldier's uniform. Hunger gnawed at me, I could see stars. A
cloud of fireflies swirled in front of my face in a sickening display of
fireworks. I let my head drop on to my knees, closed my eyes, forced
myself to think of something important, joyful, tender. But the same
images kept coming back: a plate piled high with sticky rice, a ham
hock braised in water, a basket of rice noodles with a bowl of shrimp
sauce. To eat! Luy's obsession had become my own.

My stomach churned. Hunger, like an open wound in every cell,
nerve, and muscle in my body. Now it twisted into spasms and I
doubled over, gasping. I found myself suddenly crumpled on the ground.
I pulled some of the dead man's shirts over my head and fell asleep. Like
a tide, time gently slipped away from me, evaporating, slowly, silently, in

a wisp of smoke. I slipped in and out of consciousness. A hand caressed my cheek... I opened my eyes, saw myself stretched out, my head on the dead man's sack, nestled in his sweater, drenched in fog. My sack at my feet. Above, motionless in the hammock, the skeleton slumbered.

The sun had risen. Its warmth on my cheeks. A tender caress of life. I contemplated the vines, translucent in the dawn, the luminous clouds. A strange desire overcame me. Under the quivering red light, my body warmed. The blood flooded back into my chest. My heart pounded with nostalgia and anxiety, as if it would soon stop beating forever. Suddenly I felt it, how much I wanted life. I didn't know what would happen to me, but I wanted to live.

I pulled myself up, felt my strength rushing back. To live, to still be alive. I raised myself. My head hit the top of the dead man's skull in a flash of pain. *Oh, brother, your skull is so hard!* I winced and gathered my belongings. The dead man's diary fell open on the ground. I deciphered a few halting words: 'Mother.' And the same cry howled through me. The whole valley seemed to sway and pitch, the echo of it reverberating toward the horizon. The sun was drowned out behind a curtain of fog and tears. 'Mother, I'm dying. I'm never coming back. There will be no-one to repair the thatch roof.'

I scanned the tortured lines in the dead man's diary. Here we were, the skeleton and I. Two single young men. In our hearts, we both worshipped the same female image, the only woman we had ever known: Mother. We had remained children.

I saw my mother's smile, her long, flowing hair. A memory of a familiar mixture of perfume and sweat overwhelmed me. I slipped the diary in among the clothes and rolled the bamboo flute up in a handkerchief. Gently, I placed it in my own knapsack. I tied the dead man's sack on to mine with a nylon string. The machine-gun and the cartridges shone on the plastic sheet. I took them, too.

Who was the bastard who invented this thing? I thought to myself. The machine gun was as heavy as the granite mortars we used to pound food. They said it only weighed 15 pounds, but it felt like a hundred. And that wasn't counting the ammunition. I would never make it, not even by sucking ginseng root for strength.

I hurled the machine gun into the bushes to my right and kicked the cartridge boxes aside to the left. In a few months, the colocassias would swallow them all. A new forest of flowers would bloom over the decomposing remains, suckled on blood and rotting flesh. They would cover the earth again with their pale, icy blooms, echoing the wind of death through the valley.

Good-bye, brother.

I gazed at the glistening skeleton in the hammock, its straight, flawless teeth. The skull no longer grinned at me; it looked almost tearful.

Resign yourself. That's life; in the end, we will all be separated. I'll bring your belongings to your mother. If by some misfortune she has left us, I'll visit her tomb, light incense, and read your diary to her from beginning to end. I won't skip a word. At least her soul will taste this sweetness, this solace. We sons are good for nothing. We make them suffer in this life and then console their ghosts.

I put my cap back on and left. I walked well into the afternoon. When I left the valley, I stumbled into a vast region of rolling hills covered with brambles and camphor trees. The wind from Laos blew here, dry, searing, sucking the body of all sweat and saliva. There wasn't a drop of water, not a grain of rice. I walked on, staggering through low drifts of clouds. I lost count of the hills I climbed. As the sun dipped behind a crest of hills, I could just make out the 'A' shape of a bunker. I didn't even have the strength left to shout out. I ran toward its mouth and collapsed there. ❑

© *Duong Thu Huong, excerpted from* Novel Without a Name, *William Morrow, 1995*
© *Translation Phan Huy Duong and Nina McPherson 1995*

HAROLDO CONTI

The art of hunting with dogs

H E LIFTED the
metal sheet
carefully and slipped
his head in through
the opening.

At first he only saw
the grimy haze of the
window wavering in the
vague distance, but after a moment the tiny holes in the sheet started to
glitter. There were at least a million of them, and they seemed full of
life. There was no reason for him to compare this with anything else,
but he felt as if he had stuck his head into the middle of the night. As a
kid, he'd sometimes stand in the vacant lot crowded with shadows, his
back to the booth, and stare at the multitudes of stars above, until they'd
start to jump from one side of the sky to the other, and make him afraid.

The holes trembled or changed position every time he moved his
head. In the meantime, the odour of damp and urine was seeping all the
way into his brain.

He stuck his head outside and gulped down a mouthful of air.

The car had been left behind the last hump of dirt. It was a
cardboard-coloured dirt, hard and bald. Between the car and the shed —
that is to say, between the shed and the street — there were a number of
these humps sprouting in the midst of the empty cans, the rotten tyres
and the tin clippings from the utilities factory he could see emerging on
the left. On the right was the pit dug up during the war to draw out the
clay with which they made the drainpipes instead of cement. Its walls
were covered with weeds and its bottom with water, and in summer it

was full of bare-assed kids running back and forth.

Sometimes he'd come and sit on one of the humps and, while smoking a cigarette, take it all in. It was different then, of course, as if he had been living at the beginning of things. Then time became slow and sluggish, and it seemed to him he could hear his mother calling at the top of her voice, while he lay at the bottom of the pit, dry mud all over his skin, sucking on a cigarette, three puffs at a time, with Beto and Fatso and Tiny Andy who got hit by a 403 while he was crossing the street, precisely for obeying his mother's call to come home.

Maldonado signalled to him from the car and he shook his hand in annoyance. Then he slipped his head again through the opening and called out in a low voice, aiming his words towards the left-hand corner.

'Pichón!'

His voice stretched across the shed and vanished somewhere above him.

'Pichón, are you there? It's me, Rivera.'

He waited a while and even though he could only hear the creaks and rumblings of the sheets, he felt that the man was there.

Then he lifted the sheet entirely and slid in the rest of his body.

He advanced gropingly to the middle of the shed, the holes rising and falling with every step. The light in the window, on the other hand, remained motionless and if he stared at it too steadily it seemed like nothing more than a glimmer in mid-air.

He turned round in the darkness and the holes all turned at the same time. The stench covered him from head to foot and the sound of the sheets was like that of an invisible crackling fire, or a large clockwork contraption grinding away slowly and delicately.

The man was in one of the corners of that darkness. He could feel him. He could feel the crouching shape of the man's body and the acid odour of the man's fear. He had a keen nose for these things.

'Pichón... It's me, Rivera. Don't be afraid.'

Maldonado was no good at this. All the damned promotions he'd had didn't help. He'd become nervous and spoil everything. Also, in these cases, Maldonado gave off a special odour. His nostrils would start to quiver, he'd tense up and then he'd reek in that particular way.

He stopped thinking about Maldonado because the indian features of Maldonado's face hanging in mid-air made him lose his grip on things. He turned again and halfway through the turn he knew exactly where the man was hiding.

He took a few steps closer without squinting, allowing himself to be led by nothing but his skin.

Now he had the man right in front of him.

He pulled out his box of matches and shook it. Then he heard Pichón's voice coming from below.

'Please, don't light it!'

'Don't be afraid. No-one's there.'

He lit one of the matches. All of a sudden the holes vanished.

When the sparks burst he managed to see the metal sheets that made up the wall. Then the yellowish circle shrunk.

The man was lying on a shipping crate, his hair dishevelled and his face distorted. He was aiming at the match with a 9mm Browning with an inlaid wooden French handle. No doubt, Maldonado would have his eyes on it. He was a greedy bastard and things like that showed he had a cheap bastard's soul.

The match faltered, but before throwing it away he lifted a broken candle and managed to light it.

'How are you doing?'

'How do you think?'

From under the jacket the man drew out a handkerchief soaked in blood. Sweat ran down the man's face in streams as if he had a fever. The man lowered the Browning, closed his eyes and seemed on the point of fainting.

'They won't be long,' the man said almost sobbing.

'Don't go so fast.'

The man opened his eyes and tried to look at him through the glare of the candle. The man's pupils dilated silently and a vortex of yellow stripes pointed towards him. The man's head was so buried in his fear that he needed to make a real effort to see anything else. The man frowned and lay there thinking.

He knew all about that. He had been able to notice it all several times, calmly and without passion which is how things are learned. First

the fear, bloating their veins and taking their breath away. Then despair. Finally cold abandonment. Then there's nothing left to do except grab them by the hair and fire.

'How did you get here?', the man asked in the end, without changing his expression.

'I jumped from the truck and ran as fast as I could.'

The man's face lit up a little.

'Did any of the others make it?'

'Viera. At least, I know he got away.'

That was true. Viera had jumped behind Pichón but after a short run they'd shot him down.

The man closed his eyes and lost courage again.

'Can't you see it's all over for us?', the man moaned quietly.

'Not so fast. Does it hurt?'

'Of course.'

'Let me see.'

'What's the use?'

The man pulled out the handkerchief and stared at it stupidly, not understanding.

'It looked as if all would be different... What happened?'

'Someone betrayed us,' he said simply.

'Who do you think?'

'I don't know, but that's the odds.'

The man wasn't getting it. The man wanted to think hard but he wasn't getting it.

A sheet creaked and the man's whole body contracted.

He didn't say a word, deliberately. He stood there staring at him.

The man looked almost pitiful. He had almost grown fond of the man, or at least grown accustomed to him in all these months during which they'd prepared the affair. Maldonado or any of the others were dirt compared to this man. But that was the danger: growing fond of men like this one. Inside they were different. It wasn't their outer appearance, it was the rotten ideas inside their head that mattered. Never should one lose sight of the inner man, so to speak — that dark and scaly shape they hid under the skin. Maldonado was as much a son of a bitch as he'd choose to be on the right occasions — and even sometimes when he didn't choose. And he and Maldonado were made of the same hard wood. Maldonado had an oily way of talking, and all the mannered gestures of upstart peasant, but deep inside Maldonado functioned much like he did. Much the same as with Fatso or Tiny Andy whose eyes would cross when they thought too hard. But they were all made of the same hard wood.

'It's the metal sheets.' He stretched out a hand and patted the man. 'Just the sheets, don't be afraid.'

The contact of his hand seemed to bring the man back to life.

'Rivera, you think we'll make it through this one?'

'Of course.'

'You sure?'

The man was going to go to pieces again, so he touched him once more with his hand.

'You want to smoke?'

He gave him a cigarette which the man grabbed avidly, almost breaking it between his fingers.

'Of course we'll make it,' he said, bringing the candle up close, just to say something.

'We can't beat them.'

'That's not true.'

'Once they peg you, you can't beat them.'

There was a hole larger than the others just above the man's head. He moved barely two inches and it disappeared.

'I'll finish the cigarette and I'm gone.'

Pichón cowered again. He opened his eyes wide and swallowed.

'Wouldn't it be better if you stayed?'

The cigarette hung in front of the man's face, held by a thin white hand that trembled slightly.

'I've got to go if I'm to get you out of here.'

He moved and the hole reappeared.

'Don't get all nervous, that won't help.'

Maldonado would be asking himself what was going on in there. Maldonado had no class, that's all there was to it. No style.

'I'll put out the candle.'

He stretched out his hand and before putting it out, he fixed his eyes on the man. He was just on the point...

He put it out.

He finished the cigarette in the dark.

'Better?'

'Yes.'

It was curious to see how the spark glowed large with each puff and then softly grew dim again. Just like the man's pupils.

He crushed the cigarette on the floor and moved away a few steps.

'Pichón...'

'Don't be long.'

He walked towards the opening amidst the dance of the holes of light. Before stepping out he turned and stared into the darkness. That's where the man was, no doubt, eyes wide open and the Browning clutched to his chest.

He lowered his head and walked out.

For a moment, the light blinded him. Then the humps of dirt appeared, the cans and the tyres.

The others were waiting by the car, squirming inside their uniforms. Sweat was pouring down from under their caps. Maldonado waved an arm impatiently.

He passed by the pit and remembered once again Fatso and Tiny Andy, and he even thought he could see them lying at the bottom, belly up to the sun.

Maldonado's head shone as if it were made out of tin. After all, he was someone you could laugh at.

'What kept you?'

Maldonado's nostrils were trembling and he was starting to give off that particular odour.

'What's the hurry?'

Maldonado stretched his neck and straightened his tie, the sort of thing a cheap bastard would do.

'So, what's happening?'

'He's in there.'

Maldonado clicked his fingers and the others started walking towards the shed. Then, with a quick movement, he loaded the first bullet in the chamber and followed them at a trot. ❏

© *Haroldo Conti*
© *Translation Alberto Manguel 1996*

GRAHAM GREENE

The last word

THE OLD man was only a little surprised, because he was by now well accustomed to inexplicable events, when he received at the hands of a stranger a passport in a name which was not his own, a visa and an exit permit for a country which he had never expected or even desired to visit. He was indeed very old, and he was accustomed to the narrow life he had led alone without human contacts: he had even found a kind of happiness in deprivation. He had a single room to live and sleep in: a small kitchen and a bathroom. Once a month there came a small but sufficient pension which arrived from Somewhere, but he didn't know where. Perhaps it was connected with the accident years before which had robbed him of his memory. All that had remained in his mind of that occasion was a sharp noise, a flash like lightning and then a long darkness full of confusing dreams from which he finally woke in the same small room he lived in now.

'You will be fetched at the airport on the 25th,' the stranger told him, 'and be taken to your plane. At the other end you will be met and a room is ready for you. It would be best for you if you spoke to no-one on the plane.'

The 25th? This is December, isn't it?' He found it difficult to keep account of time.

'Of course.'

'Then it will be Christmas Day.'

'Christmas Day was abolished more than 20 years ago. After your accident.'

He was left wondering — how does one abolish a day? When the man left he looked up, half expecting an answer, to a small wooden crucifix which hung over his bed. One arm of the cross and with it one arm of the figure had been broken off — he had found it two years before — or was it three? — in the dustbin which he shared with his neighbours who never spoke to him. He said aloud, 'And you? Have they abolished you?'

The missing arm seemed to give him the answer, 'Yes.' There was in a way a communication between them as though they shared a memory between them.

With his neighbours there was no communication. Since he had returned to life in this room he had not spoken to one of them, for he could feel that they were afraid to speak to him. It was as if they knew something about him which he didn't know himself. Perhaps a crime committed before the darkness fell. There was always a man in the street who could not be regarded as a neighbour, for he was changed every other day, and he too spoke to no-one at all, not even to the old lady on the top floor who was inclined to gossip. Once in the street she had used the name — not the name on the passport — with a sideways look which took in both of them — the old man and the watcher. It was a common enough name, John.

Once, perhaps because the day was warm and bright after weeks of rain, the old man had ventured a remark to the man in the street as he went to fetch the bread, 'God bless you, my dear fellow,' and the man winced as though struck by sudden pain and turned his back. The old man went on to fetch his bread which was his staple food and he had long been aware that he was followed to the shop. The whole atmosphere was a bit mysterious, but he was not deeply disturbed. Once he remarked to his only audience, the damaged wooden figure, 'I think they want to leave you and me alone.' He was quite content, as though somewhere in that dark forgotten past he had suffered an immense burden from which he was now free.

The day which he still thought of as Christmas arrived and so did the stranger — 'To take you to the airport. Have you finished packing?'

'I haven't much to pack and I have no case.'

'I will fetch one,' and so he did. When he was gone the old man wrapped the wooden figure in his only spare jacket which he put in the case as soon as it was brought and covered it with two shirts and some underclothes.

'Is that all you have?'

'At my age one needs very little.'

'What are you carrying in your pocket?'

'Only a book.'

'Let me see it.'

'Why?'

'I have my orders.'

He snatched it from the old man's hand and looked at the title page.

'You have no right to this. How did it come into your possession?'

'I have had it since childhood.'

'They should have seized it in the hospital. I will have to report this.'

'No-one is to blame. I kept it hidden.'

'You were brought in unconscious. You weren't capable of hiding.'

'I expect they were too busy saving my life.'

'I call it criminal carelessness.'

'I think I remember someone did ask me what it was. I told them the truth — a book of ancient history.'

'Forbidden history. This will go to the incinerator.'

'It's not so important,' the old man said. 'Read a little of it first. You will see.'

'I shall do no such thing. I am loyal to the General.'

'Oh, you are right of course. Loyalty is a great virtue. But don't worry. I haven't read much of it for some years. My favourite passages are here in my head, and you can't incinerate my head.'

'Don't be too sure of that,' the man replied. They were his last words before they reached the airport, and there everything strangely changed.

A N OFFICER in uniform greeted the old man with such great courtesy that he felt as though he were returning to a very distant past. The officer even gave him a military salute. He said, 'The General asked me to wish you a comfortable journey.'

'Where are you taking me?'

The officer made no reply to his question, but asked the civilian guard, 'Is this all his luggage?'

'All, but I took away this book.'

'Let me see it.' The officer turned to the title page. 'Of course,' he said, 'you were doing your duty, but all the same give it him back. These are special circumstances. He is the guest of the General, and anyway there's no danger in a book like this now.'

'The law...'

'Even laws can become out of date.'

The old man repeated his question in another form. 'What line am I travelling on?'

'You too, sir, are a little out of date. There is only one line now —
The World United.'

'Oh dear, oh dear, what changes there have been.'

'Don't worry, sir, the time of change is over. The world is settled and
at peace. No need for change.'

'Where are you taking me?'

'Only to another province. A mere four hours flight. In the General's
own plane.'

It was an extraordinary plane. There was what one might call a sitting
room with ample armchairs, sufficient for only six people, so that they
could be transformed into beds: through an open door as they passed he
could see a bath — he hadn't seen a bath for years (his small studio had
only a shower) and he felt a strong desire to spend the hours that
followed stretched out in the warm water. A bar separated the chairs
from the cockpit, and an almost cringing steward offered him a choice
from what appeared to be the drinks of all nations, if one could speak of
all nations in this United World. Even his poor clothes did not seem to
diminish the steward's respect. Presumably he cringed to any guest of the
General however unsuitable he might think one to be.

The officer took his seat at some distance as though he wished to
leave him discreetly at peace with his forbidden book, but what he felt
was a deeper desire for the peace and the silence. He was tired out by
the mystery of things: the mystery of the small studio which he had left,
of the tension coming from God knew where, this luxury plane and
above all of the bath... His mind, as it so often did, went in pursuit of
his memory, which stopped abruptly at this startling crack of sound and
the darkness which followed it...how many years ago? It was as if he had
been living under a total anaesthetic which was only now beginning to
wear thin. Suddenly he was frightened in this great private plane of what
memories might await him if he woke. He began to read his book; it
opened automatically from long use at a passage he knew by heart: 'He
was in the world and the world was made by him and the world knew
him not.'

The steward's voice sounded in his ear, 'A little caviare, sir, or a glass
of vodka, or would you prefer a glass of dry white wine?'

Without looking up from the familiar page he said, 'No, no thank
you. I am not hungry or thirsty.'

The clink of the glass the steward removed brought back a memory. His hand of its own accord tried to lay down something on the table before him, and for a moment in front of him he saw a host of strangers with bowed heads, there was a deep silence and then came that startling crack and the darkness which followed...

The steward's voice woke him. 'Your safety belt, sir. We shall be arriving in five minutes.'

A NOTHER officer awaited him at the bottom of the steps and led him towards a large car. The ceremony, the courtesy, the luxury stirred the hidden memories. He felt no surprise now; it was as though he had experienced all this many years before: he gave mechanically a deprecating movement to the hand and a phrase slipped from his mouth, 'I am a servant of the servants' and remained unfinished as the door slammed.

They drove through the streets which were empty except for a few queues outside certain stores. He began to say again, 'I am a servant.' Outside the hotel the manager was awaiting them. He bowed and told the old man, 'I am proud to receive a personal guest of the General. I hope you will have every comfort during your short stay here. You have

only to ask...'

The old man looked up with astonishment at the 14 floors. He asked, 'For how long are you keeping me here?'

'You are booked, sir, for one night.'

The officer broke hastily in, 'So that you may see the General tomorrow. He wants you to have a good rest tonight after your journey.'

The old man searched his memory and a name came back. It was as though memory were returning to him in broken pieces. 'General Megrim?'

'No, no. General Megrim died nearly 20 years ago.'

A uniformed doorkeeper saluted him as they entered the hotel. The concierge was ready with the keys. The officer said, 'I will leave you here, sir, and tomorrow morning I will come to fetch you at 11. The General will see you at 11.30.'

The manager accompanied him to the lift.

After they had both gone safely away the concierge turned to the officer. 'Who is this gentleman? The guest of the General? He looks a very poor man from his clothes.'

'He's the Pope.'

'The Pope? What's the Pope?' the concierge asked, but the officer left the hotel without making any reply.

WHEN the manager left him the old man was aware of how tired he was, but all the same he examined his surroundings with astonishment. He even felt the deep succulent mattress of the great double bed. He opened the door of the bathroom and saw an array of little bottles. The only thing he bothered to unpack was the wooden statuette he had so carefully hidden. He propped it up against the mirror on the dressing table. He threw his clothes on a chair and then as though obeying an order lay down on the bed. If he had understood anything of what was happening, perhaps he would have found it impossible to sleep, but understanding nothing he was able to sink down on the deep mattress, where sleep came immediately, and with it a dream, parts of which he remembered on waking.

He had been talking — he saw it all clearly — in some sort of immense barn to an audience of not more than a few dozen people. On one wall hung a mutilated wooden cross and a figure without an arm, like the one hidden in his case. He couldn't remember what he had been saying, for the words were in a language — or several languages — which he didn't know or couldn't remember. The barn slowly decreased in size until it was no larger than the little studio which he had left, and in front of him knelt one old woman with a small girl beside her. *She* did not kneel, but looked at him with a look of contempt which seemed to express a thought as clearly as if she had spoken aloud, 'I don't understand a word you're saying and why can't you speak properly?'

He woke to a terrible sense of failure and lay awake on his bed desperately trying to find a way back into the dream and utter some words which the child might understand. He even tried out a few of them at random. 'Pax,' he said aloud, but that would be as foreign a word to her as it had been to him. He tried another, 'Love'. It came more easily to his lips, but it seemed to him now too commonplace a word with its contradictory meaning. He found that he didn't really know what it meant himself. It was something he was not sure he had ever experienced. Perhaps — before the strange crack and the darkness which followed — he might have had a hint, but surely if love had any real importance a small memory of it would have survived.

His uneasy thoughts were interrupted by the entrance of a waiter who brought him a tray with coffee and a variety of breads and croissants he had never seen at the small bakery which served him with the only meals he took.

'The colonel asked me to remind you, sir, that he will be here at 11 to take you to the General and that your clothes for the occasion are in the wardrobe. In case you forgot to pack them in your rather hurried departure you will find razor and brushes and all that is required in the bathroom.'

'My clothes are on the chair,' he told the waiter and he added a friendly joke, 'I didn't come here quite naked.'

'I have been told to take them away. All you require is there,' and he pointed at the wardrobe.

The old man looked at his jacket and trousers, his shirt, socks, and not for the first time, as the waiter picked them gingerly up, the thought came to him that they were indeed in need of a wash. He had seen no reason in all the last years to waste a little of his small pension at the cleaners when the only people who saw him regularly were the baker, the men sent to watch him and occasionally a neighbour who would avoid looking in his direction and even cross the street to avoid him.

Clean clothes might be a social need for others, but he had no social life.

The waiter left him and he stood in his underpants brooding on the mystery of things. Then there was a knock on the door and the officer who had brought him entered.

'But you're not dressed yet, and you've eaten nothing. The General expects us to be on time.'

'The waiter has taken my clothes.'

'Your clothes are in the wardrobe.' He flung the door open and the old man saw a white surplice and a white cape hanging there. He said, 'Why? What are you asking? I have no right...'

'The General wishes to do you honour. He will be in full dress uniform himself. There is even a guard of honour waiting for you. You must wear your uniform too.'

'My uniform?'

'Be quick and shave. There will almost certainly be photographs for the world's press. The United World Press.'

He obeyed and in his confusion cut himself in several places. Then unwillingly he put on his white robe and the cape. There was a long mirror on the wardrobe door and he exclaimed with horror: 'I look like a priest.'

'You were a priest. These robes have been lent by the World Museum of Man for the occasion. Hold out your hand.'

He obeyed. Authority had spoken. The officer slipped a ring on one of his fingers. 'The Museum', he said, 'was reluctant to lend us the ring, but the General insisted. This is an occasion which will never be repeated. Follow me please.' As they were about to leave the wooden object on the dressing table caught his eye. He said, 'They should never have allowed you to bring that with you.'

The old man had no wish to bring trouble to anyone. 'I hid it carefully,' he said.

'Never mind. I dare say the Museum will be glad to have it.'

'I want to keep it.'

'I don't think you will need it after you have seen the General.'

THEY drove through many strange, empty streets before they reached a wide square. In front of what might once have been a palace a line of soldiers was drawn up and there the car stopped. The officer told him, 'We descend here. Don't be alarmed. The General wants to show you proper military honours as a former head of state.'

'Head of state? I don't understand.'

'Please. After you.'

The old man would have tripped on the robe if the officer had not grasped his arm. As he straightened there was a crack of sound and he nearly fell again. It was as though that sharp crack which he had heard once, before the long danger had wrapped him in its folds, was now multiplied a dozen times. The crash seemed to break his head in two and into that gap the memories of a lifetime began to seep in. He repeated, 'I don't understand.'

'In your honour.'

He looked down at his feet and saw the fold of the surplice. He looked at his hand and saw the ring. There was a clash of metal. The soldiers were presenting arms.

THE General greeted him with concern and came directly to the point. He said, 'I want you to understand that I was in no way responsible for the attempt to kill you. It was a grave mistake by one of my predecessors, a General Megrim. Grave mistakes are easily made in the later stages of a revolution. It has taken us a hundred years to establish the world state and world peace. In his way he was afraid of you and the few followers you still had.'

'Afraid of me?'

'Yes. You must realise that your Church has been responsible throughout history for many wars. At last we have abolished war.'

'But you are a General. I saw outside a number of soldiers.'

'They remain as the preservers of world peace. Perhaps in another hundred years they will cease to exist just as your Church has ceased to exist.'

'Has it ceased to exist? My memory failed me a long time ago.'

'You are the last living Christian,' the General said. 'You are an historic figure. For that reason I wanted to honour you at the end.'

The General took out a cigarette case and offered it. 'Will you smoke with me, Pope John. I'm sorry I forgot the number. Was it XXIX?'

'Pope? I'm sorry I don't smoke. Why do you call me Pope?'

'The last Pope but still a Pope.' The General lit a cigarette and continued. 'You must understand we have nothing at all against you personally. You occupied a great position. We shared many of the same ambitions. We had a great deal in common. That was one of the reasons why General Megrim considered you a dangerous enemy. You represented, as long as you had followers, an alternative choice. As long as there was an alternative choice there would always be war. I don't agree with the method which he took. To shoot you in such a clandestine way as you were saying — what do you call it?'

'My prayers?'

'No, no. It was a public ceremony already forbidden by law.'

The old man felt himself at a loss. 'The Mass?' he asked.

'Yes, yes, I think that was the word. The trouble with what he arranged was that it might have turned you into a martyr and delayed our programme not a little. It's true that there were only a dozen people at that — what do you call it? — Mass. But his method was risky. General Megrim's successor realised that, and I have followed the same quieter line. We have kept you alive. We have never allowed the press to make even an occasional reference to you, or to your quiet life in retirement.'

'I don't altogether understand. You must forgive me. I'm only beginning to remember. When your soldiers fired just now...'

'We preserved you because you were the last leader of those who still called themselves Christians. The others gave up without too much difficulty. What a strange pack of names — Jehovah's Witnesses,

last word

Lutherans, Calvinists, Anglicans. They all died away one by one with the years. Your lot called themselves Catholic as though they claimed to represent the whole bunch even while they fought them. Historically I suppose you were the first to organise yourselves and claim to follow that mythical Jewish carpenter.'

The old man said, 'I wonder how his arm got broken.'

'His arm?'

'I'm sorry. My mind was wandering.'

'We left what was left of you to the last because you still had a few followers and because we did have certain aims in common. World peace, the destruction of poverty. There was a period when we could use you. Use you to destroy the idea of national countries for the sake of a greater whole. You had ceased to be a real danger, which made General Megrim's action unnecessary or at any rate premature. Now we are satisfied that all this nonsense is finished, forgotten. You have no followers, Pope John. I have had you watched closely over the last 20 years. Not a single person has tried to contact you. You have no power and the world is one and at peace. You are no longer an enemy to be feared. I am sorry for you, for they must have been very long and tedious years in that lodging of yours. In a way a faith is like old age. It can't go on forever. Communism grew old and died, so did imperialism. Christianity is dead too except for you. I expect you were a good Pope as popes go, and I want to do you the honour of no longer keeping you in these dreary conditions.'

'You are kind. They were not so dreary as you think. I had a friend with me. I could talk to him.'

'What on earth do you mean? You were alone. Even when you went out of your door to buy bread you were alone.'

'He was waiting for me when I came back. I wish his arm had not been broken.'

'Oh, you are talking about that wooden image. The Museum of Myths will be glad to add it to its collection. But the time has come to talk of serious things, not of myths. You see this weapon I am putting on my desk. I don't believe in people being allowed to suffer unnecessarily. I respect you. I am not General Megrim. I want you to die with dignity. The last Christian. This is a moment of history.'

'You intend to kill me?'

'Yes.'

It was relief the old man felt, not fear. He said, 'You will be sending me where I've often wanted to go during the last 20 years.'

'Into darkness?'

'Oh, the darkness I have known was not death. Just an absence of light. I am grateful to you.'

'I had hoped you would take a last meal with me. As a kind of symbol. A symbol of friendship between two born to be enemies.'

'Forgive me, but I am not hungry. Let the execution go ahead.'

'At least, take a glass of wine with me, Pope John.'

'Thank you. I will take that.'

The General poured out two glasses. His hand shook a little as he drained his glass. The old man raised his as though in salute. He said in a low voice some words which the General could not properly catch, in a language which he did not understand. 'Corpus domini nostri...' As his last Christian enemy drank, he fired.

Between the pressure on the trigger and the bullet exploding a strange and frightening doubt crossed his mind: is it possible that what this man believed may be true? ❏

© *Graham Greene, reprinted from* The Last Word and Other Stories, *Heinemann, 1990*

EDWAR AL-KHARRAT

The accusation

'I don't know who I love
and I don't know his name
I don't know who it is
that I hold close to me' Ibn Arabi

I WOKE up on Sunday afternoon.
The final notes of a sad song seemed to linger on in my heart, sung
by an unknown voice under high Mamluke domes in a mosque's
spacious courtyard.

The lethargy of waking up from an afternoon sleep, the sweetness of
indolence...

My room was warm and all the windows were closed but I sensed the
summer wind off the sea stirring behind the the glass doors of the
balcony. The late afternoon light filtered through the wooden shutters
making me think of a distant sun.

Ambiguous feelings came to taunt me, then escaped me. Like my
thoughts they were sly and elusive, seductive images which slipped away
without warning. I focused all my attention on them in vain and lay
there staring vacantly, heavy-hearted and disturbed by a longing without
an object or a centre.

So here I was, aimless once again, bored and unproductive. Why this
dissatisfaction, this overwhelming uncertainty, this undefined anxiety? A
depression, but not serious, a feeling of unease with no obvious cause.
The shadows never deepened into real darkness, but never lifted either.

What should I tell myself? 'No, there's no way to stop feeling bowed
down by my troubles.'

Or should I not take myself so seriously? 'Come on! Come on! Death
is very sweet!'

Without moving from under the crumpled sheet which had wound itself tightly round me, I considered different ways of spending the late afternoon. I could go pigeon shooting at the Tiro in Silsila, or catch the last race at the Sporting Club, or maybe get drunk at the Atheneus. But I'd be on my own, unless I met Antoine somewhere, or Philippe Nakhla or Fattouh Qaffas. I could always go to Manshiya first and take Odette along to the six o'clock performance in the Fouad Cinema, and maybe Arlette too. They're showing a film called *Marie Chapdelaine*. People say it's good.

Then I said to myself, 'I could go and visit my cousin in the house next to Ladies Lane.'

Did she think I loved her? That exceedingly pale-skinned woman with soft, loose flesh, large breasts and thin legs, who liked to wear satin dresses without sleeves, revealing upper arms more reminiscent of thighs or joints of veal hanging in the butcher's shop. But I couldn't deny that she was amusing when she looked at me furtively, her small eyes downcast in ardent passion. I told myself that I ought to be ashamed, and respect a virgin's tender heart, not to mention her thighs, as I'd been brought up to do.

On second thoughts it might be better to go to the Crystal, and if Abd al-Qadir Nasrallah was there we could have a game of backgammon.

What should I do, where should I head for at the end of this never-ending day?

I had a sense of guilt which made me feel I wanted to go somewhere, anywhere, and at the same time prevented me moving, and I didn't know how to be free of it. Impatience, lack of resourcefulness, uncertainty and isolation, all combined to sap my strength. I found myself intoning a complaint in the words of my beloved poet Abu'l-Ala al-Ma'arri: 'I say farewell to my day, knowing that it will never return and that my life is a passing cloud, at the mercy of fate, and a gift to death.' Or something of the sort.

Odette was sitting on my right, with Arlette beside her, some distance away in the calm cave-like interior of the Fouad Cinema. The lamps on the blank, unadorned walls glowed faintly, their small, muted globes giving out a pale yellow light. Odette didn't stop me taking hold of her hand and placing it on my lap. I moved it gently down, bit by bit, bringing it to rest on the tension in my trousers. She touched it eagerly at first, then rested her hand gently beside it, then seized it excitedly and kept on and on until I had to move her discreetly off me to lessen the pressure a little, so that the explosive blaze died down to a steady, contained flame. In the translucent gloom I noticed Arlette's long, soft hair covering part of her pale face which floated in the flickering light and shadow.

When we came out of the cinema, we turned off behind Nabi Danyal Street through Attarin. Behind the elegant buildings and lighted shop windows in the summery streets, where a handful of pedestrians ambled peacefully, were the little streets of low, old houses which still gave an impression of strength and vigour, the legacy of the years. At street level — courteous, quiet and friendly as ever — were the bookbinders, cycle repair shops, panel-beaters, fast food stalls and grocers. Here was still the savour of hard work and public service and the honest camaraderie of decent poverty. People were ready to labour far into the night if the job demanded it and there was no cheating or cutting corners. A sense of pride persisted in the trade: the expertise acquired over many years, the traditional skills and the craftsmen's honour.

In a courtyard open to the sky and the road, where the bright streetlight shone harshly down on to the packed sand, a group of workers was having supper. The smell of the sea hit us suddenly by an old tree, whose huge, blackened trunk was partly lit up, leaving the other side in shadow, as if the tree had been sculpted into a new shape. The tree's thick lower branches had been pruned and jutted out like amputated limbs, while on the slender upper branches, stirring gently in the breeze, were distant crowns of fresh bright green leaves, shot through with shafts of light.

They were using sheets of *Al-Ahram* as a cloth — in those days the ink didn't run — and had placed large flat loaves of warm bread on it, whose rich smell whetted the appetite. On the ground were shallow tin plates filled to the brim with *ful* beans cooked with tomato puree and cumin and drowning in hot oil, and bunches of huge, whiskery radishes with broad dark leaves. They were eating with all the zest of people sharing a meal in good company. Unhesitatingly, they asked us to join them, their voices switching between solemnity and banter, conventional politeness and spontaneous generosity: 'Please join us! Please! By the Prophet, by the life of Sidi Abu'l-Abbas al-Mursi. You and the young ladies, sir. It's not much, but please...this is a serious invitation. We're not just being polite. Sweets for the sweet!'

I answered half-smiling, half-serious, 'No thank you, gentlemen. *Bon appetit*, my brothers. Good luck to you!'

We came out on Khedewi Street and took the clanking, rattling, shaking tram to Manshiya as if we were off on an excursion.

The army had erected their little tents in the garden in the middle of the square, right in front of the statue of Saad Zaghloul. A few soldiers were lined up in their round helmets with flattened edges, their baggy shorts to the knee and dull yellow puttees. Nearby an artillery battery was positioned, the cannon aimed out to sea, the English-made Ford truck loaded with soldiers who were plainly tired and bored. The young officer sitting on a wicker chair in the garden looked at us indifferently.

On the same day, the 24th of July, the newspaper *Al-Basir* published the following report: 'A woman living in Ladies Lane was treated for severe burns in the government hospital after she had been set on fire. The lawyer in charge of the investigation has been named as Mr Ismail Fahmy Farag. The woman has accused a neighbour and her two young daughters, O. and A., of conspiring with her cousin, a university employee, to start the fire. However the investigation has sought to establish that the victim had a relationship with the accused, her cousin, and had seen him frequenting her neighbour's house and accompanying her two daughters to expensive cinemas on a number of occasions, and believed that he was intending to marry one of the daughters. She therefore set herself on fire in a fit of jealousy, and to take her revenge on the two girls and their mother. The enquiry continues.'

On the same day thieves broke into the Singer factory in the town of Shirbin and made off with the entire contents of the building situated opposite the main police station. Persian rugs were on sale in Nahman stores starting at five Egyptian pounds, large china dinner plates in Ghandour stores for 11 piastres; 75 piastres for summer pyjamas with cord edging; 28 for jersey swimming costumes and 30 for a long-sleeved tricolene shirt. That night the comedy of manners *Safe Journey*, directed by Ibrahim Lama, was showing in the Gozy Cinema in Cairo, and I didn't go to see Walter Pidgeon and Ann Harding in the Nick Carter film at the Metro in Alexandria.

As night fell the usual misgivings came to trouble me again and I listened to the swish of car wheels on asphalt in the silence of the street, straining to hear whether they kept going or whether they stopped at the door. I said to myself, 'There's the big car coming for me.' I thought I heard the muffled squeal of brakes. I waited for the sound of heavy shoes crunching up the stairs. But they didn't come. Nothing.

I had begun to breathe faster — I only realise these things now — and my fears were suffocating me, pressing down on me. I felt completely helpless, my spirit paralysed, my resolve gone, and I was almost resigned to accepting whatever happened to me.

I had a pair of pyjamas ready, two clean shirts, two changes of underwear, shaving gear, a little mirror and a tablet of Lux soap, slippers, toothpaste and toothbrush, and then I threw in a book of English poetry, just in case. I didn't think they would object to English poetry. I packed the things in a small overnight bag and left it ready, open to add last-minute items. If they came, when they came, at least I'd be prepared.

I said to myself, 'Aren't the days of underground revolutionary activity over, the constant fear of arrest and imprisonment things of the past?'

Then: 'Who knows? The old files are still there. All they have to do is consult them.

'This business with my cousin. Who would have thought she'd set fire to herself?

'But even if she did, they don't come in the middle of the night for that type of thing. They notify you officially and give you an appointment, in broad daylight... Who knows? Who knows what could happen with them?'

Suddenly I heard the feet. Mounting the stairs, slowly and determinedly. There weren't many of them. I must have missed the noise of the car. I listened, without emotion. I didn't feel any fear now, just anticipation.

The feet kept climbing. They passed my door and the sound slowly faded. 'Who can that be? It's after two in the morning. The people upstairs, of course. Coming back from an evening out, or working late. What's odd about that?'

Then I said to myself, 'Why don't they go right to the limit with their violence? Show their victims no mercy? There doesn't seem to be a perfect machinery of repression here, like elsewhere. Are we different? Here they go so far, then stop. Except for prisons and camps like Abu Zaabal, Mahariq and the Oases where they often show no such restraint, it seems. But perhaps these are exceptions to the rule. The rule says that some instinct learnt in childhood prevents them from going all the way. Or could it be an unexpected surge of brotherly compassion, a twinge of unacknowledged shame in the depths of souls troubled by the ferocity of the orders they have received?

'I know that when a wheel starts to turn, the movement of the cogs has to carry on till the process is completed, according to its own law. But with us, something disrupts this perfect mechanism halfway through. An old policeman, in exchange for a couple of coins and more especially a few pleasant words, the same man who was beating you as hard as he could the day before, will take a message to your wife — "to the family", as you put it — or make a phone call for you and tell you what the answer is.

'It's true, there's still something countrified about us.

'With you — yes, you, since you've entered the system — the chain of power and dominance has reached its final link: either this old policeman, or sometimes the most vicious beast alive who beats you mindlessly for hours on end, but then suddenly stops, brought up short by some obscure barrier.

'Who knows? It could be that I no longer have firm convictions, that I don't believe in anything now. God help me!'

Again I listened to the sound of the cars going by in the street, trying to guess the make or size of the vehicle, the purpose of its journey, how fast it was going, until I fell asleep.

When I discovered that I was awake again, I breathed deeply, acknowledging the new day, as if to say that in daylight nothing would happen.

I said, 'Is there really a kind of complicity between victim and torturer, whatever the type of violence? Whether it's delivered through words, blows, physical or psychological torture, sex or even indirect manoeuvring. As if there's a comradeship between the beast and its prey, a shared involvement, a kind of love affair, turned on its head maybe, but definitely there.

'Can you, who have been abused with or without your consent, make your abusers, your oppressors, your killers into your lovers?

'Something in your spirit — or in your land — makes you above oppression, lust, death. Even above the meaning of love and the essence of justice. What is that eternal, undying element in you which is incorporeal and at the same time is there in your brown, red, pure body, your soft earth, your coarse sand, your running waters, and the traces left by your violator-lovers?

'You, never deviating, invulnerable, we love you as you are, as you embrace your river which, with the sperm it constantly pours into you, fertile and destructive at once, sets you back on your feet, restores you and revives you time and time again, despite all efforts to tame and restrain it.'

I was now passing through some kind of tunnel hewn out of the soft rock of Dikhaila, a little way underground. Light filtered in through distant openings and I smelt the fresh breeze which seemed to come from an enormous air-conditioner, invisible and silent.

I descended over the rough uneven surfaces of the rocks. Sometimes I had to climb a little and would have been in constant danger of slipping if my feet — inside my shoes — hadn't found cracks in which to anchor themselves.

I often had to step aside to avoid the bodies of slaughtered beasts. I could make out enormous camels, spindly goats, calves flayed white. I tried to think who they reminded me of, without success. They were branded with circular or hexagonal marks, the red dye from them running into the sheath of bleached, slightly shiny gristle.

As I went further underground I felt that I was secure for the moment.

It was as if the Bedouin women whom I left at the entrance to this cave-tunnel, this natural cellar cut in the grey stone, were still there waiting for me. They had broad red girdles wrapped around their stomachs, over black gallabiyyas lovingly emboidered and adorned with gold pieces which jangled and glittered on full, firm-looking breasts. They wore rings with serrated edges through their noses and their brown lips were tattooed with a dark blue line straight down the middle. I said to myself, 'What would it be like to kiss them? I'll never know.' Although now I do.

The body was lying in front of me, now covered up.

I remembered having seen the plump, pale face, charred and burnt, the eyes looking blindly at me with an unanswered accusation. Long thin strips of dead blackened skin hung off her naked back, revealing raw pinkish flesh, from which oozed white threads of pus.

'Did I do this?' I asked.

She was covered up now. And I was indifferent. I felt nothing.

The police lieutenant, elegant in his black uniform with a gold star on his shoulder, wrote up the report showing little concern. Routine questions and answers, blanks filled in, and the time and date to round it off. 'Do you have anything else to say?' Then the whole thing was over.

Was it really over?

Are things ever really resolved?

The boy, alone under the tree, was eating light brown balls of falafel off the newspaper and a loaf with a blistered dry crust, breaking off one scorched chunk after another. For the first time I saw the fine green slender shoots growing right near the ground, below the sawn-off stumps. Were these outbursts of new life strong enough to survive? Would they be crushed by hurrying feet? The wind blew in from the sea, smelling of iodine, while cars passed by the courtyard, beyond Attarin, and the bells jingled softly on the horse-drawn carriages.

All this because of the old love which was still powerful, and impossible to satisfy.

I said to myself, 'It's no use. Should I go back to Dikhaila? Are the frontier regiment's camels still dipping their long liquid necks to drink from the limestone troughs?'

The mannequin in the shop window in Fouad Street was naked, her joints obvious narrow cracks at the shoulders, the knees, the waist, the meeting of the thighs and also at the wrists, as she raised her hands in a wooden gesture of seduction with a fixed stare. Her dry blonde hair was dead and dull. The mound of her slit was flat, closed and totally sterile.

She was screaming. A piercing, continuous scream issuing from an indescribable pain. Nobody was taking any notice.

My love was enduring and everlasting.

The policemen in black came looking for me, rifles aimed at me, fixed bayonets naked and sharp-edged. They advanced towards me resolutely, their heads bowed.

The bayonet pierced me, burning, but not causing the slightest pain.

The stones in my heart refused to break.

The accusation still stands. ❏

© *Edwar Al-Kharrat 1996*
© *Translation Catherine Cobham 1996*

KEN SARO-WIWA

The new beggars

THE TIMES had made beggars of men. You met
the regular ones in the usual places — at
street corners or in the snarled traffic — with
begging bowls in their shrivelled hands. The
other variety turned up in offices or at airport
lounges, good-looking, well-dressed, a tale of
woe on their lips, a prayer for help in their eyes
and empty pockets bulging with hope. I often thought how some of
these latter would have made successful short-story writers, if only they
knew how to reduce the children of their imagination to the printed
page. They had to be para-psychologists to identify a likely donor and
they knew that unfailing element of a good story — surprise — which
knocked you off your feet and sent your soft heart to your purse. I know
that well enough, being something of an artist myself.

I had arrived at the airport early that morning to find that my flight
had been delayed. I had planned a day trip. I thought what the delay
would mean to my business associates waiting at the other end of my
journey. The departure lounge at the airport was chock-a-block, the din
of human chatter threatening to snuff out the crackle of the hidden
loudspeakers with their wailing music. Men and women walked past me
and flopped into the hard, steel seats ranged in rows in the wide hall.
Hawkers sang their wares between the rows of seats. Shoe-shine boys
offered their services and a man clicking a pair of scissors offered
everyone a manicure.

So lost in thought was I, I did not know when he sat opposite me. It
was his cough, or his hint of a cough which drew me out of my
thoughts and brought him to my attention.

'I am Mr Landa,' he said familiarly, extending me his right hand. I
took it involuntarily. I noticed the parcel in his left hand, placed on his
knee. He coughed again, this time, much longer.

'Forgive me,' he said. 'I have been suffering from chest pain for over 15 years.'

'You ought to see a doctor,' I sympathised with him.

'I have. Dozens of them. I've been in and out of all the hospitals you can think of.'

I thought of two or three. Not too many, I felt.

'The funny thing is, all the sophisticated equipment available found nothing in my chest.'

'Then you're probably not ill.' He might be a hypochondriac, I thought to myself.

'I was advised to see a Chinese acupuncturist. I did. All those needles in my chest and arms did not cure me. So, in the end, I had to go to a traditional healer.'

'And that didn't cure you either?'

'Do you really want to know what happened?' He coughed and then chuckled gently.

I have to admit that I became curious. The delayed flight went into the recesses of my mind. I looked at him steadily. Mr Landa was a short, chubby man. The hair stood in black spirals on his head, his beard had a touch of grey and his eyes were small, sunken into his chubby face. His shirt collar was dirty, caked with the sweat of a week or thereabouts and the shirt itself was rumpled.

'You see, I have met over 90 traditional healers in the past 10 years. The most interesting one of them came from across the border. He was a very famous man, a Kotonkoli man from Togo Republic. Fagamundoli was his name. The day I and my mother travelled to his village, they would not let us in for 24 hours.'

'Why not?'

'We were told we couldn't see him or talk to him until he had drunk himself silly.'

'Why not?'

'Because his magical powers did not ever work while he was sober. And so we camped outside the village, my distressed mother and I, all that night. The next morning, nothing happened. It was not until late the next day that we were led to his presence. Fagamundoli was seated in a chair, drinking a local beer while drummers pounded away on huge drums behind him. He belched loudly in my face as I sat, by his instruction, opposite him. After telling him the object of my mission, he

touched my head with a cow's tail and pointed another cow's tail at my painful chest. Then he belched again. "Young man," said he, "there is a sorcerer in your village who has bewitched you," he intoned. I had to believe him. No-one had ever told me that. And since neither acupuncture nor European medical skills had been able to cure me, he had to be correct. At least I hoped so, in the interest of my health. And he added, "There is some human meat in the ceiling of your house. We need to go there so I can remove it and cure you for ever.'"

I found the story very absorbing and forgot the noise in the departure lounge. I even began to hope that the plane would be further delayed.

Mr Landa pulled out a photograph from the parcel he had in his left hand. Thrusting it into my hand, he said, 'This is the photograph of Fagamundoli as he sat that day in his village.' I looked at the picture and beheld a man dressed in a colourful robe with a great beard and a drooping moustache. He had bleary eyes; beside him was a bottle of beer, in his hand a fly-whisk. He looked formidable.

I was still staring at the photograph when Mr Landa continued his story: 'We returned to my village, arriving there after a tiring day and a half. As soon as we got to my house, Fagamundoli started searching the ceiling of my house. He retrieved a parcel therefrom, claiming that it was human flesh. Right before me there, he began to eat it. He gave me a chunk of it, but I could not bring myself to eat it. I asked if he would allow me to keep it. He said he did not mind. Then he promised to use his powers to invoke a sorcerer who would come to neutralise the charms which had been used to bewitch me.

'Meanwhile, he installed himself in my house and quaffed beer by the gallon. After three days, he informed me that he had summoned the sorcerer who would be arriving at my house at midnight that day.

'The sorcerer did arrive, dancing and chanting, a load of charms dangling from both arms. I was frightened. So were the other villagers who had gathered to see him at work. No sooner did he arrive than he entrusted me with all his charms as though he had known me before. I was dumbstruck. The man did not come from our village; I had never seen him before in all my life. Why did he trust me that much? I was convinced that he was indeed a sorcerer of great powers. Here is a photograph of him as he danced before the villagers that night.'

Mr Landa thrust another photograph into my hand. I had not ever seen a sorcerer and I was fascinated by the photograph.

'I hope I'm not wasting your time?' Mr Landa asked.

'Oh, no. The plane is delayed and your story is most interesting,' I replied.

'After the sorcerer had given me the charms, Fagamundoli the healer called to him, "Fingo, do your duty now!" This was how I came to know that the sorcerer's name was Fingo.

'Fingo slapped me several times on the face, then he beat my chest and placed more charms around my neck. Thereafter, he declared me healed. He said I would find my condition altered within a week. I was very pleased. And I paid without demur the sum of 10,000 naira and a radio for which they charged me. It was all the money I had in my life. I even had to sell some of my farmland and all my cattle to pay Fagamundoli.

'The news of Fagamundoli and Fingo was soon all over the village and all those who were sick or who thought they had been victims of witchcraft sought their assistance. Fagamundoli drank ever more beer and grew much richer. He charged his clients one cow and 3,000 naira each.

'One man, Mr Kazabuga, could not pay the money and offered his daughter to Fagamundoli for a wife. The healer happily married the girl. Another man, Mr Ugema, who had been suffering from tuberculosis for a long time, offered Fagamundoli a bull. It was a really beautiful bull and Mr Kazabuga asked for it from his new son-in-law, Fagamundoli, in exchange for a cow. Fagamundoli happily obliged.

'I am sure that Fagamundoli really enjoyed himself in the time he spent in the village. He killed and ate all the cattle he was paid for his services and drank a lot of beer. Every day was a great festival for him. Soon his fame spread throughout the area. Other villages began to invite him to healing sessions.

'Meanwhile, I was not getting any better. The pain in my chest persisted. The same appeared to apply to all those Fagamundoli and Fingo claimed to have healed. Mr Ugema was very upset at what had happened to him. His relatives demanded a return of the bull they had paid to the healer. But Fagamundoli told them that he had killed and eaten the bull and there was no way he could return it. However, Mr Ugema's relatives saw the bull in Mr Kazabuga's yard. They were puzzled. Fagamundoli had said that he had slaughtered the bull. They demanded the bull.

'But Kazabuga was determined not to give back the bull. A bitter quarrel ensued. Kazabuga asked the Ugema family to sort the matter out with the healer, as they had exchanged his cow for the bull and considered it his rightful property. He said he would rather die than give away the bull. Already, Fagamundoli was in another village.'

Here Mr Landa paused to pass me another photograph.

'Here is a photograph of the bull which Ugema gave to Fagamundoli who exchanged it for a cow from Kazabuga.

I took the photograph and gazed at the bull. I was impressed by its beauty. Mr Landa allowed some time before he returned to his story. He seemed to enjoy watching me look at the photograph.

'When the Ugema relations found that they had been cheated, they went to the Criminal Investigation Department and filed a report. Two investigators traced Fagamundoli to a neighbouring village and began to quiz him.

'The two investigators were Mr Bingo and Mr Lunga. They really knew their onions. They pretended to need Fagamundoli's services.

'And, as usual, he told them the same story he had told me and offered to remove the human flesh from the ceilings of their houses. They took him to a house in the village and Fagamundoli did his usual thing. Then he began to eat the "human meat" in the presence of everyone.

'"Is that human flesh, Fagamundoli?" asked Mr Bingo.

'"Yes. It is human meat."

'"So you do eat human flesh?" queried Mr Lunga. He was dressed in a European-styled suit and looked very impressive.'

'"Oh yes, I do. In the interest of my clients," replied Fagamundoli.

'"From where do you get the human flesh?" asked Mr Bingo.

'"Always from the ceiling of the houses of my clients."

'"Who puts it there?"

'"The sorcerers. You don't know how wicked they are. Can I have some beer? The mere mention of a sorcerer makes me thirsty."

'"Yes, have all the beer you want, Fagamundoli," replied Mr Bingo. "You need it to wash down the meat you have just eaten."

'"Exactly," replied Fagamundoli, quaffing some beer.

'"How do you suppose sorcerers get their human flesh?"

'"They are wicked murderers and assassins."

'"Do you know any sorcerers at all, Fagamundoli?" demanded Mr

Lunga of the healer.

'"Oh, yes. My man Fingo is certainly one of the best sorcerers around. Very wonderful man."

'"And does he know how to obtain human flesh?"

'"Surely. He is the best of them all. I only move with the best. I'm going to ask him to cure you of the witchcraft which left the human meat in your ceiling."

'So saying, he whistled for Fingo who appeared promptly. When questioned, he confirmed that Fagamundoli did eat human flesh. Pressed to say how the human flesh came to be, he said sorcerers often used their victims in that way. Asked if as one of the best sorcerers in the world he was also in the habit of cannibalising people, Fingo could not bring himself to confess to such evil.

'In the end, he confessed that, in truth, he was no sorcerer. That he was the paid servant of Fagamundoli who was no healer and had, indeed, healed no-one. He complained that he had not been paid regularly by his master and that the meat which Fagamundoli ate was not human flesh but beef.

'The investigators took the drunkard Fagamundoli away.'

And again Mr Landa paused to give me another photograph showing the man Fagamundoli being led away by two plainclothes policemen. He gave me time to admire the photograph and then he pursued his story.

'Fagamundoli was taken to court and sentenced by the magistrate to six months' imprisonment. But he had spent all that he took from all of us in that area. He left me terribly poor and diseased.'

Landa coughed a long at the end of his tale. I felt very sorry for him.

At that moment my flight was called and I stood up, ready to leave. Mr Landa's photographs were in my hand. I offered to return them to him.

'Keep them,' he said.

'Why?'

'I don't need them. They may remind you of my unfortunate self and of man's cruelty to man.'

'But I don't need them.' I handed them over to him.

'Thank you,' he said, receiving them from me. 'Can you find __ me some money to help me obtain a cure for the pain in my chest?'

The final departure call was made over the loudspeaker; the departure lounge was a beehive of activity. Mr Landa stood helpless before me, coughing, his head on his chest.

I pulled out my purse and found 200 naira. I gave him the money. He received it with fawning gratitude, calling upon the Almighty to bless me for ever and make my journey peaceful, safe and prosperous. We parted on that note.

As the aircraft winged its way through the skies, it suddenly occurred to me that I had been duped by one of the new-style beggars that had inundated our cities. Surely what I had heard and which had touched my heart was but a tall tale? How had Mr Landa taken all those photographs which he had shown me? He couldn't have made a pictorial record of all the events as they happened? He could not have thought from the very beginning that he would have to tell that story to some stranger some day? And as to his claim to have had acupuncture and consulted over 90 traditional healers, it was probably all hogwash. I had lost money to a confidence trickster! Yes, I had been fooled! Obviously I did not know the new beggars as well as I thought I did.

But I had to confess that Mr Landa had worked hard for what he earned that morning. It took something to tell such a silly story and earn money for it. How he had succeeded in fooling me, I could not explain. I laughed at myself.

When I returned later that evening from my trip, Mr Landa was still at the airport, sitting beside another unwitting victim, this time a lady. He had the bundle of photographs in his hand. At sight of me he fell into a coughing fit, and I could see that he was doing everything to avoid me, my eyes.

I knew then that I would have to record the event, write his story for him. I would be his amanuensis. Which is what every writer is to the storyteller, the story?

I did write the story after a while and then I hawked it about from editor to editor, publisher to publisher. As it returned to me through the post, I thought ruefully how clever Mr Landa had been.

He had been paid for his story on the instant. I would keep begging and hoping that one day... ❏

© *The Executors of the Estate of the late Ken Saro-Wiwa 1996*

JANE RULE

Puzzle

Even in her late seventies Ella Carr was still trying to put her life together like a puzzle which, when she'd finally managed it, she could live in terms of, a character out of Mary Poppins walking into the completed picture. Some of the pieces of it were not difficult. The largest part had always been her work, and it was central — husband, children, lovers all at the hard edges. Oh, there were dark areas, moments when she wished she had made other choices, to write well instead of successfully, not to write at all so that she could have been the wife her husband expected, the mother she hired for her children instead. But Ella Carr was too accomplished an entertainer far too handsomely rewarded to sustain serious regret, even about the several fortunes less generous people might have said she'd squandered on the children, on friends, and on herself.

At the height of her career, magazine sales tripled while one of her novels was being serialized. Airlines paid her to fly for the use of her name. She had never kept track of foreign translations or even movie rights. To the well over a hundred books credited to her name had to be added as many again which she had written under a pen-name or ghosted. Writing was her compulsion. Her first novel had been published when she was 17, and, though her work was now suffering the shift of popular tastes her publishers tended to complain about her ability to change with the times rather than about her outdated plots.

'You can't have homosexual characters in a book of yours,' they protested. 'What will your readers think?'

'All my readers are dead,' Ella Carr replied.

In her prime, she had turned out three books in a summer and was paid $100,000 apiece for them. 'In the thirties,' she'd remind you, 'that was a lot of money.'

Now she managed, against failing energy and eyesight, only one book a year and worried about doctor's bills and taxes, because advances were small, sales a meager 10,000. People still knew who she was, though more and more often it was expressed in surprise not only that she was still writing but still alive. One young reviewer dealt ungenerously with her latest book as if it were a posthumous work. She sent a postcard which read, 'Don't speak ill of the dead,' and signed it Ella Carr.

She had had her own television program. The great movie stars had been her friends. Her fan mail hadn't stopped.

She could still fall in love, her chief diversion since she could remember. When she was hardly more than a child, Ella had herself written fan letters, love letters not only to actors and actresses, dancers, singers, concert pianists, but to any attractive friend of her parents, to her school teachers. She was rarely ignored, for those who present themselves to the world, even so unlikely a part of it as the classroom, do so to be admired and loved whatever other motive their modesty requires. To be out of love now and then, sometimes for weeks at a time, was for her like a serious illness. Ella had to be in love to get anything done. All the paraphernalia of that, the signed programs and photographs, the notes and letters, had long since gone to university archives waiting for a biographer she hoped would be less impressed than amused at the times beyond number she had offered her heart and other parts to a tasteless range of the accomplished. Though Ella enjoyed her celebrity and treated her own fans with attentive kindness, what inspired her still was other people's gifts. At the moment she was corresponding with the most promising tenor at the Met, her son's new law partner, and a young starlet whose fortune was probably in her legs.

'I've never tried to resist a good-looking woman,' she was the first to admit now that she was old and the world had begun to catch up with her.

Those infatuations, though occasionally alarming and inevitably disappointing whether requited or not, went on being as necessary to her as they had been when she was 13. Now in her old age they had the quality of those first loves, involving far more ardor than appetite. Recently without the least envy or regret, Ella had seen her thrice-divorced daughter marry a man she was in love with herself. Ella suspected it was a gesture of gallantry toward herself since he knew how she fretted over that child, who, no matter which way she was turned, had never fitted into her mother's life.

Children don't, even the ones who do as you tell them and grow up to correct all your own mistakes. Ella had a daughter like that, too, who loved being a mother and didn't believe in hiring other people to do your dirty work for you. She was quite a good painter, but it was a hobby, nothing more. Her real name was Rebuke. In fact, she was proud of her mother's accomplishments and ready to be daily dutiful even through a long dying.

When her own mother was dying, Ella was taking up nearly a floor at the Savoy in London. She was in China when her father died. She wasn't at home even when her first-born son was killed in an automobile accident. The only one she had been there for was her husband, but, holding him in her arms, they both knew it was years too late.

'How did we miss it?' he asked.

He had walked out, for obvious reasons: he couldn't stand the demands of four children under five years old; he was jealous of her work; he was sexually deprived. She could not stand to have him come into the same room. She began to shake.

Years later, a doctor said, 'There's nothing abnormal about that. You were exhausted. You had to protect yourself. Four children in five years is too many, particularly now that they all live.'

If Ella had had the pill, there might never have been children. She might have had her marriage instead. But could he have shared her with her work before he'd established his own place in the world? She doubted it. She wouldn't have found it easy to give up children, but for him she could have done it. Writing, no. What she gave up as involuntarily as she shook was her husband. Free of his support, writing and motherhood could not be in conflict. She had to support the children.

'Every writer needs a wife. Sex hasn't anything to do with it,' Ella Carr had repeated in too many interviews, as if confessing would protect her from judgment.

No-one paid the slightest attention. She was a woman 'alone' with four children.

'I might as well not exist!' Tudy cried.

In public, yes, but holding Tudy up to private scrutiny revealed her as the essential fact of life. How many successful men felt the same resentful humiliation when they recognized their success depended on the sacrifice of their wives? At least Ella hadn't sacrificed her husband. Perhaps somewhere he had pensioned off his own guilty discard as she had hers. And bought her silence.

Ella had supervised the burning of the letters because they would have brought at least $10,000 to the archives since they covered the 20 years of Ella's life when she had been the most sought after, probably the most highly paid writer in the world. After the first three years, they were love letters only out of duty, but no-one could have mistaken the nature of the relationship. Ella, who had never in her life written an explicit love scene, had been graphic in letters home to a woman she no longer desired but could not live without.

The children never knew. Tudy was for them their caretaker and tyrant, who could also, but incidentally, reduce their mother to tears. They called her Tudy, one of those inexplicable, nearly interchangeable children's names for people whose power they would like to soften. If she appeared in Ella's biography, she would be the excellently paid, intermittently resented children's nurse and sometimes housekeeper who, aside from nervous breakdowns, served faithfully until she was retired with a generous pension to Arizona.

Once, after her husband died, Ella almost called Tudy back, thinking she would go mad alone with all her losses, but she kept remembering how bitterly difficult it had been to get rid of Tudy, something neither of them could go through again.

'Oh Mother,' her motherly daughter agreed, 'Tudy's too old now to be any help. If you're lonely, borrow one of your grandchildren for a while.'

Instead Ella wrote a novel about an old woman, saintly in her love for her possessive and ill-tempered nurse/jailor. One of the secrets of Ella's success was to write lives she could not have lived. In the month it took to write, she confirmed that she could work again and be alone. Work had always been her rationalization.

The guilt, however, was never more than dormant, woke as she increasingly did in the dark hours of the morning and stank like something dead but undisposed of in the house. It was so unlike what she felt for her husband and her son, whom she missed and regretted and tried to call back from the dead. Ella was secretive about the seances except among a small group of like-minded people as unresigned as she was to losing those they loved.

Her husband and she had been the great loves of each other's lives. They had not divorced, neither of them having any reason to. Once the shock of separation settled to being the catastrophe they had not been able to avoid, each reached out to the other across the necessary distance. He never remembered the children's birthdays; he never forgot hers. She sent him congratulatory notes as his own successes became a matter of public record. When he read she was giving a speech in Chicago, he suggested they have dinner. They met like that a couple of times a year. When she was 40, two months after a hysterectomy, they became lovers again. Tudy had her second nervous breakdown, part of her cure a promise that she would never be betrayed again. That promise was not kept. Meetings between husband and wife became elaborately secret, a weekend stolen from a lecture tour, a fictitious business meeting in New York with agents and publishers. They were far better lovers than they had been, and they were still in love. When the last child left, he said to her, 'I want to come home.'

Ella never explained about Tudy. He was intuitive and tactful. He had to wait two years for Ella to bully and buy Tudy out of the house to make room for him to return. A month after he finally came home, he had a stroke. In a year he was dead.

Ella could not lay him to rest. She had too recently got him back. Though she believed they would finally be reunited in the eternal marriage only imperfectly managed in this life, she could not wait.

The child named Rebuke, when she found out about the seances, said, 'Well, if it's any comfort to you, why not?'

It was, though Ella was never certain she had any direct contact. Trying gave her something to wait for other than death.

Ella's first born had been her favorite, perhaps only because she'd been able to pay absolute attention to him for the first year of his life. She knew him as she never knew the others. He was the only one Tudy hadn't taken over. He was the only one who didn't fiercely resent Tudy once he was grown. He had married a girl Ella was hardly less in love with herself. Visits to them had to be nearly as clandestine as those with her husband.

'It's not unnatural for me to want to see my grandchildren,' Ella argued.

'It's not them. It's her you want to see...and him,' Tudy answered sullenly, accurately.

'Of course, I do. Why not?'

'I've shared you with four children. I've shared you with the world. I put up with your fans. I've put up with your infatuations, your lies, your dirty weekends. I've given up my own family, my own life...'

'I didn't ask you to.'

'You didn't have to ask. I *gave*.'

'What do you expect? What do you want?'

'You.'

'Don't you have me? Do you have to lock me in a cage as well?'

'Sometimes I'd like to.'

Tudy had been a pretty woman, but like so many who spent their days with peanut butter sandwiches, donuts, and chocolate milk, their nights awake with one sick child or another, she was 30 pounds overweight, and her hair was permanently frizzy and limp from all the steaming for croup and asthma. What made her and so many like her unattractive was a face deprived of gratitude.

Ella was grateful. She could not have lived her life without Tudy. A present for Tudy was more important than presents for the children when Ella came home from a trip. Tudy treated any gift as insufficient and suspect.

'You haven't known my size for 15 years,' about a sweater that didn't fit. 'When would I have time to read?' about a book. The closest she came to being pleased would be when she said something like, 'Well, you must have had quite a time!'

Ella was guilty. She tried to make life easier for Tudy, hired maids Tudy nearly always fired, bought household gadgets Tudy refused to use, sent the children to camp so that she and Tudy could take holidays together, catastrophes because Tudy could be jealous of a palm tree if Ella admired it, and Ella's fans were everywhere, discovered her even when she traveled under another name.

'I can't help having a recognizable face!' she protested.

'You can't live without attention.'

Since Ella couldn't avoid it, was it such a crime to enjoy it? The cost, Tudy's hour-long crying jags, from which she recovered enough to continue accusations, was too high. Their only peace was at home when

Ella was working 12 hours a day and needed to be guarded against all interruptions, even a child's broken arm.

'Don't whine for your mother. She's got to pay for it,' Tudy would say, stern and matter-of-fact.

It was Tudy who left their bed to tend the nightmares and earaches. 'You need your rest.'

Ella did spend time with the children, special time, like any loving and normally busy and preoccupied father. She could make that loss up to them but Tudy had to be their mother.

'She did the best she could,' Rebuke admitted. 'It was just that we wanted you, and you always seemed to be away or working.'

Ella never gave way to the temptation to justify herself to the children. Tudy did that for her as well, of course. She reminded them that their mother paid for the food on the table, the roof over their heads, the clothes on their backs. If they weren't appreciative then, they grew up to be pleased by cars and trips to Europe. Ella bought them houses when they married, paid their psychiatrist's bills, paid for their children's dental hardware, paid and paid and paid.

It was Tudy they finally learned to understand and forgive. All three of her surviving children still wrote to Tudy, sent her Christmas presents, even sometimes went to visit her.

'She was there,' Ella's younger son explained. 'We took her too much for granted.'

Her thrice-divorced and recently married daughter said, 'If she'd adored us, we might have forgiven her sooner. She didn't. Like all the world, she adored you.'

Alert even now for betrayals, Ella knew Tudy would never discuss her own feelings with the children. She had not even been able to confide in the very sympathetic psychiatrist called in to help her through her second crack-up. It was Ella who told him. He had comforted Ella, but whether he had ever importantly reached Tudy Ella doubted.

It wasn't the sex that was wrong but the claims made as a result. Ella, who had decided she was not only frigid but hysterical about any adult body within 20 feet of her was wonderfully surprised and comforted by Tudy's lovemaking, which gave her surer pleasure than she had found in her marriage bed and a new arrogance in the pleasure she could return.

Ella concluded that she should have been a man. Should she have seen instead that no-one should be a woman? It was a question she had made sure her biography would never include the information to pose. For herself, she still hoped she would not be required to answer it.

Ella wanted to remove Tudy from her life in such a way that there was no hole, or, if Ella had to look at that jagged emptiness, she'd rather have others to blame, the children who had played with the puzzle of her life and lost some of the pieces, Tudy herself who had changed in those years out of all recognition until there simply was no place for her in Ella's life, which had also changed.

'People outgrow each other,' Ella said to herself and then revised, as she rarely did in her work, to 'one person outgrows another.' Still, the betrayal is basically inadvert. Ella had not meant to grow away from Tudy any more than she had meant to shrink from her husband. If only she and he had had more than his dying year, their love might have closed over those intervening years, healed the interlude with Tudy until it ached only before occasional thunderstorms. As it was, her marriage could bracket but not bridge either Tudy or the children, who acknowledged their father as he lay dying only out of obedience to Ella. He handed out his blessings in the same spirit.

'There were always so many of them,' he said, tired and weakened by the thought.

For Ella there were only three. She had buried their first-born son two years before his father died, who had not been at her side. Tudy was.

When Ella saw her at the airport, she understood the Greek custom of murdering the bearer of bad news. Fate and feeling are outside the laws of justice.

'I don't want you at the funeral!' Ella shouted. 'Gloating!'

Of course, Tudy went, and if her tears were more for Ella than for the boy, there was no malice in her even for the young widow. She opened her arms to the next generation of fatherless children, grandchildren who had long since abandoned Ella as had their mother for a new husband, but they still saw Tudy without knowing she had ever been a threat to them.

'Nobody's abandoned you, darling,' Rebuke reassured her. 'Look at all these birthday cards and presents.'

From fans, from old lovers, from children and grandchildren, but there was none from Tudy.

'Once I leave this house, don't expect me to be like him, sending you stupid roses. Once I leave this house it's over; it's dead. When you find out you can't live without me, *tough!'*

Tudy also assured Ella there would be no meeting in the next world. 'It's bunk!'

'Maybe it is,' Ella had agreed bitterly. 'We've had hell enough in this one.'

Now she badly wanted husband or son to send some message that they were there waiting, would be, when the time came, on her right hand and on her left, to hold and protect her at last from the fiery call if it came. There was, however, no more message from them than from Tudy.

One day there was no mail. For the next week Ella could not work, waiting for it to happen again. Then her daughter was ill and did not come to see her for 10 days. Even the television, which she saw inadequately anyway, flickered and blurred.

'The world is going out,' she confided in herself. 'Surely that isn't dying.'

Dying is gathering up the pieces, the bright and the dark, fitting them together, puzzling out the true picture, seeing it at last. Ella couldn't any longer see. There was no-one there to help her.

'Isn't anyone going to show me how? Isn't anyone going to teach me?'

The last sentence Ella Carr wrote might have been the title for her next book, 'Death is not that Kind of Lover,' for it modified the truth, that death is no lover at all, as she had always been able to in fiction, as she had not managed to in life. ❏

© *Jane Rule, reprinted from* Inland Passage *(Naiad Press, 1985) with permission of the author and publisher*

BAI HUA

Su Qin carrying his sword

I gaze at her window. In the past, it was pasted over with black paper; now a cloth curtain with tiny blue flowers hangs there.

AGAIN the time had come for me to take my medical report to the farm. As I shut my eyes and reminisced on the bus, the scenes and images flashing through my memory were all associated with Gui Renzhong. Nothing else could intrude, no matter how interesting or sensational: Old Gui following a herd of cows, each with eyes of grief and loyalty just like his. Old Gui looking up at the lofty statue of Mao with boundless faith. Old Gui prostrating himself on the ground out of sheer joy and excitement at his five-day leave. Old Gui raising a shrivelled hand to get a chance to ask questions at the meeting. Old Gui massaging my back with his gentle hand while holding his broken leg. Old Gui wearing a brand-new suit and moving slowly toward me like a paper doll. Old Gui being forced to put his fingerprint on the marriage certificate like Yang Bailao. Carrying Jane's ashes, he follows me out of the villa, a playhouse designed for foreigners, his face showing no trace of misery or humiliation, only the relaxation of a shy actor who finally gets off the stage. The moment I thought of him, my heart was wrenched with pain as if a vulture were tearing out my entrails with its talons. His life would be an endless tragedy caused by his personality, or rather by his ignorance. But could one possibly call an internationally renowned scholar ignorant? Still, I found it hard to explain the series of tragedies caused by his ignorance. He was a man of freedom in the realm of chemistry, an expert on chemical combinations, not a high school student who merely knew that H_2O=water. Why, then, did he remain such a childish simpleton? I believe a child being stolen at infancy and raised by a pack of wolves could grow into a wolf child and feed on carrion. But could an adult — and a sophisticated, top intellectual to boot — also become a wolf man? I was puzzled by this strange phenomenon. Although the Chinese, almost without exception, were being wolfified and pigisised to various degrees, until today there were few men like old Gui who had deteriorated so much and still continued to bump their heads against walls without realising they needed to turn around. I felt he needed someone to enlighten him, like a bodhisattva, someone to drop purified water on his brow from a willow twig to wake him up at the edge of the cliff, someone to make him understand that 'if a man cannot speak like a man in front of men, a man will never speak like a man in front of Satan.' He needed someone to let him know that the statue was high because its steel frame was large and so it consumed more cement. But who was here to enlighten him? A bodhisattva was merely a Buddhist god that did not really exist as a physical being in this universe; therefore, he could not be produced by way of chemistry. I alone could save old Gui, and I felt obliged to bring him out of the wilderness. To refuse to save him would be inhumanly cynical and cruel. He had suffered enough. Now it was time for me to help him swim the bitter sea.

With these thoughts, I felt a shining halo over my head, and my noble sentiments so thrilled me that my eyes filled with warm tears. It would be difficult to catechise him face to face. Better to write it out so he could read it over and over. I took out a notebook from the satchel and wrote the following:

Old Gui:
I have been worried about you for some time. How are you? You aren't doing fine, I know that, because you are too naive, far too naive. Although no irregularity in a chemical reaction can escape your eye, when confronted with the false phenomena of the sacred in life, particularly with certain wooden idols, you quickly lose your power of perception. Worse still, you exalt those false images with a dreamlike enthusiasm. Each of us has a prison in his mind, but yours is much more fortified. Why don't you try sticking your head through the iron bars to see the vast sky beyond the prison? Sometimes just one more step will lead to a new world. I sincerely hope you accept my advice. Turn it over and over in your mind, pondering it like the tables, formulas, and equations you have mastered before. You will understand my message. May one opening (insight) lead to one

hundred openings.
Your loving student,
Liang Rui
Month x, Date x, Year x

I folded the message into a butterfly bow and thrust it into old Gui's hand as I was leaving the farm. I whispered, 'A letter for you.'

'A letter?' He reacted strangely.

'For you alone to read.'

'Me alone?' His expression grew even more strange; he stared at me pitifully.

'Yes. Read it several times. Think things over. Then burn it...'

'Burn it?' His voice became as dry as withered leaves.

I asked him another three times to burn the letter before I walked away with a relieved heart. I was lucky in having to wait only a minute before a bus came. As I dozed during the ride, I wore a broad smile because I had made progress. A beautiful new world was unfolding under my feet. I was imagining how old Gui looked on his awakening: his forehead must be radiating wisdom and his eyes becoming clear like a fountain, his face washed by tears of gratitude for me.

The screech of the bus sent me flying to the roof and then dumped me back into the seat. My head and buttocks hurt badly. An accident? A two-car crash, or someone run over? The moment I straightened myself out, the door opened and in stepped two men. To my surprise, one was the defence leader of our farm; the other was his guard. The farm's defence office was like the state's Department of Police, plus the Department of Security, plus court and prosecutor. Its leader had the power of minister plus judge plus prosecutor. All four eyes sized me up. 'Liang Rui, get off the bus!'

'What's happened?' I stood up.

'*You* can ask that?' The leader was in a rage. 'No nonsense now, roll yourself out of here!' Roll? Of course I actually walked out. As soon as I was off the bus, they snapped handcuffs on me. They used a fashionable new method: pulling my right hand over my shoulder and twisting my left behind my back, they locked my two hands together. I don't know why I asked them, 'Why shackle me like that?'

The guard said, 'This is called "Su Qin Carrying His Sword". What a bumpkin you are.' Of course I was a bumpkin; after all, not everybody has the right to exercise dictatorship over others. The Chinese, with their high culture, love to do everything in style. The Western Lake in Hangzhou has 10 scenes of beauty. So everywhere in China people try to imitate it, as if without 10 scenes a place would not be worth seeing. Refined literary names for the beautiful scenes stimulate a man's appetite for sightseeing. The bodies of a cat and a snake roasted together carries the name Dragon Fighting the Tiger. The body of a butchered chicken decorated with a tomato is called Phoenix Facing the Sun. Inventing beautiful names to match cuisine is understandable, because the names may serve as appetisers.

But why did they need a heroic name for the manner in which they shackled me? Could that also stimulate people's appetites? It certainly seemed to. Although it didn't take long to shackle me and push me into the jeep, in that short time I attracted a large crowd. There were no villages on either side of the highway, so where did they come from? Did they spring out of the ground? China has certainly earned its fame as a country with a large population. The onlookers were excited to see that I, who was being devoured by the beast of power, was not one of them. Their happiness seemed to show their favour for the power and their complicity in the act of devouring.

The jeep returned along the route it had come. It took at least a mile to throw off the onlookers. The springy seats of the jeep could by no means be compared with those in a luxury car. In less than five minutes I tasted the heroism of Su Qin Carrying His Sword. My wrists, elbows, and back ached intolerably. I started groaning, as I tried to guess what crime I had committed. Had they discovered my illness to be false? No, impossible. As long as that head doctor was still in power, he would take responsibility. Even if they had found out the true nature of my illness, did they need to stop a passenger bus to arrest me? Had my affair with Yunqian been discovered? No, even more unlikely. We were always hidden in our cocoon. Who would bother worming into it to catch us? Even if we were discovered, at most we should only be criticised for behaving immorally before marriage, a defect that can be corrected through education. I sorted through my entire short history but failed to find any crime, mistake, or even an error of omission for which I deserved to be arrested. I was certain they had made a mistake in arresting me, producing another miscarriage of justice. Yet they had to have some reason to arrest me! Yes — suddenly it came to me in a flash.

Perhaps the message I had passed to old Gui had fallen into the wrong hands. No, impossible. Absolutely impossible. After all, I told him the letter was for him alone to read. Even if the message upset his three loyalties and four infinite loves, he would not report me so fast. I had repeatedly told him: 'Read it several times. Think things over. Then burn it.' If he had read it twice and thought things over for three minutes before reporting, they still could not have arrested me so fast. Unless he reported me the moment he read the first line, as if he had discovered a dagger on unfolding the sheet. I thought it utterly impossible — a hundred times impossible, a thousand times impossible, 10 thousand times impossible.

But the facts taught me that it was possible — a hundred times possible, a thousand times possible, 10 thousand times possible.

Before the jeep arrived at the farm, the huge shed had already been prepared for a large criticism meeting. Their experience in handling such meetings was truly admirable. When I was escorted to the shed, I looked up and saw an extra-large banner hanging across the stage: *Criticise the Active Counter-revolutionary Liang Rui*, which already determined the nature of my crime and put a tall criminal's hat on me. Therefore, as soon as I entered, like a famous Beijing Opera actor striking a pose as the embroidered curtain rises, I received an uproarious welcome. Slogans showered down on me like a storm and hundreds of fists were raised in my direction, stretching and withdrawing like cannon barrels. Being denounced by the pointing fingers of thousands gave me the sense of being a star. Suddenly I felt like a great president with a sky-scraping hat. Swarms of people on tiptoes, squeezing and nudging each other, pushed forward to catch a glimpse of me. I was escorted to the stage. Holding my head high, I stood there in the heroic pose of Su Qin Carrying His Sword. Hysterical shouting distorted everyone's voice; I could not make out what they were shouting. When my head was thumped by a fist, I guessed they were shouting for me to lower my head. So I lowered my head, unable to see anything but my toes.

The solemn voice of the PLA rep rose above the din: 'Chairman Mao teaches us: "When the old reactionaries are wiped out, new ones will grow. If we lose our vigilance, we will suffer a great loss." "The trees want to be still but the wind will not stop." "Never be so bookish and naive as to treat complex class struggle as a simple matter." From the quotations he recited I could tell the ordeal I was about to go through, and my body froze from the inside out. The PLA rep continued in a voice quivering with indignation: 'Comrades, revolutionary comrades! Don't some of you think the Cultural Revolution has carried on too long? Don't some believe that all cow ghosts and snake-spirits have been wiped out? And don't some blame us for shooting mosquitoes with cannons or creating a storm in a teacup? I hope those comrades will draw a lesson from this native counter-revolutionary. Comrade Gui Renzhong, would you please come to the stage?'

The words *comrade* and *please* used by the PLA rep created a disturbance in the meeting. I was unable to see but could well imagine: being surprised by the favour, Gui Renzhong's legs turned soft. It took a long time for him to reach the stage. The PLA rep said to him, 'Please read to our comrades the reactionary manifesto of the active counter-revolutionary Liang Rui!' Manifesto? If I weren't shackled, I'd have dashed over to tear him into pieces. When did I ever write a reactionary manifesto?

Gui Renzhong started in a funereal tone. 'Comrades! Active counter-revolutionary Comrade Liang Rui — No! He is not a comrade but an enemy. Taking advantage of us being bedmates, he wrote me a letter in an attempt to shake my revolutionary belief. Before I had read it through, I smelled something fishy and immediately handed it over to the PLA rep. Now I'll read this reactionary manifesto — '

Old Gui's reading shocked me. Did I really write that? How could I have written something like that? Could I have been so careless as that? Now even *I* was finding the message to be extremely reactionary. Before old Gui had finished it, I was already soaked in sweat. Then the model fighters of the farm vied to take the stage. Nearly all of them became professional speakers, delivering elegant criticisms with associations, allusions, political theories, and class guidelines. Each heightened his speech with a grave face, harsh tone, and grandious terminology, as well as with physical gestures such as beating the chest, stamping the feet, and spraying saliva in all directions. Although I had expected such expertise, I could not help shouting bravo in my mind for their penetrating analyses and apt associations. Let me give you some samples:

'Comrades, my revolutionary comrades! Listen, what kind of words are these: "How are you? You aren't doing fine, I know that. Because you are too naive, far too naive." Do these words sound strange or new? No. They smell reactionary. Chairman Mao teaches us, "Reactionaries are waving their hands at you." What does *waving their hands* mean? The message "How are you? You aren't doing fine, I know that. Because you are too naive, far too naive" is a typical example. The author cunningly hid the supplement to the sentence. Too naive with whom? It is obvious that his spear is aimed at our great leader Chairman Mao, at the great, glorious, and flawless Chinese Communist party, and at the revolutionary masses. The beginning of his message exposes his inveterate hatred toward them.' At this moment, the speaker could not help shouting from the bottom of his heart: 'Long live our great leader Chairman Mao. Long, long, long may he live!' The audience echoed his words with the force of thunder and lightning.

Another example: 'The phrase *irregularity in a chemical reaction* sounds exactly like the counter-revolutionary Hu Feng. Is the author *really* talking about chemistry? No. Counter-revolutionaries know the importance of putting politics in command. Some of our comrades are naive enough to complain that we have overemphasised politics. The counter-revolutionaries have done it much more than we have! The author then talks about the false phenomena in life, particularly those of the sacred! Attention, comrades! What are these false phenomena of the sacred in life? What else if it is not our loyalty to the great leader and our belief in revolution? But he does not stop there. Listen to the next line: "You exalt those false images with a dreamlike enthusiasm." Notice the arrogance of this counter-revolutionary, who assumes the reactionary intellectual's pose of "I alone wake while the whole world sleeps." He is slandering the great, stormy, revolutionary movement we are currently carrying out as the false dream of a single individual. How vicious he is! If we tolerate *him*, who can we not tolerate? Down with the counter-revolutionary Liang Rui!' Another wave of slogans resounded in the shed.

Another example: 'This counter-revolutionary is extremely vicious. He attacks every happy man living in our socialist China for having a prison in his mind. What does the mind prison refer to? It refers to the fundamental principles of Marxism-Leninism-Mao Zedong thought. He has issued a reactionary call for us to step out of the prison, saying "just one more step will lead to a new world." What new world is he really talking about? No doubt, the so-called Free World. This counter-revolutionary Liang Rui must be a running dog of US imperialism. We can be certain, without any investigation, that he is a spy of the American FBI. Down with US imperialism! Down with Soviet revisionism!' US imperialism and Soviet revisionism were a matching pair. Each phrase sounded incomplete without its partner, even in slogans.

Another one: '"May one opening lead to one hundred openings." What does that mean? No doubt it is a reactionary password. Be open to whom? His first opening seems to be toward Taiwan and Taiwan's spy organisations. This first opening will then lead to US imperialism, French imperialism, British imperialism, Soviet revisionism, and so on: more than a hundred openings. How dangerous one opening is, my comrades!'

Yet another: 'The reasons Liang Rui joined the American FBI and Chiang Kai-shek's spy networks to sabotage our socialism can be traced to his class background.' When did I join these spy organisations? How did I join them? Did I have contacts to introduce me? Who? Where? I searched my mind in earnest. 'Both his parents were reactionary intellectuals. The moment the great Cultural Revolution started, they committed suicide to resist the revolutionary campaign and to show their deep-seated hatred for the Communist party. Liang Rui has buried hatred in his heart because of his late parents and has attempted to revenge them at every possible turn. Now he is honing his sword. Shouldn't we hone ours?!'

There were too many wonderful speeches to display them all here. But they unexpectedly calmed me down, and I pondered them with pleasure. But old Gui was scared almost to death; I could hear him shivering. His report on me, his vigilance and his loyalty had won him little forgiveness: nearly a third of the criticism speeches were directed at him. For instance: 'Why did the counter-revolutionary choose you? You must have something in common, stinking together.' 'How did you collaborate with him? Why did he call himself a student of yours? Why? You must have taught him his counter-revolutionary schemes.' 'It is to your credit that you exposed him in time and regained your political head. However, the fact that he chose you and you alone proves what a dark reactionary soul you have.' 'Your relationship with him has exposed your ugly soul to the broad daylight. Don't entertain the idea that you are different from him. You and he are wolves of the same pack!'

Although my hands were shackled, I took pity on old Gui, fearing he would be too scared to live this thing through. It was true that the PLA rep had a higher understanding of policy, for he said in a conciliatory tone: 'Comrade Gui Renzhong.' The term *comrade* dragged old Gui from the enemy side over to the ranks of the people. It was a reprieve from death. 'Of course, he has made his own mistakes. But mistakes are different from crimes. Everyone makes mistakes. But he has performed a meritorious deed by trusting in the strength of the party and helping to root out a counter-revolutionary.' I heard old Gui give a sigh of relief. 'However, he must undertake serious self-criticism in order to cast off his birthmark and his old bones.' Could old Gui cast off his birthmark? Could his old bones be remoulded? I doubted it.

That night I was sent to the second prison, along with the evidence of my crimes — the message I had written and all the criticism speeches delivered at the meeting. My way to prison seemed simple: no delay caused by red tape, no torture to obtain a confession. Everything — all the procedures from arrest to incarceration — was boiled in one pot. If only other matters in our country could be performed in such an efficient manner. After they checked my ID card and the evidence against me, the prison gate clanked open. I was driven in a prison car for quite a few minutes before reaching the cell allotted to me. The prison was obviously a big one. Two guards walked me to a changing room, where they ordered me to strip. As I took off my shorts, the two suddenly jumped me, kicking and pummelling me. I only had time to give a desperate cry: 'Hey, I have TB!'

'We wouldn't spare you if you had cancer!'

I gaze at her window. In the past it was pasted over with black paper; now a cloth curtain with tiny blue flowers hangs there. ❑

© *Bai Hua, excerpted from Chapter 14 of* The Remote Country of Women, *University of Hawaii Press, 1994*
© *Translation Qingyun Wu and Thomas O Beebee 1994*

MOHAMED CHOUKRI

The poets

THE CROWD was waiting for the procession of poets to arrive. On the pavement of the big street was a platform with a table on it where piles of books were arranged, each bearing a poet's number, and next to the table was a dustbin. The crowd was silent and tightly packed. They leaned forward, craning their necks to look along the street. They moved closer together, jostling one another on the edge of the pavement, and talking in low voices.

The procession of poets came into view, surrounded by guards.

'Six poets.'

'Seven.'

'No, eight, nine. There are nine of them.'

The crowd looked into the poets' eyes and the poets looked back.

'Look at their beards and their long untidy hair!'

'They must have been shut up somewhere with hardly any sunlight or air.'

There had never been such a large crowd before and their silence was more humane that day. Even the footsteps of the poets and their escort could be clearly heard. The crowd hardly believed what they saw and the children were silent too, open-mouthed beside their parents. A little girl began to cry and the woman with her put a hand over her mouth in the hope of quietening her.

The poets wore black jackets with large white numbers back and front. Four guards climbed the wooden steps up to the platform, leading the procession of poets, and the rest of the guards brought up the rear. The guards formed a line and faced the crowd. After a moment's silence the chief guard summoned poet number one.

'Step forward and throw your books in the dustbin.'

The poet didn't move. The guard summoned him a second time in a louder voice, and then a third time. The poet stayed where he was. The guard looked at him menacingly, then signalled to the garbage collector, who went forward and took out two books bearing a black label with a white number one on it and threw them in the dustbin with disgust.

The chief's voice grew steadily angrier as he called out one poet's number after another. The garbage collector spat on the books before he threw them in the dustbin. The crowd roared their indignation. Children cried. Voices were raised in protest. The chief whispered something in the garbage collector's ear. All the poets refused to obey. There was silence again. The poets looked into the crowd's eyes and the crowd looked back.

Then the poets descended from the platform and went back where they'd come from. ❏

© *Mohamed Choukri 1973*
© *Translation Catherine Cobham 1996*

M T SHARIF

The letter writer

For Mansoureh

A DERVISH who stopped in the town for a loaf of *barbari* saw
Haji the letter writer and proclaimed, 'Mark my words.
Today that man inscribes cards and papers. Yet he will live in a
seven-columned house. And seven concubines will attend him.
And seven servants will obey his every wish.' Saying this, he
gathered his bundle and disappeared.

Gossip spread faster in Rostam Abbad than lice on a
donkey's testicles; the dervish's words created a sensation.
Drinking tea in coffeehouses, people of different persuasions
debated the issue hotly. All referred to the one house of
opulence they knew, the Shah's summer mansion, Shady
Palace. Though no-one approached it to peer through its gates,
in this shady place in the mountains, the informed assumed,
there were many rooms, many columns, many mirrored *darbars*.
Here the consensus ended and arguments ensued. Some said,
'Haji has eyes the size of hubcaps, we tell you. Made for ogling
over extravagances, we tell you.' Others said, 'You propose that
he will occupy a home resembling the King's?' The local
pundit said, 'Haji's a fool. He cannot tell a *mullah* from a mule.'
So the rumours persisted and his future intrigued people.

Haji ignored the sudden interest in his affairs, muttering. 'A
businessman has little time for chatter.' Then he looked right
and left, and startled passers-by with a lusty call: 'Hurry. Hurry.
Petitions. Affidavits. Money orders drafted here.'

His professional apparatus consisted of a few pens and quills,
some papers, a Quran, and coloured picture of the Prophet.
Resorting to these pictures, citing the holy book, waving his
material in the air, all day he accosted people. '*Agha*. Yes, you,

chewing beet leaf. Are you deaf? Commission a card for your wife, children, or mother-in-law.' He coaxed another, 'Madame. Lady in the see-through veil. Are you married? Have you a father? What would he say if he saw you dressed like this? A postcard for your suitors?'

He scolded those who obstructed his view. He concocted, for a few *toomans*, a eulogy or a curse letter. He directed traffic. At all times he advertised an impressive array of services: 'Hurry. Hurry. Checks. Wills. Notarised papers. By special arrangement, green cards and diary entries.' Thus Haji held court in a corner of Cannon Square.

Salty sceptics watched him transacting business and said, 'The man is a public nuisance. One cannot cross the square safely anymore.' Haughty gossips said, 'We hear that he consorts with all sorts of evil creatures.' Cucumber-fingered cynics said, 'God willing, rivals will trim that malicious tongue of his.'

Indeed, Haji's was a competitive calling. In the narrow square professionals of all arts vied for attention. Vendors of bitter almonds, tyre thieves, and junk sellers hawked their wares. Liver cooks and beet merchants praised their produce. Bankers, bakers, and butchers jostled one another. Also a typist hovered about, hiding in dark corners, ready to spring forth and set up shop the minute Haji averted his head.

Amidst this mêlée, Haji crouched, observing the bustle with that yearning look of a camel upon cotton seeds. If shoppers snubbed him, if regulars slighted him, if the typist snatched a customer and settled down to punch his machine, Haji appealed to the store owners directly. 'Brother vendors. Neighbour businessmen. I ask of you, is there room for more than one author in this square? Instruct your patrons to frequent my establishment.'

He raised prices and reduced them, he cursed and cajoled, he hurled unsolicited advice in the general direction of onlookers, until, cornering some hesitant customer, coercing the fellow to sit cross-legged on the ground, he said, 'Enunciate properly. Who is to receive this letter?' This was just the first in a series of questions. For half an hour he interrogated his patron on the content and purpose of the piece, the desired tone, diction, style, and format. Then he licked his pen, raised his brow, blew *Allah Akbar* in the air, and wrote, 'May I be your slave and servant, the carpet beneath your feet. Allow me to forward my salaam and prayers. My father forwards his salaam and prayers. My mother forwards her salaam and prayers. My other kith and kin forward their salaam and prayers.' Later he ended a letter in a similar vein. 'May your shadow never diminish. May I make a balcony from my head for your steps. This green leaf is from your slave and servant.' Between these ceremonial introductions and conclusions, space permitting, he squeezed in a word or two uttered by the client.

Question the soul, however, who requested a sight alteration, abbreviation, or rephrasing. Pity the person who protested that he had no father or mother. Such impertinence angered Haji. He cast pen and paper aside and roared, 'Why, sir, you know better? Take your business elsewhere. Find that typist. He has operated a grocery, dabbled in gynaecology, proceeded to geographical astrology, and is now a writer of mail. Save for a few flowery maxims he is practically illiterate. But he will suit you better.'

Now Haji neglected his customer. He chewed a *nabat* and gurgled. He cleaned his nails, scrubbed his feet. He napped; he drank a tumbler of tea. Now, abruptly, eyeing the letter seeker, he said, 'Sir. You are still here? I ask of you, if a man lets his donkey graze on the land of a friend and pays for this service, and it so happens that his donkey becomes pregnant, who, sir, does the offspring belong to — the owner of the animal or the proprietor of the land? You do not know? May I suggest to you, then, to leave important matters to your elders.' With half a dozen riddles of this nature he thoroughly cowed the customer. Then he licked his pen, raised his brow, blew *Allah Akbar*, and said, 'Tell me, who is this to be sent to and what do you propose to say?'

The inquisitive asked him, 'Haji, why bother asking folks what they want said?'

'Your excellencies,' he responded. 'These are uneducated people. They tell me what they generally feel and I fashion that into acceptable prose.'

His reasoning confounded friends, but it scarcely convinced foes. Arm-in-arm cucumber cynics and salty sceptics paced the square and said, 'The blackguard robs simple, poor villagers. His whole family ought to find themselves honourable professions.' Damning information had it that an elder brother of Haji's, a self-proclaimed 99-year-old chemist, palm reader, and beggar, led a flourishing practice in the main mosque feigning epileptic seizures.

Glib rumours of this sort pained him. 'How do I know who goes where masquerading as my brother?' he remarked. 'I have no kith or

kin. Probably the man is cross-eyed and cannot see straight. Why else would he be sitting in a house of worship pleading for alms? I assure you, mosque beggars are the most suspicious personalities.'

He marked the passage of time by the movement of schoolchildren. They passed him on their way to the Dabestan at eight, taunted him during recess, and raced home after four. By then he had exhausted his clientele, collected various copper coins, and stuffed them in his socks.

In due course the din of Cannon Square subsided. Shopkeepers closed their *megazehs*. Beggars, vendors, hired hands, went their separate ways. Haji followed suit, assembled his apparatus, and found shelter in the doorway of a house or the threshold of a shop.

No doubt he conducted a valuable service. No doubt he enjoyed wooing patrons, sparring with foes. No doubt he would have continued, to the hour when milk sprouts in the nipples of eunuchs.

One day, a day neither hot nor cold, at the most ordinary hour, the appointed hour, as the horizon resembled a sheet of charcoal dotted by camphor, Rostam Abbad discovered the Revolution. Word hummed down the dusty Tehran Road. Wise beards and white beards heard it. The local pundit heard it. In the shade of walnut trees, playing backgammon, reciting Ferdousi, men heard it. Soaking their hot feet in cool streams, children heard it.

Certain citizens feared the whole affair. Half a dozen sold their belongings and immigrated to Cleveland. Others appointed themselves Revolutionary Guards. They patrolled streets; they stopped cars; they searched houses. Also they liberated Shady Palace. This caused much commotion. Some folks organised an expedition and toured the property, noting watery gardens of *maryam* and narcissus, and many columns, and many rooms. They rushed home and said, 'There are many things to see.' The next day a larger crowd scaled the mountain and sought entry. An old officer wearing a new khaki stopped them at the gates and shouted, 'Go back.' For the guards had bolted the windows, wired the walls, inaugurating Rostam Abbad's Revolutionary Committee for Public Grievances.

Perched in his usual corner in Cannon Square, Haji witnessed the twists and turns of history. He wrote his letters. He kept to his own affairs.

A fortnight after that ordinary day, uniformed guards seized him and said, 'Haji, Haji, what have you done?'

'What have I done, sirs?'

'Do not be coy with us, Haji. Your brother spied for the anti-Revolution.'

'Brother? I have no brother.'

'He painted all sorts of leaflets in the main mosque and God knows what else. Do you know him?'

'That beggar? I have heard of him. What of it? For the past 15 years he has claimed kinship to me.'

'Come with us.'

'Why, sirs? Just because some rabble calls himself my relative? Besides, I never saw the man.'

'Enough, Haji. Provide evidence and you will be freed.'

Meekly he followed them. The palace brimmed with people. Guards ran to and fro. Relatives of detainees cried here and there. 'Sit,' the guards ordered. He sat and marvelled, a finger of amazement in his mouth. Even the most exaggerated accounts left him ill-prepared for this. A chandelier hung in every room. Oak doors connected room to room. While the authorities rushed back and forth, opening, shutting doors, Haji counted 40 chandeliers above 40 carpets smooth as a woman's moustache. These luxuries he saw on the first floor. Perhaps there was a second, he reasoned, a third and a fourth, since the winding staircase that linked floor to floor spiralled to the sky.

Hours later the guards returned and dragged him to a hall where thousands of books lay in glass shelves. There the authorities dared him. There they blamed him. Again and again he said, 'I am no traitor. That man is not my brother.' He spent the night in a cellar alongside Communists and pickpockets.

In the succeeding months he maintained his innocence. He cursed. He reeled. He swore. He petitioned the municipality, the different committees, the president of the republic. Each and every time the authorities informed him, 'Your brother has confessed and is serving time in Tehran.'

'That good for nothing character is not my brother.'

'You are implicated in his affairs.'

'Gentlemen, do not believe him. Mosque beggars are highly unreliable.'

'Either admit to your crimes or show us proof.'

'How am I to do that? Am I a biographer or a writer of birth certificates?'

'Take this fool away,' they said.

Date-eyed and afraid, every day, handcuffed Loyalists, Royalists, and other assorted anti-Revolutionaries marched forth and met their colleagues in the cellars of Shady Palace. These suspects the authorities processed swiftly. A few were flogged. A few were freed. Crammed in trucks, the rest were forwarded to Tehran. None remained incarcerated longer than Haji. The authorities told him, 'We have not harmed you, not sent you to the capital, where you could be tortured. Come, come. Tell us what you know.'

'I know nothing,' he said. 'Nothing.' He clamoured. He complained. A year or two passed. He said nothing. As the carpets wore thin, he said, 'I know nothing.' As the grass *maryam*, and narcissus grew waist-high in the untended garden, he said, 'I know nothing.' As the roof leaked and the tiled columns dulled, he said, 'Nothing. Nothing.' As the palace, trampled by numerous feet, prey to the dust and the wind, adapted a less splendorous look, he said, 'That man is not my brother. I know nothing.' And he clamoured. And he complained.

THE authorities sympathised with his predicament. 'Haji,' they said. 'Stop this racket. There is no peace in this compound because of you.' They transferred him to a spacious room on the second floor and said, 'Now be content. You have your very own room, table, chair, and view of the garden.'

'Pray, how long?' he asked. 'How long?'

'It is not in our hands. Tehran demands a confession from all political prisoners. Ages ago you should have repented.'

A friendly official hit upon an ingenious idea. He ordered a stack of magazines brought up to Haji's room from the library and said, 'Haji, look here. There are pictures of women in these pages. American women. English women. They are misled, misinformed. Their hair is uncovered. They wear sleeveless shirts and low-cut dresses. Make good use of your time. Cover their nakedness. We plan to distribute these papers to the public.'

'Am I a painter?' he retorted. But his days were long, his nights dreary. Presently he picked a pen, chose a magazine, and sat by the window. Glossy pictures filled this foreign text; not a word could he decipher. There were so many pictures, though. Most required prompt attention. From cover to cover he searched the paper, applying the ink at necessary junctures, draping exposed knees and bare arms. Something in the act soothed him. He moved to another text. When he had sorted through the whole bundle he called on the guards for a second supply.

L ATE spring the buffalo gazed westward, hiding one foot, hoping for rain. Midsummer the grape burned bright as a lamp; on strings spiders seemed too hot to hunt. Autumn arrived heavily, fattened like a persimmon, riper and riper, then retreated, ushering in the winter snow. Beyond the window-panes the years breezed away and Haji worked.

He woke at dawn and toiled past dusk. To the authorities he said, 'I have fallen behind. Do not expect to distribute these papers yet. I am working night and day to finish.' He worked slowly. Each paper, each page, every photograph, posed a new problem, a fresh challenge.

He found women in a variety of positions, in all shapes and sizes. Some reclined on cars. Some rested on cushions. Some held objects and grinned. Some grimaced. Some were sweet as *halva*. Some sour as a saw. Some looked plump. Some looked thin. Some young. Some old. Some felt smooth to the touch. Some tough and taut.

Before tackling the task at hand, Haji examined his subjects, considered their flaws. Then he licked his pen and wove his veils. He clothed their sinewy legs and dyed nails. He blotted their necks. He covered their wrists and exposed chests. With the tip of his pen he stroked them, shaded their naked limbs from strange and shameless eyes. Those he liked he treated this way. But those whom he judged disreputable, he attacked and tore apart.

The authorities visited him once a month. Each and every time he shuddered and said, 'I am yet to finish. I am a few weeks behind and am working night and day.'

One day they told him, 'Your brother has died.'

'He was not my brother.'

'Nevertheless, we will plead your case with Tehran.' He nodded. They returned and said, 'A recalcitrant lot. But do not despair. We have other means.'

Nowadays he wandered around the palace freely. There were few prisoners left. The building was in desperate need of repair. Plaster flaked off the ceiling. Walls sagged. Columns cracked. 'This place is uninhabitable,' the authorities argued. They built a modern facility nearby and told Haji, 'Tehran is adamant. They want a confession.'

'Stranger things, I hear,' Haji said. 'I hear that typist fellow went out of business because masons, vendors, villagers, all have learned to read and write. Anyway I have much to do.'

When the authorities prepared to evacuate the palace they explained, 'We will contact them once more, Haji. Do not lose hope. In the meantime we will take you to our new facilities.'

'Why, sirs? Are you dissatisfied with my performance? I will work harder. Only allow me to stay. The books, the papers, are here.'

In this manner Haji and an old revolutionary guard became the sole occupants of Shady Palace. His jailer cooked for Haji, did his wash, and every morning hauled a bundle of magazines to the second floor. Pen in hand Haji greeted him and said, 'Am I to go to the well and return thirsty again? If the authorities so inquire, inform them that I am working ceaselessly.'

Snowy seasons, he toiled indoors. The yellowed, worm-eaten pages crumbled in his hands. The mold and dust irritated his eyes, itched his nails. He worked and worked. For after he clothed them, after he draped, after he veiled, traced their every curve, suddenly, their withered faces shone, their eyes loomed larger, and their lips quivered, promising perpetual enchantment.

Melon days and summer nights, his jailer placed a chair on one of the numerous balconies and there too Haji laboured. Sometimes old salty sceptics and cucumber cynics saw him on these crumbling *eivans*, pointed him out to their grandchildren, and said, 'During the Revolution, it is recorded, he was a spy and killed many. The Revolution, dear ones, have you heard of it? Do you know about that great turmoil?' ❏

© *M T Sharif, reprinted from The Agni Review, 1989*

ROSARIO CASTELLANOS

Death of the tiger

THE BOLOMETIC tribe consisted of families of the same blood. Their protecting spirit, their *waigel*, was the tiger, whose name they were entitled to bear because of their courage and their daring.

After immemorial pilgrimages (fleeing from the coast, from the sea and its suicidal temptation), the men of this race finally established themselves in the mountainous region of Chiapas, in a plateau rich in pastures, woods and water. There prosperity made them lift their heads up high, and filled their hearts with haughtiness and greed. Frequently the Bolometic would come down from the mountains to feed on the possessions of the neighbouring tribes.

With the arrival of the white men, known as *caxlanes*, the belligerent and fiery Bolometic leapt into battle with such force that they dashed themselves against the invading iron and crumbled to pieces. Worse than vanquished, aghast, the Bolometic felt for the first time in their own flesh the rigours of defeat. They were stripped of their belongings, thrown into jail, forced into slavery. Those who managed to escape (their newly acquired poverty inspired them, made them invisible to their enemies' fury) sought refuge at the foot of the hills. There they stopped to look back and see what the calamity had left them, and there they began a precarious life in which the memory of past greatness slowly vanished, and history became a dying fire that no-one was capable of rekindling.

From time to time, a few of the bravest men would climb down to the neighbouring settlements and trade in their harvest; they would also visit the sanctuaries, praying to the Higher Powers that They cease tormenting their *waigel*, their tiger, whom the shaman could hear, roaring and wounded, high above in the thicket. The Bolometic were generous in their offerings, and yet their prayers were not answered. Their tiger was

yet to receive many more wounds.

The *caxlanes*' greed cannot be stifled either by force or with gifts. It sleeps not. It watches, wide awake, within the white men, within their children, within their children's children. And the *caxlanes* march on, never sleeping, trampling the earth with the iron hoofs of their horses, casting around their hawk's eyes, nervously clicking their whips.

The Bolometic saw the advancing threat but did not run, as before, to lift the weapons they no longer had the courage to wield. They drew together, trembling with fear, to discuss their own conduct, as if they were about to appear before a demanding and merciless tribunal. They would not defend themselves: how could they? They had forgotten the art of war and had not learnt that of arguing. They would humble themselves. But the white man's heart is made of stuff that does not grow soft with prayers. And mercy is a fine plum on a captain's helmet, but does not dust the sand that dries the clerk's legal documents.

'In this speaking paper all truth is set. And the truth is that all this land, with its hillsides good for the sowing of corn, with its pine forests to be felled for logs and fire-wood, with its rivers good for mills, is the property of Don Diego Mijangos y Orantes, who has proven direct lineage from that other Don Viego Mijangos, conquistador, and from the later Mijangos, respectable slave traders. Therefore you, Sebastian Gomez Escopeta, and you, Lorenzo Perez Diezmo, and you, Juan Dominguez Ventana, or whatever your name is, you're not wanted here, you're taking up room that doesn't belong to you, and that is a crime punished by the law. Off with you, you good-for-nothings. Away.'

Centuries of submission had deformed that race. Quickly they lowered their faces in obeisance; meekly they turned their backs to run. The women went ahead, carrying the children and a few necessary utensils. The elderly men followed on slow feet. And further back, protecting the exodus, the men.

Hard days, with no goal in sight. Leaving one place because it was unfriendly, and another not to fight over it with its owners. Provisions and vittuals were scarce. Those whom hunger bit more cruelly than others dared to sneak out at night, near the maize fields, and under cover of darkness would steal a few ripe stalks of grain, a few edible leaves. But the dogs would sniff out the strangers and bark their warning. The guards would arrive whirling their machetes and making such a racket that the intruders would flee, panic-stricken. But they would carry on their quest, starving, in hiding, the long hair bedraggled and the clothes in shreds.

Misery ravaged the tribe, badly protected from the harsh weather. The cold breathed upon them its lethal breath and shrouded them in a whitish, thick fog. First the children, who died without understanding why, their little fists tightly clenched as if trying to cling onto the last wisp of heat. Then the old people, huddled next to the campfire ashes, without uttering a single moan. The women hid themselves to die, with a last display of modesty, as in the happy old days they had hidden themselves to give birth.

These were the ones who stayed behind, those who would never see their new homeland. They finally set up camp on a high terrace, so high that it cut in two the white man's cold breath, a land swept by hostile winds, poor, scorned even by the vilest weeds and creepers, the earth showing its barren entrails through the deep cracks. The brackish water lay far away.

A few stole pregnant ewes and herded them in secret. The women set up a loom, waiting for the first shearing. Others ploughed the land, the inflexible, avaricious land. The rest set off on long journeys to pray for divine benevolence in sanctuaries set aside for holy worship.

But times were grim and hunger was on the rampage, going from house to house, knocking at every door with its bony hand.

The men, after meeting in council, decided to leave. The women forewent the last mouthful so as not to hand them an empty basket. And at the crossroads they said their farewells.

On and on. The Bolometic never rested, even at night. Their torches could be seen snaking down the blackness of the hills.

Now, in Ciudad Real men no longer live according to their whims or their needs. In the planning of this city of white men, of *caxlanes*, what ruled was the intelligence. The streets cross each other in geometrical patterns. The houses are of one and the same height, of one and the same style. A few display on their facades a coat of arms, because their owners are the descendants of those warriors — conquistadores, the first colonisers — whose deeds still ring with an heroic peal in certain family names: Marin, De la Tovilla, Mazariegos.

During the colonial centuries and the first decades of independence, Ciudad Real was the provincial seat of government. It boasted the opulence and abundance of commerce, it became the beacon of culture. But in the years to come, only one high function still kept its seat in Ciudad Real: the bishopric.

Now the city's splendour was a thing of the past. Decay gnawed at its very innards. Men with neither temerity nor vision, full of their own importance, deep in the contemplation of the past, gave up the political sceptre, let go the reins of commerce, closed the book of intellectual endeavours. Surrounded by a tight ring of indian communities, all silently hostile, Ciudad Real always maintained with them a one-sided relationship. The systematic plunder was answered by a latent grumbling that a few times exploded into bloody uprisings. And each time Ciudad Real seemed less capable of stifling these by itself. Neighbouring towns — Comitan, Tuxtla, Chiapa de Corzo — came to its aid. Towards them flew the wealth, fame, command. Ciudad Real became nothing but a presumptuous and empty shell, a scarecrow that only scared the indian soul, stubbornly attached to fear.

The Bolometic crossed the first streets amid the silent disapproval of the passers-by who, with squeamish gestures, avoided brushing that offensive misery.

The indians examined the spectacle before their eyes with curiosity, insistence, and lack of understanding. The massive walls of the *caxlanes'* temples weighed upon them almost as if they were obliged to carry that weight on their shoulders. The exquisite beauty of the ornaments — certain iron railings, the detailed carving of some of the stones — awoke in the Bolometic the desire to destroy them. They laughed at the sudden appearance of an object whose purpose they could not guess: fans, porcelain figures, lace clothing. They remained in ecstasy in front of a photographer's samples: postcards in which a melancholy lady appeared, meditating next to a broken column, while in the distant horizon sunk the also melancholy sun.

And people? How did the Bolometic see the people? They did not recognise the pettiness of these little men, short, plump, red-cheeked, the lees of a full-blooded, intrepid race. In front of their eyes they only saw the lightning which, in the past, had struck them down. And through the ugliness and decadence, the superstitious soul of the defeated could still make out the mysterious sign of the omnipotent *caxlan* god.

The women of Ciudad Real, the *coletas*, shuffled along the streets with small reticent steps, like doves; the eyes lowered, the cheeks blushing under the rough stroke of the wind. Silence and mourning went with them. And when they spoke, they spoke with that moss-like voice which puts tiny children to sleep, comforts the sick, helps the dying. The voice of those who watch the men go by from behind a window-pane.

The marketplace attracted the foreigners with its bustle. Here was the throne of plenty. Here was corn which stuffed the granaries with its yellow gold; here were red-blooded beasts, slaughtered, hanging from enormous hooks. The mellow fruits, delicious: peaches with their skins of eternal youth; bananas, strong and sturdy; the apple that, at times, tastes like the blade of a knife. And coffee, fragrant from a distance. And sweet preserves, baroque, christened with faraway tribal names: *tartaritas, africanas*. And bread with which God greets man every morning.

This was what the Bolometic saw, and they saw it with an amazement that was not touched with greed, that destroyed any thoughts of greed. With religious amazement.

The policeman in charge of watching over the marketplace was strolling aimlessly among the stalls, humming a song, waving away, here and there, a stray fly. But when he noticed the presence of the bunch of ragged loafers — he was accustomed to seeing them on their own, not in a group and with a leader — he automatically became suspicious. He gripped tight onto his stick, ready to swing it at the first attempt to steal, or to break that long and nebulous article of the law which he had never read but in whose existence he believed: causing public disturbances. But the Bolometic's intentions seemed to be peaceful. They had left the marketplace and were now looking for an empty spot among the pews of the Church of La Merced. On their haunches, the indians patiently began to pick off their fleas and eat them. The policeman watched them from afar, pleased because contempt was on his side.

A gentleman who kept hovering around the Bolometic decided at last that he would speak to them. Fat, bald, full of forced merriment, he said to them in their own tongue:

'So, you there. Are you looking for work?'

The Bolometic looked at each other quickly and in panic. Each one left upon the other the responsibility of answering. Finally, the one who looked the most venerable — he was the most respected of the group because of his age and because he had once before been to Ciudad Real — asked:

'Can you find us work? Are you a "collector"?'

'Exactly, my good fellow. And known to be fair and honest. My name is Juvencio Ortiz.'

'Ah yes. Don Juvencio.'

The comment was less an echo of his fame than a sign of good manners. Silence spread upon them like a stain. Don Juvencio drummed his fingers on the curve of his stomach, at the height of the waistcoat button where the watch chain should have hung. Remembering that he did not yet own a watch chain made him dig his spurs into the conversation.

'Well, then? Do we have a deal?'

But the indians were in no hurry. There is never any hurry to fall into a trap.

'We came down from our lands. There's not much there, sir. The crops won't give.'

'Exactly my point. Let's go to the office and sort out the details.'

Don Juvencio began to walk, certain that the indians would follow. Hypnotised by his assurance, the indians went after him.

What Don Juvencio so pompously called his 'office' was a dirty circular room on one of the streets off the marketplace. The furniture consisted of two wooden tables — more than once the splinters of their badly smoothed top had torn the sleeves of the only suits Don Juvencio and his associate possessed — a shelf full of papers, and two chairs of unsteady legs. On one of them, perched with the provisional attitude of a bird, was Don Juvencio's associate; a large profile, protected by a green plastic visor. He croaked as the visitors appeared before him.

'What good things are you bringing us, Don Juvencio?'

'Whatever I could get hold of, my dear friend. Competition is tough. "Collectors" with fewer merits than mine — and I have a lawyer's degree, given by the Law School of Ciudad Real — and less experienced than myself, steal our clients away.'

'They use other methods. You've never made use of drink, for instance. A drunk indian never notices what he does or what he agrees to do. But skimping on drink...'

'Not at all. But taking advantage of these poor souls when they are unconscious is, as His Illustrious Don Manuel Oropeza would say, a despicable thing to do.'

Don Juvencio's associate showed his teeth in a wicked little smile.

'Well, your morals make our fortune. You were the one who said that everything might be lacking in this world, but there would always be indians to spare. So we'll see. The farms that have put us in charge of their management run the risk of losing their crops for want of workers.'

'Wise men change opinions, my dear partner. I also used to say... But anyway, no need to complain. Here they are.'

Don Juvencio made a wide gesture with his arm, like a magician unveiling his bag of tricks. But his associate's admiration remained undaunted.

'These?'

Don Juvencio saw himself obliged to change his tone of voice.

'These? Don't use that tone of voice with me... What's wrong with them?'

Don Juvencio's associate shrugged his shoulders.

'They've got vultures pecking at their back, that's what's wrong. They'll never endure the climate on the coast. And you, who are so particular...'

Don Juvencio drew close to his associate, lifting a finger in mock anger.

'You... No wonder they call you a Jonah! Just remember, dear friend, the saying about minding one's own business. Is it our responsibility whether these indians stand up or not to the climate? Our only obligation is to see that they arrive alive at the farm. What happens afterwards is none of our business.'

And to avoid further discussion he moved towards the shelf and took out a pile of papers. After handing them over to his associate, Don Juvencio turned towards the Bolometic and ordered:

'Come on now, get in line. One by one, go up to this gentleman's desk and answer his questions. No lies, because the gentleman is a sorcerer and can hurt you badly. You know why he wears that visor? So as not to burn you with his eyes.'

The Bolometic listened with ever-growing anguish. How would they be able to keep on hiding their true name?

They waited. But they knew it was useless.

And this is how the Bolometic placed the name of their *waigel,* the wounded tiger, under the will and command of those ink-stained hands.

'Pablo Gomez Bolom.'

'Daniel Hernandez Bolom.'

'Jose Dominguez Bolom.'

Don Juvencio's associate drilled the indians with useless suspicion. As usual, he thought, they were making fun of him. Afterwards, when they escaped from the farms without paying their debts, no-one would be able to find them, because the place they said they came from did not exist, and the names they gave as theirs were false.

But no, in the name of the Holy Virgin of Caridad, enough! Don Juvencio's associate banged his fist on the table, furious. His knowledge of the indian tongue was not enough to allow him to argue. Grumbling, all he said was:

'Bolom! I'll give you "bolom"! Let's see the next one.'

As soon as they had finished the associate let Don Juvencio know.

'Forty. What farm shall we send them to?'

'We'll service Don Federico Werner once and for all. He's the most urgent. Write down "Coffee Plantation El Suspiro." In Tapachuela.'

As he wrote, his eyes protected by the green visor, Don Juvencio's associate insisted:

'Forty's not enough.'

'Not enough? Forty indians to pick the coffee beans on one farm? Worse is nothing. Not enough?'

'The forty won't reach the farm. They won't last the journey.'

And Don Juvencio's associate turned the page, satisfied he was right.

WITH the advance money they had received, the Bolometic began their journey. Gradually, they left behind the wilderness of the hills and were shrouded in a sad, gritty breeze that broke into their misery. They could smell in the breeze sweet things. And they felt restless, like dogs on the trace of an unknown prey.

The height, leaving them so abruptly, shattered their eardrums. They were in pain, they bled from their ears. When the Bolometic reached the sea, they thought that its immense fury was mute.

The only presence that never left them was the cold, unwilling to abandon the bodies it had always held in its grip. Every day, at the same time, even when the tropical sun hit the grey stones, the cold would uncoil like a repulsive snake and slither over the Bolometic's bodies, stiffening their jaws, their arms and legs, with a terrible trembling. After that, the Bolometic would feel faint, shrunk, as if little by little the cold were shrivelling them in order to better fit in their awaiting tomb.

Those who survived that long journey were never able to return. The debts would form a cage, link after link, chaining them to their new master. In the eardrum scars there echoed, more and more faintly, the voices of their women, calling them, and of their children, dying out.

The tiger in the hills was never heard of again. ❏

© *Rosario Castellanos, reprinted from* Ciudad Real, *1960*
© *Translation Alberto Manguel 1985*

NEDIM GÜRSEL

The graveyard of unwritten books

BEFORE moving to Paris, Rue du Figuier or Figtree Street, I thought writing was a way of life. I haven't changed my mind but, since settling on this street lined with old buildings, the writing craft (which implies being in touch with the world and with its people, taking the pulse of the sea, streets, cities, children and trees, earth and birds, day and night, that is to say, nature and human society — that opening towards the Other), transformed itself, first into complete solitude and then, progressively, into an authoritarian domination. I'm no longer as I used to be, tender and free in my relationship to words. I no longer abandon myself easily to the words circling over my head, like the small moths that are drawn to my lamp at night, through the open window. Instead of savouring their exquisite shapes — the iridescent glitter of their wings, the sounds they make as they fly about — instead of overcoming my longing for my country and my mother tongue by caressing them with my eyes, I take on the role of an implacable and crafty hunter.

I don't believe that there is a direct link between my new address and the obligatory change in my conception of what the writer's craft should be. At least, that was my belief until the day when, out of curiosity, I began to research the history of my street and the origin of its name. Earlier on, I had lived in Paris in similar lodgings, small bedsitters or single rooms under the eaves where, bent over white sheets of paper spread out over my desk, I would constantly stare at the overcast sky, at the blackened walls, or at the television antennae standing erect across from me like a field full of scarecrows. I have more or less the same kind of view from here. But the Hôtel de Sens, flanked by its turrets that rise up at the level of my new flat, adds a new dimension to the scene. I can't tear my eyes away from the courtyard of this astonishing building, surrounded by high walls. Whatever time I choose to sit down and write, I see the words scatter away instead of lining up neatly on the blank space of the page in front of me, and then take wing towards the courtyard of the Hôtel de Sens which, with its corner turrets, its loopholes, its gargoyles, its newly built porch reminiscent of a ruined drawbridge, resembles more a fortress than a sixteenth-century mansion, so common in this old neighbourhood of Paris. All my efforts are in vain! I can no longer make the words obey me nor can I exercise control over them, as I used to in the past. Even if I catch a few words in mid-flight to imprison them on paper, others succeed in escaping. And yet, in earlier times, a robust understanding existed between us, since my freedom as a writer depended on their will to serve me. Until now, placed, displaced, crossed out, lined up according to grammatical rules, they had always been under my yoke — under my command I should say — when I wrote my books. They had never behaved in such an unruly manner, even when I'd try to invent new narrative procedures, thereby upsetting their syntax; I still had a good grip on them. Letters too. They didn't use to make me lose my temper as easily as they did now, splitting off from one word to attach themselves to another and, through various acrobatic acts, dispel the meanings with which I tried to infuse the words. Now, however hard I try to write, they proclaim their freedom from my guardianship and their will to do as they please. As the pressure on them increases, they tend ever more forcefully towards revolt and defiance. Our agreement, the interdependence born from the relation between master and slave, has changed into a bizarre game of pursuit. Even though I appear, in the eyes of most readers, to be a respectable writer, I've become a pitiful blindfolded fool in a game of blind-man's-bluff. I could certainly not have guessed, when writing out the working-title of this story, that an *L* would escape from the word it was in, to come and dislodge the *R*. But that is exactly what happened. And the rest followed. Once *The Well of Rocks* changed into *The Well of Locks*, the other letters followed the steps of the first mutineers and stopped listening to me once and for all. I was obliged, whether I wanted to or not, to change the text according to their whims. Now the words, whose mastery I'd lost since my moving to Rue du Figuier, began to detach themselves from the sentences and then, as I continued to write my story, started to swim up to the surface like air bubbles in

water, floating off towards the Hôtel de Sens. At first I imagined that
their flight was caused by the peculiar name of the building, Hôtel de
Sens, which would translate as 'The Mansion of Meaning' in English.
They might indeed have been attracted by such an eloquent title. How
could I have known that the Hôtel de Sens, rising before me as if out of
another world and whose draughts of medieval air, winding their way
through the gloomy maze of corridors, made me shiver, owed its name
to Tristan de Salazar, Archbishop of Sens, who ordered its construction?
Where could I have learned that what was capturing my words — my
dear words plucked with a thousand and one difficulties from the
uttermost recesses of my memory and from the most sensitive folds of
my being, to be offered to my readers — happened to be a disaffected
well in the courtyard of the Hôtel de Sens?

That afternoon, I worked until late at the library. Since the sixteenth
century, the Hôtel de Sens had been the residence of several old French
families; now, for the past three decades, it was in use as a library. After
having concealed so many secrets, passions, dead loves and terrible
crimes, it now housed thousands of printed volumes. In the ancient
ballroom where, in times gone by, under the light of flaming torches, the
noblemen of the kingdom had danced and made merry with their ladies,
a few passionate booklovers such as myself now sat so absorbed in their
reading that they failed to notice that, behind the stained-glass windows,
it was growing dark.

I stayed at the library until late, oblivious that the Parisian night had
fallen suddenly on the roofs. A hand touched my shoulder, making me
jump. It was the librarian saying that the closing time was long past, that
seeing me read without once lifting my head from the book in which I
was immersed, he hadn't wanted to disturb me, but that now I had to
leave. If I wished, I could borrow the book I was reading. After
thanking him for his understanding, I left carrying the book. As I was
walking down the stairs, he shouted after me:

'The doorman has locked the entrance gate. Go across the courtyard,
you'll be able to exit through the back door.'

As far as I know, the Hôtel de Sens has no entrance other than the
portico resembling a drawbridge. To avoid further disturbing the
librarian, I didn't ask him where exactly was the back door. I quickly
walked down the stairs and found myself in the courtyard. Night had
fallen, and it was pitch dark. A ray of yellow light filtering through the

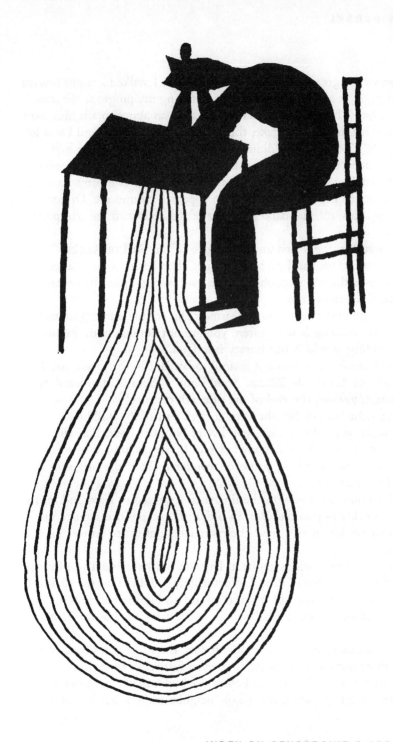

windows of the great hall fell on the courtyard. I walked straight towards it, lifted my eyes and saw the librarian watching my progress. We stared at each other. Then, all of a sudden, just as I was about to ask him, with gestures, what direction to take, the light was switched off and I was left in the dark. The city lights didn't reach the courtyard over the high walls. I decided to climb back upstairs and look for the librarian who had just switched off the lights, and then leave in his company. As I was about to retrace my steps, the librarian appeared behind me. Directing his flashlight towards the darkest corner of the courtyard, he whispered in my ear:

'This way, Sir. We'll pass under the gate of the Well of Rocks.'

There was no well and no rock in sight. The beam of light, after sweeping over the rough cobbles of the yard, shone upon the cement. He noticed my hesitation.

'Sir, I quite understand your uneasiness,' he continued. 'Apparently, in spite of your coming here so often, you are not familiar with the history of the building in which our library is lodged.'

'True, I knew nothing about it until today. But in that book you lent me I read that Tristan de Salazar, Archbishop of Sens, had ordered its construction towards the end of the fifteenth century.'

'I meant the history, Sir, the very ancient past of the building. According to your library card, you live at Number Four, Rue du Figuier. Let us say that your knowledge of history is limited to a few centuries. In that case, have you ever wondered about the origin of the name of your street?'

I had no time to chat with the librarian. I wanted to leave and return home as quickly as possible. But, in order not to appear discourteous after his earlier kindness, I nevertheless made an effort to answer his question:

'Had I not been curious about it, I would not have asked you for the book called *The Streets of Paris*. Unfortunately, I didn't find the slightest information in it on the history of the Rue du Figuier before the sixteenth century. It was probably built at the same time as the Hôtel de Sens.'

'No. According to irrefutable documents, the street dates back to the thirteenth century. But let us go back even further in time. I'm convinced that several centuries before the building of the Hôtel de Sens, even in an age when this whole neighbourhood didn't exist and

subscribe today!

[UK: one year for only £36*]

Name

Address

Postcode

*Overseas orders (exc US/Canada) should add £6 for postage.

Payment: £ _____ total. ❏ Cheque (£) ❏ Visa/Mastercard ❏ Am Exp

Card No.

Expiry   Signature   B6A6

❏ I do not wish to receive mail from other companies.

INDEX 33 Islington High St, London N1 9LH *last word*
Fax: 0171 278 1878 E-mail indexoncenso@gn.apc.org

subscribe today!

[US: one year for only $50*]

Name

Address

Postcode

*Overseas orders (exc US/Canada/UK) should add $9 for postage.

Payment: £ _____ total. ❏ Cheque (US$) ❏ Visa/Mastercard ❏ Am Ex

Card No.

Expiry   Signature   B6B6

❏ I do not wish to receive mail from other companies.

INDEX 708 Third Avenue, 8th Floor, New York, New York 10017
Fax: 0171 278 1878 E-mail indexoncenso@gn.apc.org

INDEX ON CENSORSHIP
33 Islington High Street
London N1 9BR
United Kingdom

INDEX ON CENSORSHIP
708 Third Avenue
8th Floor
New York, NY 10164-3005

Paris, called then Lutetia, was a walled fortress on the Ile de la Cité of some 20,000 inhabitants, there was a figtree growing among rocks exactly there where this street now lies. Later, a well was dug among the rocks at the foot of the tree, so that those who wanted to rest in the tree's shade could also refresh themselves with a drink from the well. In fact, the well was used mainly for watering the crops, since the area was farmed for marshland produce. The well still exists. The figtree is long since dead, but the water from that well served to mix the mortar used in the building of the Hôtel de Sens. And Queen Margot, after ordering the execution of her overnight lovers, had them thrown into this same well.'

I was starting to itch with impatience. All this talk didn't interest me in the least.

'Please excuse me,' I said. 'I have an urgent meeting elsewhere. What if we chatted about this some other day? I'll be back tomorrow. Right now, let us get out of here.'

'I understand your haste, Sir, but you should indeed pay attention to my story. Our leaving depends to some degree on the Well of Rocks.'

'I don't understand. A while ago you said I would be able to leave by the back door.'

'Yes, but in order to reach it, we must climb down into the bottom of the well, since the gate I mentioned isn't here, but in the inner courtyard.'

'How is that possible?', I asked anxiously. 'Look over there; I live on the top floor of the building opposite. From my window I can see the whole of the Hôtel de Sens. If there were a courtyard other than this one, it would certainly not have escaped my notice.'

'I know you spend the night writing to the light of your lamp, and that you often lift your head from your papers to look at the Hôtel de Sens. I've been watching you since you moved here. But you can't learn anything from such a great height. I've been working in this library for the past 20 years and it is only recently that I've discovered this inner courtyard.'

'Impossible. In the oldest documents which I've consulted in the archives, on the most detailed plans of the building, there was never any mention of such a courtyard. You must have seen a mirage.'

He didn't answer. He simply smiled superciliously. I was on the point of losing my patience.

'If you don't mind, I want to get out of here at once,' I insisted.

'It cannot be done.'

'Why?'

'We must first climb down into the Well of Rocks.'

He asked me to follow him and he started to lead the way. At the end of the courtyard, we stopped by the wall. Pointing the beam of his flashlight towards one of the mossy stones, he said:

'We'll make our way through here.'

In the light, I saw the stone move on its base. In front of us a passage opened, big enough for a small child. The librarian climbed through it first, then he lit my way with his flashlight. I found myself inside a narrow and gloomy gallery. Crouching as we walked, we reached at last the inner courtyard. In the very centre of this secret courtyard, which I guessed was surrounded by the inside walls of one of the corner turrets, there was indeed a well. We approached it. The librarian began to climb down the rope ladder that lost itself in its depths. I followed. Curiously, I didn't feel the least anguish. There was no room in me for even the slightest unease. Everything seemed rather natural to me. My earlier absent-mindedness while I was reading in the library the documents relating to the Rue du Figuier, my conversation with the librarian, my arrival close behind him in this secret courtyard, our descent into a dry well by means of a rope ladder — all seemed quite commonplace, just as if every night I followed this route on my way home to my workdesk. Nothing disturbed me: neither the librarian's sententious words, nor the insects scuttling away in the beam of his electric flashlight, not even the spider webs clinging to my feet during the descent. At last we reached the bottom of the well. In front of us stretched a gallery with a higher ceiling and we were able to proceed with ease. We walked for a long while inside that dark tunnel with dripping walls, when suddenly we began to hear the sound of rattling chains. The further we went, the louder the sound grew. We stopped in front of an iron door. The librarian knocked. The door creaked open and, as soon as we stepped inside, I was blinded by the light. We were inside an immense storeroom lit with spotlights. Attendants in official uniforms moved feverishly in all directions. As soon as my eyes grew accustomed to the spotlights, I saw a pile of books in the middle of the room. The attendants were picking them up by the armful and placing them on metallic shelves that towered all the way up to the ceiling; once the shelves were full, they prevented access to the books by securing them with chains.

'We are now in the Well of Locks,' said the librarian. 'Please hide the book you just borrowed. If the attendants see it, it too will be secured under lock and chain.'

I slipped the book I was holding into the inside pocket of my jacket, and we followed the line of shelves. No-one paid any attention to us. They were all busy stashing away on the shelves the books that were being thrown from above into the middle of the storeroom, and then chaining them in.

'These are the books banned by the authorities,' the librarian continued. 'Don't pay attention to their number. If you were to count them, you'd realise they are hardly more than a hundred. But when a book is banned, all editions of that book are also pulled out of circulation. They are then brought here to be placed under lock. Sometimes I'm called upon to help draw up the lists of banned titles.'

So the librarian was in fact an informer! This fake scholar, this hypocrite who earned his living thanks to the books he lent to readers, spent his nights compiling blacklists!

'How can you take part in such shameful activities!', I shouted at him.

'Don't be angry, my dear Sir,' he answered in a mocking tone, 'I have a passion for books, I'm mad about books. I love books and therefore I punish them. They're like my children to me.'

'But books don't need to be taught manners!'

'Why not? Like human beings, they are born, they grow up and they can turn out good or bad. Then, my dear Sir, they die. Their pages fall out and they disappear like corpses rotting underground.'

'No! Books are immortal! Human beings die, but not books!'

'Some die even before seeing the light of day. Your own, for instance.'

'My own?'

'Yes, a few of your books, those placed here in chains, are first among the books that were aborted or stillborn. And you didn't even know it.'

The librarian's words turned my blood to ice. The Ministry of Justice had only just lifted the ban on certain books of mine. So what did the librarian mean? Noticing my astonishment, he stopped one of the attendants hurrying past us and asked him to put down his armload of books. The attendant did so, as if obeying the orders of a superior. After having clicked his heels and saluted, he hurried away. The librarian chose a book from the pile and handed it over to me.

'Look, here's your latest book.'

I trembled as I saw my name on the cover. It carried the title of one of the stories I had tried in vain to write without ever being able to see its end. It was a beautiful edition, carefully printed. As I leafed through it, I felt terrified. Here were all the stories I had planned to write since my move to Rue du Figuier.

'Before martial law was proclaimed in the country, this was the graveyard of unwritten books,' the librarian explained. 'Then the banned books were added to them. You have several books in both categories. Gradually, as judges who support freedom of thought authorise the reissuing of your censored volumes, the number of your unwritten books increases. In a sense, it is you yourself who bans them. I only do my duty. Deep down inside, I'm fond of writers. If you wish to continue to write, leave your new lodgings at once. Don't bother with words that rebel against you and that will no longer listen to you. When you have moved far away from the Well of Rocks, drifting once again towards the light of your lamp, they will most certainly return, as if by miracle, to find you once again.'

I felt an irresistible impulse to escape from the cursed graveyard as quickly as possible. The repulsive man who called himself a librarian was obviously the graveyard's caretaker. And, what was worse, he was also a loathsome gravedigger! I didn't allow him to accompany me to the door. I started to run after my words fluttering towards the Hôtel de Sens. I crossed the iron door and, after it had creaked shut behind me, I made up my mind to write the tale of how my last story, which I had wanted to call *The Well of Rocks*, had become *The Well of Locks* and, finally, *The Graveyard of Unwritten Books*. As I ran, I felt I was being pursued by the sound of rattling chains. Then the damp walls of the gallery shook, as if the shelves loaded with books were collapsing behind me. ❏

© *Nedim Gürsel,* Son Tramway, *1990*
© *Translation (from the French) Alberto Manguel 1996*

URSULA K. LE GUIN

The diary of the rose

30 August

D R NADES recommends that I keep a diary of
my work. She says that if you keep it carefully,
when you reread it you can remind yourself of observations you made,
notice errors and learn from them, and observe progress in or deviations
from positive thinking, and so keep correcting the course of your work
by a feedback process.

I promise to write in this notebook every night, and reread it at the
end of each week.

I wish I had done it while I was an assistant, but it is even more
important now that I have patients of my own.

As of yesterday I have six patients, a full load for a scopist, but four of
them are the autistic children I have been working with all year for Dr
Nades's study for the Nat'l. Psych. Bureau (my notes on them are in the
cli psy files). The other two are new admissions:

Ana Jest, 46, bakery packager, md., no children, diag. depression,
referral from city police (suicide attempt).

Flores Sorde, 36, engineer, unmd., no diag., referral from TRTU
(Psychopathic behavior — Violent).

Dr Nades says it is important that I write things down each night just
as they occurred to me at work: it is the spontaneity that is most
informative in self-examination (just as in autopsychoscopy). She says it
is better to write it, not dictate on to tape, and keep it quite private, so
that I won't be self-conscious. It is hard. I never wrote anything that was
private before. I keep feeling as if I was really writing it for Dr Nades!
Perhaps if the diary is useful I can show her some of it later, and get her
advice.

My guess is that Ana Jest is in menopausal depression and hormone therapy will be sufficient. There! Now let's see how bad a prognostician I am.

Will work with both patients under scope tomorrow. It is exciting to have my own patients, I am impatient to begin. Though of course teamwork was very educational.

31 August
Half-hour scope session with Ana J. at 8:00. Analyzed scope material, 11:00-17:00. N.B.: Adjust right-brain pickup next session! Weak visual Concrete. Very little aural, weak sensory, erratic body image. Will get lab analyses tomorrow of hormone balance.

It is amazing how banal most people's minds are. Of course the poor woman is in severe depression. Input in the Con dimension was foggy and incoherent, and the Uncon dimension as deeply open, but obscure. But the things that came out of the obscurity were so trivial! A pair of old shoes, and the word 'geography'! And the shoes were dim, a mere schema of a pair-of-shoes, maybe a man's maybe a woman's, maybe dark blue maybe brown. Although definitely a visual type, she does not see anything clearly. Not many people do. It is depressing. When I was a student in first year I used to think how wonderful other people's minds would be, how wonderful it was going to be to share in all the different worlds, the different colors of their passions and ideas. How naive I was!

I realised this first in Dr Ramia's class when we studied a tape from a very famous successful person, and I noticed that the subject had never looked at a tree, never touched one, did not know any difference between an oak and a poplar, or even between a daisy and a rose. They were all just 'trees' or 'flowers' to him, apprehended schematically. It was the same with people's faces, though he had tricks for telling them apart: mostly he saw the name, like a label, not the face. That was an Abstract mind, of course, but it can be even worse with the Concretes, whose perceptions come in a kind of undifferentiated sludge — bean soup with a pair of shoes in it.

But aren't I 'going native'? I've been studying a depressive's thoughts all day and have got depressed. Look, I wrote up there, 'It is depressing.' I see the value of this diary already. I know I am over-impressionable.

Of course, that is why I am a good psychoscopist. But it is dangerous. No session with F. Sorde today since sedation had not worn off.

TRTU referrals are often so drugged that they cannot be scoped for days.

REM scoping session with Ana J. at 4:00 tomorrow. Better go to bed!

1 September
Dr Nades says the kind of thing I wrote yesterday is pretty much what she had in mind, and invited me to show her this diary again whenever I am in doubt. Spontaneous thoughts — not the technical data, which are recorded in the files anyhow. Cross nothing out. Candor all-important.

Ana's dream was interesting but pathetic. The wolf who turned into a pancake! Such a disgusting, dim, hairy pancake, too. Her visuality is clearer in dream, but the feeling tone remains low (but remember: *you* contribute the affect — don't read it in). Started her on hormone therapy today.

F. Sorde awake, but too confused to take to scope room for session. Frightened. Refused to eat. Complained of pain in side. I thought he was unclear what kind of hospital this is, and told him there was nothing wrong with him physically. He said, 'How the hell do you know?' which was fair enough, since he was in straitjacket, due to the V notation on his chart. I examined and found bruising and contusion, and ordered X-ray, which showed two ribs cracked. Explained to patient that he had been in a condition where forcible restraint had been necessary to prevent self-injury. He said, 'Every time one of them asked a question the other one kicked me.' He repeated this several times, with anger and confusion. Paranoid delusional system? If it does not weaken as the drugs wear off, I will proceed on that assumption. He responds fairly well to me, asked my name when I went to see him with the X-ray plate, and agreed to eat. I was forced to apologise to him, not a good beginning with a paranoid. The rib damage should have been marked on his charge by the referring agency or by the medic who admitted him. This kind of carelessness is distressing.

But there's good news too. Rina (Autism Study subject 4) saw a first-person sentence today. Saw it: in heavy, black, primer print, all at once in the high Con foreground: *I want to sleep in the big room.* (She sleeps alone because of the faeces problem.) The sentence stayed clear for over five seconds. She was reading it in her mind just as I was reading it on the holoscreen. There was weak subverbalisation, but not subvocalisation, nothing on the audio. She has not yet spoken, even to herself, in the first person. I told Tio about it at once and he asked her after the session, 'Rina, where do you want to sleep?' — 'Rina sleep in the big room.' No pronoun, no conative. But one of these days she will say *I want* — aloud. And on that build a personality, maybe, at last: on that foundation. I want, therefore I am.

There is so much fear. Why is there so much fear?

4 September
Went to town for my two-day holiday. Stayed with B. in her new flat on the north bank. Three rooms to herself!!! But I don't really like those old buildings, there are rats and roaches, and it feels so old and strange, as if somehow the famine years were still there, waiting. Was glad to get back to my little room here, all to myself but with others close by on the same floor, friends and colleagues. Anyway I missed writing in this book. I form habits very fast. Compulsive tendency.

Ana much improved: dressed, hair combed, was knitting. But session was dull. Asked her to think about pancakes, and there it came filling up the whole Uncon dimension, the hairy, dreary, flat wolf-pancake, while in the Con she was obediently trying to visualise a nice cheese blintz. Not too badly: colors and outlines already stronger. I am still willing to count on simple hormone treatment. Of course they will suggest ECT, and a co-analysis of the scope material would be perfectly possible, we'd start with the wolf-pancake, etc. But is there any real point to it? She has been a bakery packager for 24 years and her physical health is poor. She cannot change her life situation. At least with good hormone balance she may be able to endure it.

F. Sorde: rested but still suspicious. Extreme fear reaction when I said it was time for his first session. To allay this I sat down and talked about the nature and operation of the psychoscope. He listened intently and finally said, 'Are you going to use only the psychoscope?'

I said Yes.

He said, 'Not electroshock?'

I said No.

He said, 'Will you promise me that?'

I explained that I am a psychoscopist and never operate the electroconvulsive therapy equipment, that is an entirely different department. I said my work with him at present would be diagnostic, not therapeutic. He listened carefully. He is an educated person and

understands distinctions such as 'diagnostic' and 'therapeutic.' It is interesting that he asked me to *promise*. That does not fit a paranoid pattern, you don't ask for promises from those you can't trust. He came with me docilely, but when we entered the scope room he stopped and turned white at sight of the apparatus. I made Dr Aven's little joke about the dentist's chair, which she always used with nervous patients. F.S. said, 'So long as it's not an electric chair!'

I believe that with intelligent subjects it is much better not to make mysteries and so impose a false authority and a feeling of helplessness on the subject (see T.R. Olma, *Psychoscopy Technique*). So I showed him the chair and electrode crown and explained its operation. He has a layman's hearsay knowledge of the psychoscope, and his questions also reflected his engineering education. He sat down in the chair when I asked him. While I fitted the crown and clasps he was sweating profusely from fear, and this evidently embarrassed him, the smell. If he knew how Rina smells after she's been doing shit paintings. He shut his eyes and gripped the chair arms so that his hands went white to the wrist. The screens were almost white too. After a while I said in a joking tone, 'It doesn't really hurt, does it?'

'I don't know.'

'Well, does it?'

'You mean it's on?'

'It's been on for ninety seconds.'

He opened his eyes then and looked around, as well as he could for the head clamps. He asked, 'Where's the screen?'

I explained that a subject never watches the screen live, because the objectification can be severely disturbing, and he said, 'Like feedback from a microphone?' That is exactly the simile Dr Aven used to use. F.S. is certainly an intelligent person. N.B.: Intelligent paranoids are dangerous!

He asked, 'What do you see?' and I said, 'Do be quiet, I don't want to see what you're saying, I want to see what you're thinking,' and he said, 'But that's none of your business, you know,' quite gently, like a joke. Meanwhile the fear-white had gone into dark, intense, volitional convolutions, and then, a few seconds after he stopped speaking, a rose appeared on the whole Con dimension: a full-blown pink rose, beautifully sensed and visualised, clear and steady, whole.

He said presently, 'What am I thinking about, Dr Sobel?' and I said,

'Bears in the Zoo.' I wonder now why I said that. Self-defense? Against what? He gave a laugh and the Uncon went crystal-dark, relief, and the rose darkened and wavered. I said, 'I was joking. Can you bring the rose back?' That brought back the fear-white. I said, 'Listen, it's really very bad for us to talk like this during a first session, you have to learn a great deal before you co-analyse, and I have a great deal to learn about you, so no more jokes, please? Just relax physically, and think about anything you please.'

There was flurry and subverbalisation on the Con dimension, and the Uncon faded into grey, suppression. The rose came back weakly a few times. He was trying to concentrate on it, but couldn't. I saw several quick visuals: myself, my uniform, TRTU uniforms, a grey car, a kitchen, the violent ward (strong aural images — screaming), a desk, the papers on the desk. He stuck to those. They were the plans for a machine. He began going through them. It was a deliberate effort at suppression, and quite effective. Finally I said, 'What kind of machine is that?' and he began to answer aloud but stopped and let me get the answer subvocally in the earphone: 'Plans for a rotary engine assembly for traction,' or something like that, of course the exact words are on the tape. I repeated it aloud and said, 'They aren't classified plans, are they?' He said, 'No,' aloud, and added, 'I don't know any secrets.' His reaction to a question is intense and complex, each sentence is like a shower of pebbles thrown into a pool, the interlocking rings spread out quick and wide over the Con and into the Uncon, responses rising on all levels. Within a few seconds all that was hidden by a big signboard that appeared in the high Con foreground, deliberately visualised like the rose and the plans, with auditory reinforcement as he read it over and over: KEEP OUT! KEEP OUT! KEEP OUT!

It began to blur and flicker, and somatic signals took over, and soon he said aloud, 'I'm tired,' and I closed the session (12.5 min.).

After I took off the crown and clamps I brought him a cup of tea from the staff stand in the hall. When I offered it to him he looked startled and then tears came into his eyes. His hands were so cramped from gripping the armrests that he had trouble taking hold of the cup. I told him he must not be so tense and afraid, we are trying to help him not to hurt him.

He looked up at me. Eyes are like the scope screen and yet you can't read them. I wished the crown was still on him, but it seems you never catch the moments you most want on the scope. He said, 'Doctor, why am I in this hospital?'

I said, 'For diagnosis and therapy.'

He said, 'Diagnosis and therapy of *what*?'

I said he perhaps could not now recall the episode, but he had behaved strangely. He asked how and when, and I said that it would all come clear to him as therapy took effect. Even if I had known what his psychotic episode was, I would have said the same. It was correct procedure. But I felt in a false position. If the TRTU report was not classified, I would be speaking from knowledge and the facts. Then I could make a better response to what he said next:

'I was waked up at two in the morning, jailed, interrogated, beaten up, and drugged. I suppose I did behave a little oddly during that. Wouldn't you?'

'Sometimes a person under stress misinterprets other people's actions,' I said. 'Drink up your tea and I'll take you back to the ward. You're running a temperature.'

'The ward,' he said, with a kind of shrinking movement, and then he said almost desperately, 'Can you really not know why I'm here?'

That was strange, as if he has included me in his delusional system, *on 'his side.'* Check this possibility in Rheingeld. I should think it would involve some transference and there has not been time for that.

Spent pm analysing Jest and Sorde holos. I have never seen any psychoscopic realisation, not even a drug-induced hallucination, so fine and vivid as that rose. The shadows of one petal on another, the velvety damp texture of the petals, the pink color full of sunlight, the yellow central crown — I am sure the scent was there if the apparatus had olfactory pickup — it wasn't like a mentifact but a real thing rooted in the earth, alive and growing, the strong thorny stem beneath it.

Very tired, must go to bed.

Just reread this entry. Am I keeping this diary right? All I have written is what happened and what was said. Is that spontaneous? But it was *important* to me.

5 September
Discussed the problem of conscious resistance with Dr Nades at lunch today. Explained that I have worked with unconscious blocks (the children, and depressives such as Ana J.) and have some skill at reading

through, but have not before met a conscious block such as F.S.'s KEEP OUT sign, or the device he used today, which was effective for a full 20-minute session: a concentration on his breathing, bodily rhythms, pain in ribs, and visual input from the scope room. She suggested that I use a blindfold for the latter trick, and keep my attention on the Uncon dimension, as he cannot prevent material from appearing there. It is surprising, though, how large the interplay area of his Con and Uncon fields is, and how much one resonates into the other. I believe his concentration on his breathing rhythm allowed him to achieve something like 'trance' condition. Though of course most so-called 'trance' is mere occultist fakirism, a primitive trait without interest for behavioral science.

Ana thought through 'a day in my life' for me today. All so grey and dull, poor soul! She never thought even of food with pleasure, though she lives on minimum ration. The single thing that came bright for a moment was a child's face, clear dark eyes, a pink knitted cap, round cheeks. She told me in post-session discussion that she always walks by a school playground on the way to work because 'she likes to see the little ones running and yelling.' Her husband appears on the screen as a big bulky suit of work clothes and a peevish, threatening mumble. I wonder if she knows that she hasn't seen his face or heard a word he says for years? But no use telling her that. It may be just as well she doesn't.

The knitting she is doing, I noticed today, is a pink cap.

Reading De Cams's *Disaffection: A Study*, on Dr Nades's recommendation.

6 September

In the middle of the session (breathing again) I said loudly: 'Flores!'

Both psy dimensions whited out but the soma realisation hardly changed. After four seconds he responded aloud, drowsily. It is not 'trance,' but autohypnosis.

I said, 'Your breathing's monitored by the apparatus. I don't need to know that you're still breathing. It's boring.'

He said, 'I like to do my own monitoring, Doctor.'

I came around and took the blindfold off him and looked at him. He has a pleasant face, the kind of man you often see running machinery, sensitive but patient, like a donkey. That is stupid. I will not cross it out. I am supposed to be spontaneous in this diary. Donkeys do have beautiful faces. They are supposed to be stupid and balky but they look wise and calm, as if they had endured a lot but held no grudges, as if they knew some reason why one should not hold grudges. And the white ring around their eyes makes them look defenseless.

'But the more you breathe,' I said, 'the less you think. I need your cooperation. I'm trying to find out what it is you're afraid of.'

'But I know what I'm afraid of,' he said.

'Why won't you tell me?'

'You never asked me.'

'That's most unreasonable,' I said, which is funny, now I think about it, being indignant with a mental patient because he's unreasonable. 'Well, then, now I'm asking you.'

He said, 'I'm afraid of electroshock. Of having my mind destroyed. Being kept here. Or only being let out when I can't remember anything.' He gasped while he was speaking.

I said, 'All right, why won't you think about that while I'm watching the screens?'

'Why should I?'

'Why not? You've said it to me, why can't you think about it? I want to see the color of your thoughts!'

'It's none of your business, the color of my thoughts,' he said angrily, but I was around to the screen while he spoke, and saw the unguarded activity. Of course it was being taped while we spoke, too, and I have studied it all afternoon. It is fascinating. There are two subverbal levels running aside from the spoken words. All sensory-emotive reactions and distortions are vigorous and complex. He 'sees' me, for instance, in at least three different ways, probably more, analysis is impossibly difficult! And the Con-Uncon correspondences are so complicated, and the memory traces and current impressions interweave so rapidly, and yet the whole is unified in its complexity. It is like that machine he was studying, very intricate but all one thing in a mathematical harmony. Like the petals of the rose.

When he realised I was observing he shouted out, 'Voyeur! Damned voyeur! Let me alone! Get out!' and he broke down and cried. There was a clear fantasy on the screen for several seconds of himself breaking the arm and head clamps and kicking the apparatus to pieces and rushing out of the building, and there outside, there was a wide hilltop, covered with short dry grass, under the evening sky, and he stood there all alone. While he sat clamped in the chair sobbing.

I broke session and took off the crown, and asked him if he wanted some tea, but he refused to answer. So I freed his arms, and brought him a cup. There was sugar today, a whole box full. I told him that and told him I'd put in two lumps.

After he had drunk some tea he said, with an elaborate ironical tone, because he was ashamed of crying, 'You know I like sugar? I suppose your psychoscope told you I liked sugar?'

'Don't be silly' I said, 'everybody likes sugar if they can get it.'

He said, 'No, little doctor, they don't.' He asked in the same tone how old I was and if I was married. He was spiteful. He said, 'Don't want to marry? Wedded to your work? Helping the mentally unsound back to a constructive life of service to the Nation?'

'I like my work,' I said, 'because it's difficult, and interesting. Like yours. You like your work, don't you?'

'I did,' he said. 'Goodbye to all that.'

'Why?'

He tapped his head and said, '*Zzzzzzt!* — All gone. Right?'

'Why are you so convinced you're going to be prescribed electroshock? I haven't even diagnosed you yet.'

'Diagnosed me?' he said. 'Look, stop the playacting, please. My diagnosis was made. By the learned doctors of the TRTU. Severe case of disaffection. Prognosis: Evil! Therapy: Lock him up with a roomful of screaming thrashing wrecks, and then go through his mind the same way you went through his papers, and then burn it...burn it out. Right, Doctor? Why do you have to go through all this posing, diagnosis, cups of tea? Can't you just get on with it? Do you have to paw through everything I am before you burn it?'

'Flores,' I said very patiently, '*you're* saying 'Destroy me' — don't you hear yourself? The psychoscope destroys nothing. And I'm not using it to get evidence, either. This isn't a court, you're not on trial. And I'm not a judge. I'm a doctor.'

He interrupted — 'If you're a doctor, can't you see that I'm not sick?'

'How can I see anything so long as you block me out with your stupid KEEP OUT signs?' I shouted. I did shout. My patience *was* a pose and it just fell to pieces. But I saw that I had reached him, so I went right on. 'You look sick, you act sick — two cracked ribs, a temperature, no appetite, crying fits — is that good health? If you're not sick, then prove it to me! Let me see how you are inside, inside all that!'

He looked down into his cup and gave a kind of laugh and shrugged. 'I can't win,' he said. 'Why do I talk to you? You *look* so honest, damn you!'

I walked away. It is shocking how a patient can hurt one. The trouble is, I am used to the children, whose rejection is absolute, like animals that freeze, or cower, or bite, in their terror. But with this man, intelligent and older than I am, first there is communication and trust and then the blow. It hurts more.

It is painful writing all this down. It hurts again. But it is useful. I do understand some things he said much better now. I think I will not show it to Dr Nades until I have completed diagnosis. If there is any truth to what he said about being arrested on suspicion of disaffection (and he is certainly careless in the way he talks) Dr Nades might feel that she should take over the case, due to my inexperience. I should regret that. I need the experience.

7 September

Stupid! That's why she gave you De Cams's book. Of course she knows. As Head of the Section she has access to the TRTU dossier on F.S. She gave me this case deliberately.

It is certainly educational.

Today's session: F.S. still angry and sulky. Intentionally fantasized a sex scene. It was memory, but when she was heaving around underneath him he suddenly stuck a caricature of my face on her. It was effective. I doubt a woman could have done it, women's recall of having sex is usually darker and grander and they and the other do not become meat-puppets like that, with switchable heads. After a while he got bored with the performance (for all its vividness there was little somatic participation, not even an erection) and his mind began to wander. For the first time. One of the drawings on the desk came back. He must be a designer, because he changed it, with a pencil. At the same time there was a tune going on the audio, in mental puretone; and in the Uncon lapping over into the interplay area, a large, dark room seen from a child's height, the windowsills very high, evening outside the windows, tree branches darkening, and inside the room a woman's voice, soft, maybe reading aloud, sometimes joining with the tune. Meanwhile the whore on the bed kept coming and going in volitional bursts, falling apart a little more each time, till there was nothing left but one nipple. This much I analysed out this afternoon, the first sequence of over 10 sec. that I have analysed clear and entire.

When I broke session he said, 'What did you learn?' in the satirical voice.

I whistled a bit of the tune.

He looked scared.

'It's a lovely tune,' I said, 'I never heard it before. If it's yours, I won't whistle it anywhere else.'

'It's from some quartet,' he said, with his 'donkey' face back, defenseless and patient. 'I like classical music. Didn't you —'

'I saw the girl,' I said. 'And my face on her. Do you know what I'd like to see?'

He shook his head. Sulky, hangdog.

'Your childhood.'

That surprised him. After a while he said, 'All right. You can have my childhood. Why not? You're going to get all the rest anyhow. Listen. You tape it all, don't you? Could I see a playback? I want to see what you see.'

'Sure,' I said. 'But it won't mean as much to you as you think it will. It took me eight years to learn to observe. You start with your own tapes. I watched mine for months before I recognised anything much.'

I took him to my seat, put on the earphone, and ran him 30 sec. of the last sequence.

He was quite thoughtful and respectful after it. He asked, 'What was all that running-up-and-down-scales motion in the, the background I guess you'd call it?'

'Visual scan — your eyes were closed — and subliminal proprioceptive input. The Unconscious dimension and the Body dimension overlap to a great extent all the time. We bring the three dimensions in separately, because they seldom coincide entirely anyway, except in babies. The bright triangular motion at the left of the holo was probably the pain in your ribs.'

'I don't see it that way!'

'You don't see it; you weren't consciously feeling it, even, then. But we can't translate a pain in the rib onto a holoscreen, so we give it a visual symbol. The same with all sensations, affects, emotions.'

'You watch all that at once?'

'I told you it took eight years. And you do realise that that's only a fragment? Nobody could put a whole psyche onto a four-foot screen. Nobody knows if there are any limits to the psyche. Except the limits of the universe.'

He said after a while, 'Maybe you aren't a fool, doctor. Maybe you're just very absorbed in your work. That can be dangerous, you know, to be so absorbed in your work.'

'I love my work, and I hope that it is of positive service,' I said. I was alert for symptoms of disaffection.

He smiled a little and said, 'Prig,' in a sad voice.

Ana is coming along. Still some trouble eating. Entered her in George's mutual-therapy group. What she needs, at least one thing she needs, is companionship. After all why should she eat? Who needs her to be alive? What we call psychosis is sometimes simply realism. But human beings can't live on realism alone.

F.S.'s patterns do not fit any of the classical paranoid psychoscopic patterns in Rheingeld.

The De Cams book is hard for me to understand. The terminology of politics is so different from that of psychology. Everything seems backwards. I must be genuinely attentive at P.T. sessions Sunday nights from now on. I have been lazy-minded. Or, no, but as F.S. said, too absorbed in my work — and so inattentive to its context, he meant. Not thinking about what one is working *for*.

10 September
Have been so tired the last two nights I skipped writing this journal. All the data are on tape and in my analysis notes, of course. Have been working really hard on the F.S. analysis. It is very exciting. It is a truly unusual mind. Not brilliant, his intelligence tests are good average, he is not original or an artist, there are no schizophrenic insights, I can't say what it is, I feel honored to have shared in the childhood he remembered for me. I can't say what is is. There was pain and fear of course, his father's death from cancer, months and months of misery while F.S. was twelve, that was terrible, but it does not come out pain in the end, he has not forgotten or repressed it but it is all changed, by his love for his parents and his sister and for music and for the shape and weight and fit of things and his memory of the lights and weathers of days long past and his mind always working quietly, reaching out,

reaching out to be whole.

There is no question yet of formal co-analysis, it is far too early, but he cooperates so intelligently that today I asked him if he was aware consciously of the Dark Brother figure that accompanied several Con memories in the Uncon dimension. When I described it as having a matted shock of hair he looked startled and said, 'Dokkay, you mean?'

That work had been on the subverbal audio, though I hadn't connected it with the figure.

He explained that when he was five or six Dokkay had been his name for a 'bear' he often dreamed or daydreamed about. He said, 'I rode him. He was big, I was small. He smashed down walls, and destroyed things, bad things, you know, bullies, spies, people who scared my mother, prisons, dark alleys I was afraid to cross, policemen with guns, the pawnbroker. Just knocked them over. And then he walked over all the rubble on up to the hilltop. With me riding on his back. It was quiet up there. It was always evening, just before the stars come out. It's strange to remember it. Thirty years ago! Later on he turned into a kind of friend, a boy or man, with hair like a bear. He still smashed things, and I went with him. It was good fun.'

I write this down from memory as it was not taped; session was interrupted by power outage. It is exasperating that the hospital comes so low on the list of Government priorities.

Attended the Pos. Thinking session tonight and took notes. Dr K. spoke on the dangers and falsehoods of liberalism.

11 September
F.S. tried to show me Dokkay this morning but failed. He laughed and said aloud, 'I can't see him any more. I think at some point I turned into him.'

'Show me when that happened,' I said, and he said, 'All right,' and began at once to recall an episode from his early adolescence. It had nothing to do with Dokkay. He saw an arrest. He was told that the man had been passing out illegal printed matter. Later on he saw one of these pamphlets, the title was in his visual bank, 'Is There Equal Justice?' He read it, but did not recall the text or managed to censor it from me. The arrest was terribly vivid. Details like the young man's blue shirt and the coughing noise he made and the sound of the hitting, the TRTU agents' uniforms, and the car driving away, a big grey car with blood on the door. It came back over and over, the car driving away down the street, driving away down the street. It was a traumatic incident for F.S. and may explain the exaggerated fear of the violence of national justice justified by national security which may have led him to behave irrationally when investigated and so appeared as a tendency to disaffection, falsely I believe.

I will show why I believe this. When the episode was done I said, 'Flores, think about democracy for me, will you?'

He said, 'Little doctor, you don't catch old dogs quite that easily.'

'I am not catching you. Can you think about democracy or can't you?'

'I think about it a good deal,' he said. And he shifted to right-brain activity, music. It was a chorus of the last part of the Ninth Symphony by Beethoven, I recognised it from the Arts term in high school. We sang it to some patriotic words. I yelled, 'Don't censor!' and he said, 'Don't shout, I can hear you.' Of course the room was perfectly silent, but the pickup on the audio was tremendous, like thousands of people singing together. He went on aloud, 'I'm not censoring. I'm thinking about democracy. That is democracy. Hope, brotherhood, no walls. All the walls unbuilt. You, we, I make the universe! Can't you hear it?' And it was the hilltop again, the short grass and the sense of being up high, and the wind, and the whole sky. The music was the sky.

When it was done and I released him from the crown I said, 'Thank you.'

I do not see why the doctor cannot thank the patient for a revelation of beauty and meaning. Of course the doctor's authority is important but it need not be domineering. I realise that in politics the authorities must lead and be followed but in psychological medicine it is a little different, a doctor cannot 'cure' the patient, the patient 'cures' himself with our help, this is not contradictory to Positive Thinking.

14 September
I am upset after the long conversation with F.S. today and will try to clarify my thinking.

Because the rib injury prevents him from attending work therapy, he is restless. The Violent ward disturbed him deeply so I used my authority to have the V removed from his chart and have him moved into Men's Ward B, three days ago. His bed is next to old Arca's, and when I came to get him for session they were talking, sitting on Arca's bed. F.S. said, 'Dr Sobel, do you know my neighbor, Professor Arca of the Faculty of Arts and Letters of the University?' Of course I know the old man, he has been here for years, far longer than I, but F.S. spoke so courteously and gravely that I said, 'Yes, how do you do, Professor Arca?' and shook the old man's hand. He greeted me politely as a stranger — he often does not know people from one day to the next.

As we went to the scope room F.S. said, 'Do you know how many electroshock treatments he had?' and when I said no he said, 'Sixty. He tells me that every day. With pride.' Then he said, 'Did you know that he was an internationally famous scholar? He wrote a book, *The Idea of Liberty*, about twentieth-century ideas of freedom in politics and the arts and sciences. I read it when I was in engineering school. It existed then. On bookshelves. It doesn't exist any more. Anywhere. Ask Dr Arca. He never heard of it.'

'There is almost always some memory loss after electroconvulsive therapy,' I said, 'but the material lost can be relearned, and is often spontaneously regained.'

'After sixty sessions?' he said.

F.S. is a tall man, rather stooped, even in the hospital pyjamas he is an impressive figure. But I am also tall, and it is not because I am shorter than he that he calls me 'little doctor.' He did it first when he was angry at me and so now he says it when he is bitter but does not want what he says to hurt me, the me he knows. He said, 'Little doctor, quit faking. You know the man's mind was deliberately destroyed.'

Now I will try to write down exactly what I said, because it is important.

'I do not approve of the use of electroconvulsive therapy as a general instrument. I would not recommend its use on my patients except perhaps in certain specific cases of senile melancholia. I went into psychoscopy because it is an integrative rather than a destructive instrument.'

That is all true, and yet I never said or consciously thought it before.

'What will you recommend for me?' he said.

I explained that once my diagnosis is complete my recommendation will be subject to the approval of the Head and Assistant Head of the Section. I said that so far nothing in his history or personality structure warranted the use of ECT but that after all we had not got very far yet.

'Let's take a long time about it,' he said, shuffling along beside me with his shoulders hunched.

'Why? Do you like it?'

'No. Though I like you. But I'd like to delay the inevitable end.'

'Why do you insist that it's inevitable, Flores? Can't you see that your thinking on that one point is quite irrational?'

'Rosa,' he said, he has never used my first name before, 'Rosa, you can't be reasonable about pure evil. There are faces reason cannot see. Of course I'm irrational, faced with the imminent destruction of my memory — my self. But I'm not inaccurate. You know they're not going to let me out of here un...' He hesitated a long time and finally said, 'unchanged.'

'One psychotic episode —'

'I had no psychotic episode. You must know that by now.'

'Then why were you sent here?'

'I have some colleagues who prefer to consider themselves rivals, competitors. I gather they informed the TRTU that I was a subversive liberal.'

'What was their evidence?'

'Evidence?' We were in the scope room by now. He put his hands over his face for a moment and laughed in a bewildered way. 'Evidence? Well, once at a meeting of my section I talked a long time with a visiting foreigner, a fellow in my field, a designer. And I have friends, you know, unproductive people, bohemians. And this summer I showed our section head why a design he'd got approved by the Government wouldn't work. That was stupid. Maybe I'm here for, for imbecility. And I read. I've read Professor Arca's book.'

'But none of that matters, you think positively, you love your country, you're not disaffected!'

He said, 'I don't know. I love the idea of democracy, the hope, yes, I love that. I couldn't live without that. But the country? You mean the thing on the map, lines, everything inside the lines is good and nothing outside them matters? How can an adult love such a childish idea?'

'But you wouldn't betray the nation to an outside enemy.'

He said, 'Well, if it was a choice between the nation and humanity, or the nation and a friend, I might. If you call that betrayal. I call it morality.'

He *is* a liberal. It is exactly what Dr Katin was talking about on Sunday.

It is classic psychopathy: the absence of normal affect. He said that quite unemotionally — 'I might.'

No. That is not true. He said it with difficulty, with pain. It was I who was so shocked that I felt nothing — blank, cold.

How am I to treat this kind of psychosis, a *political* psychosis? I have read over De Cams's book twice and I believe I do understand it now, but still there is this gap between the political and the psychological, so that the book shows me how to think but does not show me how to *act* positively. I see how F.S. should think and feel, and the difference between that and his present state of mind, but I do not know how to educate him so that he can think positively. De Cams says that disaffection is a negative condition which must be filled with positive ideas and emotions, but this does not fit F.S. The gap is not in him. In fact that gap in De Cams between the political and the psychological is exactly where *his* ideas apply. But if they are wrong ideas how can this be?

I want advice badly, but I cannot get it from Dr Nades.

When she gave me the De Cams she said, 'You'll find what you need in this.' If I tell her that I haven't,

it is like a confession of helplessness and she will take the case away from me. Indeed I think it is a kind of test case, testing me. But I need this experience, I am learning, and besides, the patient trusts me and talks freely to me. He does so because he knows that I keep what he tells me in perfect confidence. Therefore I cannot show this journal or discuss these problems with anyone until the cure is under way and confidence is no longer essential.

But I cannot see when that could happen. It seems as if confidence will always be essential between us.

I have got to teach him to adjust his behavior to reality, or he will be sent for ECT when the Section reviews cases in November. He has been right about that all along.

9 October
I stopped writing in this notebook when the material from F.S. began to seem 'dangerous' to him (or to myself). I just reread it all over tonight. I see now that I can never show it to Dr N. So I am going to go ahead and write what I please in it. Which is what she said to do, but I think she always expected me to show it to her, she thought I would want to, which I did, at first, or that if she asked to see it I'd give it to her. She asked about it yesterday. I said that I had abandoned it, because it just repeated things I had already put into the analysis files. She was plainly disapproving but said nothing. Our dominance-submission relationship has changed these past few weeks. I do not feel so much in need of guidance, and after the Ana Jest discharge, the autism paper, and my successful analysis of the T.R. Vinha tapes she cannot insist upon my dependence. But she may resent my independence. I took the covers off the notebook and am keeping the loose pages in the split in the back cover of my copy of Rheingeld, it would take a very close search to find them there. While I was doing that I felt rather sick at the stomach and got a headache.

Allergy: A person can be exposed to pollen or bitten by fleas a thousand times without reaction. Then he gets a viral infection or a psychic trauma or a bee sting, and next time he meets up with ragweed or a flea he begins to sneeze, cough, itch, weep, etc. It is the same with certain other irritants. One has to be sensitized.

'Why is there so much fear?' I wrote. Well now I know. Why is there no privacy? It is unfair and sordid. I cannot read the 'classified' files kept in her office, though I work with the patients and she does not. But I am not to have any 'classified' material of my own. Only persons in authority can have secrets. Their secrets are all good, even when they are lies.

Listen. Listen Rosa Sobel. Doctor of Medicine, Deg. Psychotherapy, Deg. Psychoscopy. Have you gone native?

Whose thoughts are you thinking?

You have been working two to five hours a day for six weeks inside
one person's mind. A generous, integrated, sane mind. You never
worked with anything like that before. You have only worked with the
crippled and the terrified. You never met an equal before.

Who is the therapist, you or he?

But if there is nothing wrong with him what am I supposed to cure?
How can I help him? How can I save him?

By teaching him to lie?

(Undated)

I spent the last two nights till midnight reviewing the diagnostic scopes
of Professor Arca, recorded when he was admitted, 11 years ago, before
electroconvulsive treatment.

This morning Dr N inquired why I had been 'so far back in the files.'
(That means that Selena reports to her on what files are used. I know
every square centimeter of the scope room but all the same I check it
over daily now.) I replied that I was interested in studying the
development of ideological disaffection in intellectuals. We agreed that
intellectualism tends to foster negative thinking and may lead to
psychosis, and those suffering from it should ideally be treated, as Prof.
Arca was treated, and released if still competent. It was a very interesting
and harmonious discussion.

I lied. I lied. I lied. I lied deliberately, knowingly, well. She lied. She
is a liar. She is an intellectual too! She is a lie. And a coward, afraid.

I wanted to watch the Arca tapes to get perspective. To prove to
myself that Flores is by no means unique or original. This is true. The
differences are fascinating. Dr Arca's Con dimension was splendid,
architectural, but the Uncon material was less well integrated and less
interesting. Dr Arca knew very much more, and the power and beauty
of the motions of his thought was far superior to Flores's. Flores is often
extremely muddled. That is an element of his vitality. Dr Arca is an, was
an Abstract thinker, as I am, and so I enjoyed his tapes less. I missed the
solidity, spatiotemporal realism, and intense sensory clarity of Flores's
mind.

In the scope room this morning I told him what I had been doing.
His reaction was (as usual) not what I expected. He is fond of the old
man and I thought he would be pleased. He said, 'You mean they saved

the tapes, and destroyed the mind?' I told him that all tapes are kept for use in teaching, and asked him if that didn't cheer him, to know that a record of Arca's thoughts in his prime existed: wasn't it like his book, after all, the lasting part of a mind which sooner or later would have to grow senile and die anyhow? He said, 'No! Not so long as the book is banned and the tape is classified! Neither freedom nor privacy even in death? That is the worst of all!'

After session he asked if I would be able or willing to destroy his diagnostic tapes, if he is sent to ECT. I said such things could get misfiled and lost easily enough, but that it seemed a cruel waste. I had learned from him and others might, later, too. He said, 'Don't you see that I will not serve the people with security passes? I will not be used, that's the whole point. You have never used me. We have worked together. Served our term together.'

Prison has been much in his mind lately. Fantasies, day-dreams of jails, labor camps. He dreams of prison as a man in prison dreams of freedom.

Indeed as I see the way narrowing in I would get him sent to prison if I could, but since he is *here* there is no chance. If I reported that he is in fact politically dangerous, they will simply put him back in the Violent ward and give him ECT. There is no judge here to give him a life sentence. Only doctors to give death sentences.

What I can do is stretch out the diagnosis as long as possible, and put in a request for full co-analysis, with a strong prognosis of complete cure. But I have drafted the report three times already and it is very hard to phrase it so that it's clear that I know the disease is ideological (so that they don't just override my diagnosis at once) but still making it sound mild and curable enough that they'd let me handle it with the psychoscope. And then, why spend up to a year, using expensive equipment, when a cheap and simple instant cure is at hand? No matter what I say, they have that argument. There are two weeks left until Sectional Review. I have got to write the report so that it will be really impossible for them to override it. But what if Flores is right, all this is just playacting, lying about lying, and they have had orders right from the start from TRTU, 'wipe this one out' —

(Undated)
Sectional Review today.
If I stay on here I have some power, I can do some good No no no but

I don't I don't even in this one thing even in this what can I do now how can I stop

(Undated)
Last night I dreamed I rode on a bear's back up a deep gorge between steep mountainsides, slopes going steep up into a dark sky, it was winter, there was ice on the rocks

(Undated)
Tomorrow morning will tell Nades I am resigning and requesting transfer to Children's Hospital. But she must approve the transfer. If not I am out in the cold. I am in the cold already. Door locked to write this. As soon as it is written will go down to furnace room and burn it all. There is no place anymore.

We met in the hall. He was with an orderly.

I took his hand. It was big and bony and very cold. He said, 'Is this it, now, Rosa — the electroshock?' in a low voice. I did not want him to lose hope before he walked up the stairs and down the corridor. It is a long way down the corridor. I said, 'No. Just some more tests — EEG probably.'

'Then I'll see you tomorrow?' he asked, and I said yes.

And he did. I went in this evening. He was awake. I said, 'I am Dr Sobel, Flores. I am Rosa.'

He said, 'I'm pleased to meet you,' mumbling. There is a slight facial paralysis on the left. That will wear off.

I am Rosa. I am the rose. The rose, I am the rose. The rose with no flower, the rose all thorns, the mind he made, the hand he touched, the winter rose. ❏

© *Ursula K. Le Guin 1976; first appeared in* Future Power, *reprinted by permission of the author and the author's agent Virginia Kidd*

CONTRIBUTORS

Reinaldo Arenas *Traitor*
Translated by Dolores M Koch
Born near Holguin, Cuba in 1943, both as a writer and an open homosexual Arenas was considered an enemy of the Cuban revolution. Released in 1976 after years in a forced labour camp and then in prison, he was forbidden to write because of his alleged disrespect for the rules of official literature and of conventional morality. By 1980, when he left the island, all his manuscripts had been confiscated. Only his novel *Celestino antes de alba* (translated as *Singing from the Well*, 1987) has ever been published in Cuba (*see also* Index *4/88, 'Profile of Reinaldo Arenas'*).

Among the other novels in English translation are *Farewell to the Sea* (1986), *The Ill-Fated Peregrinations of Fray Servando* (1987), *The Graveyard of the Angels* (1987), *The Doorman* (1988), and *The Assault* (posthumous, 1993). A long poem about his labour camp experiences was published in English as *El Central: A Cuban Sugar Mill* (1984). His memoirs *Before Night Falls* were published posthumously in 1993. Arenas died in Manhattan, New York in 1990. This is the first English translation of his short story, 'Traitor', published as 'Traidor' in *Adios a mama* (De La Havana a Nueva York) Ediciones Altera Barcelona 1995.

Bai Hua *Su Qin Carrying His Sword*
Translated by Qingyun Wu and Thomas O Beebee
Bai Hua was born Chen Youhua in Xinyang, Henan Province, China in 1930. He has been a cause célèbre because of his dissidence and his involvement in the human rights movement in China. His screenplay *Bitter Love* (filmed in 1980 as *The Sun and Man*) prompted Deng Xiaoping to target him as the chief victim of the first post-Mao Campaign Against Spiritual Pollution in 1981 (*see* Index *4/81, 2/82*). He has remained in China, residing in Shanghai since 1985.

Official attitudes toward liberal authors hardened again in early 1996, and it would seem China is now in the midst of another Campaign against Spiritual Pollution. In June 1996, Bai Hua was held incommunicado under the pretext that he lived a 'socially unacceptable lifestyle'. Presumably this was meant as a warning to 'avant-garde intellectuals'.

The selection symbolically titled 'Su Qin Carrying His Sword' is excerpted from Bai Hua's important novel *The Remote Country of Women*, published in China, Taiwan and Hong Kong in 1988 and translated into English and published by University of Hawaii Press in 1994.

Italo Calvino *The General in the Library*
Translated by Tim Parks
Novelist, short story writer, essayist and journalist, Italo Calvino was born in Santiago de Las Vegas, Cuba in 1923 and grew up in San Remo, Italy. He was a member of the Partisan movement during the German occupation of northern Italy in World War II. The book that resulted from that experience, published in English as *The Path to the Nest of Spiders*, was highly acclaimed. Other works of fiction include *Cosmicomics*, *Invisible Cities* (1974), *The Castle of Crossed Destinies* (1976), *If on a Winter's Night a Traveller*, (1981) and *Mr Palomar* (1985). Non-fiction includes *Six Memos for the Next Millennium* and *The Uses of Literature*, collections of literary essays and the anthology *Italian Folktales*. He died in Siena in 1985. 'The General in the Library' is taken from his posthumous collection of writings, *Primal che tu dica 'Pronto'* (Arnoldo Mondadori, 1993), translated in English as *Numbers in the Dark* (Jonathan Cape, 1995).

Rosario Castellanos *The Death of the Tiger*
Translated by Alberto Manguel
Rosario Castellanos was born in Mexico City in 1925. She grew up on a ranch near the Guatemalan border and later in Comitan, Chiapas, a region of centuries-old conflicts between the Tzotzil indians and the landholding families. In 1950 she received a master's degree in philosophy from the National University of Mexico, her thesis 'On Feminine Culture' presaging a lifelong concern with women's place in society and with the reversal of myth imposed on female experience, as reflected in her poetry (two selections of her poetry were translated into English: *Looking at the Mona Lisa*, 1981, *Meditation on the Threshold*, 1988, and her complete poetry up to 1971 appeared in Spanish under the title *Poesía no eres túm*, 1972); novels (*Balún-Canian*, 1958); plays (*El Eterno Femenino*) and essays.

She died in an accidental electrocution in Tel Aviv, Israel in 1974.

The short stories in *Ciudad Real* (1960) — from which 'Death of the Tiger' was taken — grew out of her work with the Indigenist Institute in 1952 and her interest in the Chamula indian culture she had first touched upon as a seven-year-old girl.

Mohamed Choukri *The Poets*
Translated by Catherine Cobham
Born in the West Rif, Morocco in 1935, Mohamed Choukri lived as a street-child for many years. He went to school for the first time in 1956 at the age of 21. His first story, 'Violence on the Beach', was published in 1966. Since then, he has become one of the leading Arabic writers of Morocco. His autobiography, published in English in two volumes, *For Bread Alone* (1993) and *Streetwise* (1996), has become a classic in the Islamic world. His work has come under criticism from the Moroccan authorities, and several of his books are not available in Arabic, or only in self-censored versions. Written in 1973, this is the first English translation.

Haroldo Conti *The Art of Hunting with Dogs*
Translated by Alberto Manguel
Haroldo Conti was born in Chacabuco, Province of Buenos Aires, Argentina in 1925. Conti was a journalist for the magazine *Crisis* and also worked in theatre and film. His stories and novels, including *Sudeste* (1962), *Alrededor de la jaula* (1966), *En vida* (1971) and *Mascaró, el cazador americano* (1975), won several prizes both in Argentina and abroad.

Though he had been under threat from the military government since 1975, he refused to go into exile. On his desk he had a sign which said, 'This is my battlefield, and from here I am not leaving.' He was abducted on 4 May 1976 by the paramilitary police and never seen alive again (*see Index 3/76, 5/81*). At the time of his kidnapping, his personal correspondence and all the manuscripts of his work were stolen. His kidnappers never knew what the sign said because it was written in Latin. This is the first English translation of this story.

Duong Thu Huong *The Labyrinth*
Translated by Phan Huy Duong and Nina McPherson
Duong Thu Huong was born in Thai Binh in 1947. During the Vietnam War, she served for seven years in a Communist Youth Brigade and was

the first woman combatant and reporter at the front during the war with China in 1979.

An outspoken advocate of human rights and democratic reform, Duong Thu Huong was expelled from the Communist Party in 1989 and imprisoned without trial for seven months in 1991 on charges of sending abroad documents containing state secrets. These documents were her own writings, including in English translation the novels *Paradise of the Blind* (1995) and *Novel Without a Name* (William Morrow, 1995), from which the excerpt 'The labyrinth' is taken. Her works sold thousands of copies in Vietnam but are no longer published in the country. A new novel, *Beyond Illusions*, is forthcoming in English translation (1997). Duong Thu Huong lives in Hanoi with her two children.

Graham Greene *The Last Word*
Graham Greene was born in Berkhamsted, UK in 1904. His novels include *The Power and the Glory* (1940), *The End of the Affair* (1951), *The Quiet American* (1955), *A Burnt-out Case* (1961), *Travels with my Aunt* (1969), *The Honorary Consul* (1973), *The Human Factor* (1978) and *Monsignor Quixote* (1982). He also wrote several volumes of short stories, republished as *The Collected Stories* (1972) as well as essays and literary criticism. His last published book was a dream diary entitled *A World of My Own* (posthumous, 1992). He died in Vevey, Switzerland in 1991.

In 1989, Graham Greene donated 'The Last Word' to PEN Canada, later published in *The Last Word and Other Stories* (Heinemann, 1990).

Nedim Gürsel *The Graveyard of Unwritten Books*
Translated by Alberto Manguel
Born in Turkey in 1951, Nedim Gürsel is the author of numerous novels, short stories and essays. His book *Uzun Sürmüs Biryaz* (1976) was awarded a prize by the Academy of Turkish Language, but was later banned in Turkey in 1981 and resulted in a four-year-long trial for 'offending the national security forces', a crime according to Article 159 of the Turkish Penal Code. His novel *Kadinlar Kitabi: öyküler* (1983) was also banned (for obscenity, according to Article 426, in 1983), but was eventually released in Turkey and won him the Ipekci Prize three years later, for 'contribution to understanding between the Greek and Turkish peoples'. One year later, in 1987 a short story published in the French edition of *Playboy* also resulted in a judicial inquiry in Turkey.

He has been awarded a prize by Radio France Internationale for Best Short Story (1990) and by Struga of Macedonia for his essays (1992). He is currently in voluntary exile in Paris where he writes, translates, and teaches at the École Nationale des Langues and Civilisations Orientales.

'The Graveyard of Unwritten Books' from *Son Tramway* (1990) is the first of Gürsel's works to be published in English translation.

Edwar Al-Kharrat *The Accusation*
Translated by Catherine Cobham
Novelist, poet, critic, translator and editor, Edwar Al-Kharrat was born in Alexandria, Egypt in 1926. His novels in English translation include *City of Saffron* (1989) and *Girls of Alexandria* (1993). He was an Associate Senior Member of St Antony's College, Oxford and lectured in Oxford and London on Egyptian fiction. Among his awards are the State Prize for his short story collection *House of Pride* in 1972, the Franco-Arab Friendship Prize in France in 1991, and the prestigious Oweiss Prize (the Arab world's largest prize for writers and intellectuals) in 1996. Doris Lessing has described his work as 'More Proust than Durrell, and I think worthy of the comparison'.

'The Accusation' is Al-Kharrat's personal choice for this anthology to depict the nightmarish conditions of a society under censorship. This is the first English translation.

Ursula K. Le Guin *Diary of the Rose*
Ursula K. Le Guin was born in 1929 in Berkeley, California. She has published over 80 short stories, two collection of essays, 10 books for children, several volumes of poetry and 16 novels, including *The Left Hand of Darkness*, *The Dispossessed* and the *Earthsea* tetralogy. She has won a National Book Award, five Hugo and four Nebula awards, the Kafka Award, a Pushcart Prize and the Howard Vursell Award of the American Academy of Arts and Letters.

Jane Rule *The Real World*
Jane Rule was born in Plainfield, New Jersey in 1931 and has lived in Canada since 1956. She involved herself in the defence of Toronto's gay magazine *Body Politic* during censorship attacks by the Canadian government in the 1970s and 1980s, and her testimony during the 1994 trial in which the Vancouver bookshop, Little Sister's, took the

government to court to end Canadian customs' harassment of gay and lesbian authors and booksellers (see *Restricted Entry: Censorship on Trial* by Janine Fuller and Stuart Blackley, Press Gang, 1995) is seen in North America as a definitive statement on the censorship of literature.

Jane Rule's books have never been officially banned in Canada and can be found in most mainstream bookshops (*see also Jane Rule 'Lesbian literature needs readers'*, Index *9/90*). *The Young in One Another's Arms* (1971) received the Canadian Authors Association Award for best novel, but it was also detained by customs, especially when ordered from the American publisher by Canadian gay bookshops such as Little Sister's. Despite a court injunction, in September 1996 the Little Sister's bookshop experienced a new wave of harassment.

Rule's other novels include *Desert of the Heart* (1964), *This is Not for You* (1970), *Contract with the World* (1980), *A Hot-eyed Moderate* (1985) and *Memory Board* (1987). Most recently Rule contributed an essay to the anthology *Forbidden Passages: Banned Writing in Canada* (Cleis Press, 1996). 'Puzzle' was first published in *Inland Passages and Other Stories* (Naiad Press, 1985).

Ken Saro-Wiwa *The New Beggars*

Ken(ule Beeson) Saro-Wiwa was born in 1941 in Bori, Rivers State, Nigeria. Though he published his first book in 1983, he is best known for his satirical *Sozaboy: A Novel in Rotten English* (1985) and a successful television series, *Basi and Company*, which he produced and wrote from 1985 to 1990. In 1990 he became president of the Movement for the Survival of the Ogoni People (MOSOP) and created a campaign to bring world attention to their plight at the hands of the military government and Shell Oil Company. In 1993 he was imprisoned, an ordeal which he chronicled in *A Month and A Day: A Detention Diary* (1995). In May 1994, after four Ogoni leaders, suspected of collaborating with the military authorities, were killed, Saro-Wiwa was again arrested, together with eight others, and charged with murder. On 2 November 1995, he and his co-defendants were sentenced to death. Despite international pressures, the executions were carried out on 10 November in Port Harcourt, Nigeria. Salman Rushdie wrote: 'He and his colleagues did not die because of his literary output, but as a result of their fight for the Ogoni people's survival and against the tyranny of the Abacha regime. That fight must now become the world's fight' (*see also* Index *6/94, 6/95,1/96*).

'The New Beggars' is a short story from the unpublished posthumous collection, *A Kind of Festival and Other Stories*.

M.T. Sharif *The Letter Writer*
Born in Iran, the writer known as M.T. Sharif has lived in exile in the USA for several years. He teaches at a university and writes in English under the pseudonym 'M.T. Sharif' in order to protect himself and his family. 'The Letter Writer' first appeared in *The Agni Review* (1989). M.T. Sharif's stories have also been published in *The Literary Review*.

Ma Thida *The Secret of Successful Transfusion*
Translated by Ohnmar Khin
Ma Thida (Sanchaung) was born in Rangoon, Burma in 1966, where she trained as a medical doctor. In 1988 she worked as campaign assistant for National League for Democracy leader, Aung San Suu Kyi. She published over 60 short stories between 1985 and September 1988; however, since the coup in 1989 by the State Law and Order Restoration Council (SLORC), her stories have been submitted to the Scrutiny Board, and many have been banned. On 15 October 1993 she was sentenced to 20 years in prison under the Emergency Powers Act for 'contact with illegal organisations, endangering public peace and distributing banned literature to foreign opposition groups'. 'The Secret of Successful Transfusion' was written on 29 September 1991 and submitted to *Pe-Hpu-Hlwa* magazine. Before it could be published (or censored) the magazine was banned in December 1991. No other magazine would take it.

Pramoedya Ananta Toer *Encounter with the Devils*
Translated by Willem Samuels
Pramoedya Ananta Toer was born in Blora, East Java, Indonesia in 1925. He has been imprisoned by each of Indonesia's three twentieth-century governments for alleged subversive political activities and writings (*see also Index 5/78 Interview, 5/81 Book Reviews, 7/87 & 9/88 Appeals*). His works in English translation include *The Fugitive* (1990) and the Buru Quartet (*This Earth of Mankind, Child of all Nations, Footsteps*, and *House of Glass*, 1990) which was conceived in stories the author told to other prisoners during his confinement without trial on Buru Island from 1965 to 1979. He received the PEN Freedom-to-Write Award in 1988 and the Raymond Magsaysay Award (the most important literary honour in Asia)

in 1995 but was not allowed to attend either ceremony. The Suharto regime still keeps him under city arrest in Jakarta where his books are banned and selling them is a crime punishable by imprisonment. The story 'Encounter with the Devils' was published in the periodical *Manoa*, Spring 1991.

EDITORS

Alberto Manguel was born in Argentina and is now a Canadian citizen. One of Canada's best-known literary figures, he enjoys an international reputation both as a translator and as editor of many acclaimed anthologies including *Black Water: The Flamingo Anthology of Fantastic Literature*, *Other Fires: Short Fiction by Latin American Women*, and *The Gates of Paradise: The Flamingo Anthology of Erotic Literature*. He is also author of the highly acclaimed novel *News From a Foreign Country Came*, winner of the 1992 McKitterick Prize. His latest book is *A History of Reading* (Harper Collins, 1996). **Craig Stephenson** is an analyst-in-training at the C G Jung Institute, Zurich and the editor of the anthologies *Between Worlds: A Collection of Writings on the Canadian Immigrant Experience* and *Countries of Invention*. Alberto Manguel and Craig Stephenson compiled *In Another Part of the Forest: The Flamingo Anthology of Gay Short Fiction* (HarperCollins, 1994).

Illustrations by **Jeff Fisher**, an artist and illustrator living in Paris.

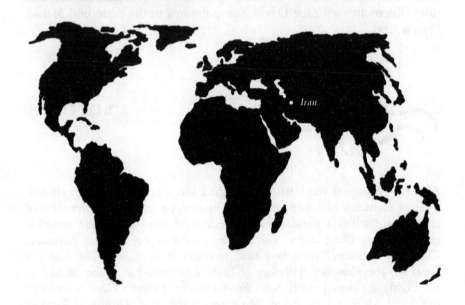

Iran

Dead men tell no tales

A BUSLOAD of Iranian writers is on its way to Armenia. They've been invited to a meeting with their colleagues in Yerevan as part of a cultural exchange programme between the two countries. Their bus is hurtling along the highway when the driver — a government-employed driver — suddenly and with complete disregard for his own safety, opens the door and leaps from the speeding vehicle, leaving the busload of writers apparently facing imminent death. One of their number, however, quicker-thinking than the rest, manages to grab the controls in the nick of time and brings the bus safely to a halt. The driver, it seems, is the only casualty of his own recklessness.

This story might be true or it might not. It supposedly took place in August, somewhere in Azerbaijan. It's hard to be completely sure of the details: according to some retellings the driver, having been found bruised but without serious injury, reboards the bus only to repeat the performance a few miles further on. But apocryphal or not — whether or not the government would really go to such baroque lengths to murder a group of writers — the story has acquired a certain mythic status on the Iranian literary scene. If not factually true in all the details, it is at least true in spirit.

Being a writer in Iran doesn't make for an easy life. Those who observe the situation from outside are used to talking about the right of authors to be politically engaged, to bring into focus, through the critical lens of their fiction, their poetry or their drama, those personal, social, cultural or economic relations which we call, broadly, 'politics'. But the other side of that coin is the right of an author to stand aside from the political, to admit of being no more or less than a teller of tales. In Iran, where the revolution has tended to politicise, or rather Islamicise, just about everything, that right is increasingly denied.

Compared with its predecessor, the Rafsanjani administration has made concerted efforts to show a more friendly face to the West. The negotiations with the European Union have even yielded an official commitment 'not to send any commandos' to kill Salman Rushdie. But aside from this concession, in many ways Iran seems to be becoming less tolerant of dissent, not more, as hardliners reassert their influence.

The Ministry for Islamic Guidance, which is responsible for vetting books prior to publication, is currently reviewing all the decisions it took in the first 12 or so years of the revolution. This means that many books by well-known authors are now being proscribed, even as they are about to go into their sixth, seventh or eighth printing. At least 10 cultural or literary magazines are also currently banned, so that writers are being denied that outlet for their work as well. Implicit in this tightening of the reins is an admission that the decisions the Ministry made in the 1980s and early 1990s were too lenient. The Ministry does not publicly accept this interpretation.

Meanwhile, the propaganda campaign to discredit leading writers and thinkers as decadent pro-Westerners continues (see page 174). The men from the Ministry, armed with cameras, burst into the German attaché's residence in August, apparently so it could film a group of Iranian writers in the middle of being wined and dined by a foreign government. Such an extraordinary breach of diplomatic protocol would be unthinkable anywhere else. In Iran, such fantastic tales are fast becoming commonplace. ❏ *Adam Newey*

A censorship chronicle incorporating information from the American Association for the Advancement of Science Human Rights Action Network (AAASHRAN), Amnesty International (AI), Article 19 (A19), the BBC Monitoring Service Summary of World Broadcasts (SWB), the Committee to Protect Journalists (CPJ), the Canadian Committee to Protect Journalists (CCPJ), the Inter-American Press Association (IAPA), the International Federation of Journalists (IFJ/FIP), the International Press Institute (IPI), Human Rights Watch (HRW), the Media Institute of Southern Africa (MISA), Network for the Defence of Independent Media in Africa (NDIMA), International PEN (PEN), Open Media Research Institute (OMRI), Reporters Sans Frontières (RSF), the World Association of Community Broadcasters (AMARC) and other sources

AFGHANISTAN

On 29 September a woman journalist working for Associated Press was barred from attending a news conference by Mullah Mohammed Rabbani, the leader of Kabul's newly formed governing council. On the same day, two women were reported to have been beaten by militiamen in a market in the east of the city centre after they were spotted wearing scarves which were not covering all their hair and faces. Since Kabul fell to Taliban forces on 27 September, Islamic law has been stringently applied. Women and girls must conform to strict dress codes and are prohibited from going to work or school. Women who

ignore the dress code are beaten. In early October it was reported that music and television have been completely banned, along with kite-flying, marbles, large wedding parties, picnics and the owning of songbirds. Restrictions were also announced on the press, including the taking of moving or still photographs of military installations or ministerial buildings, in addition to previous bans on pictures of people in Taliban-controlled parts of the country. Journalists are also barred from reporting 'sensitive' incidents on the grounds that they might be distorted and used the discredit the Taliban. (*Times, Independent, Guardian,* Reuters)

ALBANIA

On 5 September the Albanian Council of Ministers approved a draft law on public gatherings. It defines different types of gatherings and outlines the conditions necessary for obtaining permission. (SWB)

On 16 September four people — **Timoshenko Pekmezi, Sami Meta, Tare Isufi and Kristaq Mosko** — were sentenced to between 12 and 18 months in prison for founding a Communist party. They were charged with 'creating anti-constitutional parties and associations in collaboration' (*Index* 3/1996). Communist parties have been banned since June 1992. The four say they will appeal. (OMRI, AI)

Recent publication: *Detention and Ill-Treatment of Government Opponents* (AI, September 1996, 24pp)

ALGERIA

On 3 September a court upheld the banning of the daily *La Tribune* for six months and imposed suspended sentences on cartoonist **Chawki Amari**, publisher **Khaireddine Ameyar**, and editor-in-chief **Baya Gacemi** for publication of a cartoon deemed to mock the Algerian flag (*Index* 5/1996). On 30 September *La Tribune* journalists began publishing their work as 'Algerian Journalists Against Censorship' on the Reporters Sans Frontières' website (http://www.calva-com.fr/rsf/). (RSF)

The popular Rai singer **Boudjemaa Bechiri** — known as **Cheb Aziz** — was kidnapped by Islamist guerrillas and murdered, after attending a wedding in Constantine on 18 September. His body was found on 20 September. He is the fourth Rai singer to have been murdered during the civil war. (Reuters)

ARMENIA

Security forces opened fire on opposition protesters in the capital, Yerevan, on 25 September after a crowd of at least 40,000 people gathered outside the Central Election Commission. One person died and around 60 were injured. It was the third demonstration in as many days by people accusing President Ter-Petrosian of vote-rigging in the 22 September presidential election. Tanks and troops were ordered on to the streets of the capital and all demonstrations against the results of the election were banned. Around

250 opposition activists are believed to have been arrested in unrest since the election. Eight members of the National Assembly — defeated presidential candidate **Vazgen Manoukian, Paruir Ayrikian, Nerses Zeynalvandian, Seyran Avagyan, David Vartanian, Sharvarsha Kocharian, Arshak Sadoyan and Ruben Hakopian** — were stripped of their parliamentary immunity and will face charges. Hakopian and Kocharian were charged on 7 October with various offences, from fomenting mass disturbances to treason. The Organization for Security and Cooperation in Europe reported early in October that 22,000 ballots had gone missing, roughly the number by which Ter-Petrosian clinched victory in the first round of voting. The European Institute for the Media, which monitored the campaign, reported that state television 'clearly favoured Ter-Petrosian through its tendentious coverage'. The opposition paper *Ayzhm*, which had not appeared for some time, resumed publication on 4 October. (*Times*, Radio Free Europe, *Express-Chronicle*, Armenian News Network, OMRI)

The chief censor, John Dickie, has introduced a list of 34 'offensive and unsuitable' words that cannot be used on magazine covers, it was reported at the end of September. Included on the list are words such as 'nympho', 'horny' and 'nunga' (derived from the Aboriginal 'nungaiyi', meaning 'wife', and which has assumed more explicit connotations). Any magazine which uses one of the listed words on its cover must be sold in an opaque wrapper. (*Age*)

In a speech on 23 September the prime minister, John Howard, said that his government will lift 'the pall of censorship' created by the previous government's adherence to 'political correctness'. There are, he said, 'lots of people who felt intimidated out of expressing their views on certain things because they felt that to do so was to have yourself branded as a racist or a bigot.' Critics immediately accused Howard of giving tacit support to the views of the independent MP, Pauline Hanson, whose controversial maiden speech on 10 September included claims that the country is being 'swamped' by Asians and that 'a multicultural country can never be strong or united.' Shortly after Howard's speech the British revisionist historian **David Irving** (whose views Hanson has publicly endorsed) announced that he will apply for a visa to enter the country. Irving has been denied entry since 1992, because of his denial of the Holocaust. (*Age, Sydney Morning Herald*)

In early October the federal government said it would support a challenge to a 1994 High Court ruling that found that freedom of expression in political matters is a right implied in the Constitution. The so-called Theophanus decision struck down restrictive defamation laws on the

activities of public figures, and was hailed as a major advance for free speech. The challenge to the ruling is being led by the Victoria state government, which is engaged in an ongoing battle with animal rights activist Laurie Levy. (*Age, Sydney Morning Herald*)

On 21 September **Abbas Salman**, a correspondent with Reuters, was summoned to the Interior Ministry. He was detained and questioned over a story he had written on the political situation in Bahrain. He was released the following day without charge. (Reuters)

There has been a series of attacks on journalists recently. On 7 September **Goutam Das**, a correspondent with *Bhorer Khagoj*, was assaulted by a policeman when he tried to report on a road accident. At least nine photojournalists were injured by activists after a meeting of the Bangladesh National Party (BNP) on 10 September in Dhaka. The home of **AKM Moqsud Ahmed**, editor of *Dainik Giridarpan*, was pelted during a demonstration supported by the BNP and Jamaat-e-Islami on 14 September. A group of demonstrators later entered the newspaper offices and threatened employees. On 16 September home-made bombs were thrown at the home of **Chita Gosh**, a correspondent with *Dainik Sangbad* in Dinajapur. **SM Shamsul Alam**, a stringer for the Voice of America and a correspondent with *Ajker Kagoj*, and

Sheik Mohammad Illias, a correspondent with *Dainik Al Mujadded*, were both run down by a timber merchant on 18 September. They had been investigating illegal timber extraction and trading. (RSF)

The trial of **Taslima Nasrin** on charges of 'insulting religious sentiments' (*Index* 10/1993, 2/1995) has once again been postponed, until mid-November. (PEN)

BELARUS

The country's last remaining independent newspapers, *Svaboda* (Freedom) and *Nasha Niva* (Our Niva), had their bank accounts frozen on the orders of the Minsk regional government at the end of August (*Index* 5/1996). Other media facing fines for alleged non-payment of tax include the independent weeklies *Belaruskaya Delovaya Gazeta* (Belarusian Business Gazette), *Imya* (Name), *Belaruski Rinok* (Belarusian Market), *Belaruskaya Gazeta* (Belarusian Gazette) and *Semida*. Also threatened are *BelaPan*, the only independent news agency in Belarus, and the newspapers *Narodnaya Volya* (The People's Will) and *Svabodnie Novosti Plus* (Free News Plus). (RSF)

On 1 September the Ministry of Communications suspended broadcasts by **Radio 101.2 FM** by severing access to its state-owned transmitter. The Ministry earlier claimed that the station interfered with government frequencies. No replacement wavelength has been allocated to the station,

which was launched in 1995 and transmits mainly music and news to the Minsk area. (RSF, AMARC)

Two leaders of the opposition Belarusian Popular Front, **Zenon Poznyak** and **Sergei Naumchik** applied for asylum in the USA on 30 September. They claim they are in danger because they have exposed human rights abuses committed by President Lukashenka and that he has ordered them to be 'neutralised'. (*Independent*)

BELGIUM

On 18 September Belgian police carried out a series of raids on the homes of Kurds and offices of Kurdish organisations allegedly linked to the separatist Kurdish Workers' Association (PKK). Among the organisations raided was **MED TV**. Police confiscated archives, interrogated staff and forcibly closed the offices. As of early October, the offices remained closed. The Turkish government accuses MED TV of being a mouthpiece for the PKK, which is banned in Belgium (*Index* 5/1996). On the same day MED TV's office in London was also raided. (Reuters, Article 19, PEN, IPI)

BOSNIA-HERCEGOVINA

The European Institute for the Media, which monitored the coverage of the election campaign from 22 July to 14 September, reports that media coverage seriously marred the fairness of the democratic process, especially in Republika Srpska and the

Croat-controlled part of the Federation. The preliminary report, released on 17 September, noted that the absence of freedom of movement meant that access to impartial information was impaired. Fair and impartial coverage was provided neither by Serbian Television, SRT, nor by the Croat television station HTM in Mostar. (European Institute for the Media)

BOTSWANA

Four staff on the independent *Botswana Guardian* were ordered to appear before Gaborone Magistrates Court on 1 October. **Professor Malema, Joel Sebonego, Tshmimologo Boitumelo** and **Horace Somanje** pleaded not guilty to charges of 'unlawful disclosure of the identity of a person still under investigation' (*Index* 5/1996). They face up to one-year imprisonment or a fine of US$667 if found guilty. (MISA)

BULGARIA

On 9 July Sofia police broke into the offices of the Flamingo Centre, a legally registered publisher of gay and lesbian erotic magazines, and confiscated all printed material. Three employees were detained for 10 hours. Also on 9 July, videotapes were seized from Comet, an erotic video centre in Sofia. (IGLHC)

On 24 September the Constitutional Court unanimously decided to rule on the Radio and Television Act which was readopted by

Parliament on 5 September despite President Zhelev's veto (*Index* 5/1996). Zhelev expressed concerns that the Act would violate consitutional guarantees of freedom of expression. (CPJ, OMRI, SWB)

Recent publication: *Children of Bulgaria — Police Violence and Arbitrary Confinement* (HRW, September 1996, 145pp)

BURMA

The sentence given to **U Win Htein** (*Index* 5/96) was doubled from seven to 14 years on 30 August. No reason was given for the increase. (Reuters)

Nine youths, described as 'juvenile delinquents' in the official press, were detained in late September and accused of distributing pamphlets designed to spread 'false anti-government rumours' at the weekly gatherings outside Aung San Suu Kyi's house. On 27 September the police set up roadblocks on the main road leading to the house. Between 26 and 29 September, at least 559 people, including 159 National League for Democracy members, were detained. The police action, which included a surprise raid on Suu Kyi's house and the detention of demonstrators in the Shwedagan Pagoda area, was taken to prevent an unauthorised congress planned for 27-29 September to mark the eighth anniversary of Suu Kyi's National League for Democracy. Over the course of the weekend the media were also subject to repression:

military intelligence officers prevented news photographers and cameramen from leaving their hotel on 28 September and one photographer had his film, shot near Suu Kyi's house, confiscated. On 8 October the roadblocks around Suu Kyi's house were dismantled and she announced that she will resume her weekly gatherings there. However, her telephone is reported to be tapped and frequently cut off by the authorities to prevent her from speaking to the international media. (A19, HRW, Reuters, SWB)

The State Law and Order Council (SLORC) announced tight new restrictions on the ownership of computers that could be used for accessing the Internet in early October. The new measure punishes unauthorised possession of a computer with networking capabilities by prison terms of between seven and 15 years. There are similar sentences for anyone found using a computer to send or receive information on various matters, including state security, the economy and national culture. (*Financial Times*)

Recent publications: *Beyond the Law* (A19, August 1996, 74pp); *The Rohingya Muslims — Ending a Cycle of Exodus?* (HRW, September 1996, 38pp); *Update on Political Arrests and Trials* (AI, September 1996, 13pp)

BURUNDI

At least 6,000 people died in violence following the coup d'état of 25 July which bought Major Pierre Buyoya to

power, Amnesty International reported at the end of August. Most were killed in massacres carried out between 27 July and 10 August by government forces in the Gitega province, but other massacres were reported in Bujumbura, Maramvya, Kayanza and Cibitoke provinces. A government spokesman denied the reports, saying: 'Amnesty International is either completely misguided or is falling into a propaganda trap... These numbers are outrageous.' (AI, Reuters, Integrated Regional Information Network)

Archbishop Joachim Ruhuna was buried on 19 September in Gitega. He was murdered in an ambush while driving north of the city the previous week. Ruhuna's body was found alongside that of a nun in a shallow grave three kilometres from the scene of the attack. The rebels and the army blame each other for the attack. (Reuters, Integrated Regional Information Network)

CAMBODIA

Former *Serei Pheap Thmey* editor-in-chief **Hen Vipheak** (*Index* 2/1995, 5/1996) was released from prison by royal decree on 30 August, one week after his sentence for libel was upheld. (SWB)

CAMEROON

Eyoum Ngangue of *Le Messager Popoli* was sentenced to a year's imprisonment and a US$600 fine on 3 October. His colleague **Pius Njawe** received a six-month sentence and a fine of US$200. The pair were charged with insulting the president and 'disseminating false news' in a satirical article published in December 1995. (World Association of Newspapers)

CENTRAL AFRICAN REPUBLIC

Marcel Mokwapi, managing editor of the weekly *Le Novateur*, was arrested on 11 September following an article criticising the slowness of the country's judicial system, with reference to an ongoing case involving the state-owned Petroca oil company. (RSF)

CHILE

Manuel Cabieses, editor-in-chief of the weekly *Punto Final*, is being tried in absentia by a military court on charges of 'inciting sedition'. Police raided the journalist's home on 10 September, as well as the offices of the weekly, with a warrant for his arrest. Cabieses is now in hiding. On 9 September 1991 Cabieses published a front-page cartoon of General Pinochet cleaning his bloody nose with the Chilean flag. The ensuing charges against Cabieses were withdrawn by the Santiago Appeals Court in 1995 and the case was dismissed. However, military prosecutors have now decided to reopen the case, shortly before the five-year limit in which the charges could be brought expired on 8 September. (RSF)

CHINA

Publication of *Economic Monthly Magazine* was suspended in late August after it printed an article critical of a privately circulated pro-Marxist tract known as the '10,000 word essay'. Earlier, magazines and newspapers were banned from reprinting two articles on economic reform by **Cao Siyuan**, also highly critical of the tract, which had appeared in the July edition of the magazine. (Reuters)

Chen Longde, currently serving three years re-education through labour (*Index* 5/1996), has been severely beaten by prison guards for refusing to sign a self-criticism. Chen reportedly broke both legs when he jumped from a third-floor window in an attempt to escape a beating in late August. (*International Herald Tribune, China Labour Bulletin*)

In early September China's Taiwan Affairs Office, Propaganda Department, and Central Overseas Publicity Group issued a joint circular detailing standardised forms of address and wording to be used with reference to Taiwan. According to the circular, journalists are prohibited from using the term 'Republic of China' and the names of Taiwan's official organs, documents, and institutions and the titles of Taiwanese officials are also banned, unless quotation marks are added. The term 'mainland' is to be avoided and in the reporting of international matters the terms 'China's Taiwan' or 'China's Taipei' are suggested alternatives. (SWB)

On 3 September the Foreign Ministry cancelled the English-language translations of its twice-weekly briefings for the foreign press. The move — described as 'irreversible' by a Ministry spokesman — will be problematic: few members of the foreign press corps speak Chinese and the government forbids foreign media to hire translators except through the official Diplomatic Service Bureau, many of whose translators are inadequately trained. (*China News Digest, Independent*)

In early September the Ministry of Radio, Film and Television implemented a new policy of annual censorship aimed at strengthening ideological control over the media. Broadcasters' adherence to regulations will be examined and certificates of quality issued to stations which meet government requirements. Those found guilty of 'political accidents' or 'major accidents through negligence' will be rectified or given 'other punishments'. (SWB)

Access to hundreds of websites, including those of human rights groups, media outlets, and politically sensitive organisations in Hong Kong and Taiwan, was blocked in the first week of September. Most Hong Kong and Taiwanese newspapers, including the pro-Beijing, Hong Kong paper *Ta Kung Pao*, found their sites blocked, as did CNN, Voice of America, *Washington Post*, *Wall Street Journal*, and *Playboy*. Human rights groups affected by the measure were

Amnesty International, Human Rights Watch, Tibet Information Network, and Human Rights in China. US-based sites catering to overseas Chinese, such as China News Digest and the homepage of the Taiwan Government Information Office, were also blocked. (*International Herald Tribune, Los Angeles Times*)

Zhang Zhong'ai went on trial in Shanxi on 16 September, indicted on charges of pledging loyalty to Taiwan authorities after the police found a letter addressed to General Wego Chiang, son of the late Chiang Kai-shek, in which he sought 'guidance and assistance' from the Taiwanese media on how to bring democracy to China. Zhang, who was detained on 3 June, was also accused of receiving US$100 from a 'hostile' overseas organisation, and charged with spreading counter-revolutionary propaganda and incitement through a letter to a friend in the USA and an interview with dissident Wang Dan. (Reuters)

Pro-democracy activist Fu Guoyong (*Index* 4/1995, 2/1996) continues to be held in police custody, having been detained in Shanxi on 26 July for illegal political activities. (Reuters)

On 5 October it was reported that Ye Xu, who works in the Beijing office of SBC Warburg, had been held since 20 September for allegedly divulging economic data contained in a circular issued by the People's Bank of China. (*International Herald Tribune*)

Dissident and literary critic Liu Xiaobo was ordered to serve three years in a camp for 're-education through labour' on 9 October. He had been detained at home the previous day by police who also confiscated books, documents, photographs and articles. His detention appears to be linked to a joint statement he made on 30 September with the writer and pro-democracy activist Wang Xizhe (*Index* 4/1996), calling on the government to honour a pledge made in 1945 to guarantee political liberties. The statement also demanded that President Jiang Zemin be impeached. (Reuters, HRW)

Xinjiang: According to reports in early September, 98 people have been detained and 19 underground religious schools closed down near Hotan city since the start of a 100-day security operation in mid-July which forms part of the ongoing 'Strike Hard Campaign' (*Index* 4/1996). Of those detained, 12 have been sentenced to labour reform, 68 have received administrative punishments, 15 are still subject to investigation and three have been released. The Religious Affairs Administrative Department in Urumqi has denied the detentions and insists that those taken into custody have been 'assembled to receive patriotic education'. (SWB)

COLOMBIA

On 2 September the government lifted the strict curbs on television coverage of recent peasant protests in the southern coca-growing region

(*Index* 5/1996). The National Television Commission said that journalists are being urged to use their 'good judgement and professional criteria' in coverage of the protests but will no longer face the threat of sanctions. The restrictions were lifted four days after a demonstration by coca cultivators in Caqueta during which five journalists were shot. The journalists, all of whom could be clearly identified by brightly coloured flak jackets marked with the names of their news organisations, are Luis Alberto Mito, Camilo Chaparro, Gloria Tisna, Jaime Orlando Gaiten, and Maribel Osorio. Several attacks against journalists have been reported since the middle of August, all of them believed to be related to attempts by the media to cover protests by coca producers against the government's eradication campaign. (Reuters, CPJ)

Communications minister Saulo Arboleda called for a wholesale laundering of Colombia's image on 29 September. Speaking at an international conference against violence in Cartagena, Arboleda called for media self-censorship to tone down negative images of Colombia as the world's foremost supplier of drugs and as the kidnapping capital of the world. (Reuters)

COTE D'IVOIRE

Abou Dramane Sangare, Emmanuel Kore and Freedom Neruda — the three journalists detained earlier this year for disrespect for the head of state (*Index*

2/1996, 5/1996) — have had their appeals for bail turned down after refusing to ask for a pardon. (*West Africa*)

CROATIA

On 3 September charges were brought against **Veljko Vicevic**, editor-in-chief of the independent newspaper *Novi List* and columnist **Tihana Tomicic**, and against **Ivo Pukanic**, editor-in-chief of the independent weekly *Nacional* and columnist **Srecko Jurdana**. Both sets of charges, brought by the ruling HDZ, came under the amended section of Article 71 of the Croatian Penal Code forbidding the publication or broadcasting of information which could injure the reputation of senior officials. A recent column in *Novi List* compared the political climate in Croatia before the 1990 elections to that of Germany before Hitler's election. Jurdana frequently criticises HDZ leaders. The libel suit against the weekly *Globus* (*Index* 4/1996) is still pending. (CPJ)

On 26 September **Viktor Ivancic**, chief editor of the satirical weekly *Feral Tribune* and reporter **Marinko Culic** were acquitted on charges of slandering President Franjo Tudjman (*Index* 4/1996). The case has been widely regarded as a test for the new press law, allowing punishment of journalists on grounds of slandering high officials or revealing state secrets (*Index* 3/1996). Judge Marin Mrcela said that the articles contained value-judgements which could not be the subject of prosecution and were not libellous. The

state prosecutor appealed against the acquittals on 10 October. (OMRI, CPJ, IFJ, SWB, *Independent*)

On 2 October Parliament enacted a new media law with measures to guarantee press freedoms according to Council of Europe standards and also to require the media to distribute 'truthful and correct' information. A new media law was one of the membership conditions stipulated by the Council. (Reuters)

Radovan Jovic (*Index* 6/1995), a Serbian former judge who was arrested and charged with 'espionage against the Croatian state' after taking part in a meeting in Tuzla organised by the Helsinki Citizens' Assembly, was released from prison on 7 October. (hCa)

CUBA

Carlos Lórez Martínez, a university lecturer arrested more than four months ago, is reported to be seriously ill in detention. He is being held in a punishment cell at the Department of State Security in Pinar del Rio province and has been denied access to a lawyer. He is believed to be under investigation for 'enemy propaganda'. (AI)

On 9 September **Joaquín Torres Alvárez**, director of the independent news agency Havana Press, and reporter **Jorge Olivera Castillo** were summoned to state security headquarters for questioning, apparently in connection with a report about sabotage at the

Cuban Radio and Television Institute. Olivera had already been questioned about the report and warned that he would continue to be questioned until he revealed the sources for his story. (RSF, BPIC)

Independent Cuban Press Bureau (BPIC) correspondent **Olance Nogueras Rofe** was expelled from the Writers' Union building on 20 September. He was attempting to address the Caracol 96 seminar, which was discussing Cuba's policy on electronic media. Nogueras Rofe was interrupted by the director of information programming for Cuban television, Danilo Cirias, who told participants that he could not allow a counter-revolutionary to take the podium. Nogueras Rofe was verbally attacked and forced to leave the premises. (BPIC)

Plans for an informal meeting to commemorate the first anniversary of the independent news agency **Cuba Press** on 23 September were disrupted by members of the Vigilance and Protection System (SUVP), an umbrella group of various civic groups tied to the Cuban Communist Party (PCC). The SUVP members threatened Cuba Press director **Raul Rivero** and other journalists with violence if they did not cancel the meeting. (CPJ, PEN)

EUROPEAN UNION

EU telecommunications ministers, meeting in Brussels on 27 September adopted a voluntary code of conduct for curbing sexually explicit material on the Internet. The self-regulatory approach is in line with the Safety-Net proposals announced in Britain on 26 September (see below): they include a hotline for users to report what they think is illegal material, and a rating system which allows parents to block offensive text or images. Legal definitions of obscenity vary considerably through the EU, however, raising doubts about the value of regional co-operation on the matter. (*Independent*)

Recent publication: *Public Policy Issues Arising from Telecommunications and Audiovisual Convergence — a Summary Report* (KPMG, 8 Salisbury Square, London EC4Y 8BB, September 1996)

FINLAND

Johan Helsingius suspended his anonymous electronic remailing service on 30 August after a Helsinki judge ruled that a court may, under certain circumstances, order him to reveal the identities of users of the service. Known as anon.penet.fi, the service enables people to send e-mail without the recipient knowing the identity of the sender. It is the largest and best-known service of its kind in the world, with an estimated half a million users. The court was ruling on a petition from the Church of Scientology, which wanted Helsingius to disclose the identity of a person who they allege to have breached the Church's copyright by posting Scientology materials on the Internet. (*Los Angeles Times*)

FRANCE

François Mitterrand's former adviser Michel Charasse and former chief of staff, Gilles Ménage, failed in their attempt to prevent publication of the book *The Elysée's Secret Wars* by Paul Barril, a former member of Mitterrand's anti-terrorist unit. A court ruled on 9 September that the book may be published on condition that the publisher put up signs in bookshops saying that certain passages in the book are contested. The book alleges that Mitterrand used a 'secret police force' to spy on political enemies, and that Charasse and Ménage ordered the murder of Mitterrand's friend and colleague François de Grossouvre, who was found dead at the Elysée Palace in 1994. (Reuters)

At the end of September an appeals court authorised the continuation of an investigation into illegal telephone tapping of journalists and politicians during the Mitterrand administration. Six former officials, including Gilles Ménage, are under investigation for alleged violations of privacy rights. (Reuters)

GERMANY

Acting on legal threats from the government, Internet providers in Germany blocked the Dutch website **Access For All** (http://www.xs4all.nl) on 18 September. The government acted because the site hosts a homepage with political content which is alleged to be illegal in Germany. (GreenNet)

GHANA

On 9 August **Cofie Ammuako-Annan**, acting editor of the *Ghanaian Chronicle*, was sentenced to 30 days' imprisonment for contempt of court. On the same charge, **General Portfolio** (the publishing company behind the newspaper) was fined US$700, although company director **Cofi Coomson** (*Index* 2/1996) was acquitted. The charge related to the *Ghanaian Chronicle's* report of a murder trial, suggesting that the trial judge had influenced the foreman to return a unanimous verdict. The High Court judge further ruled that no reporting of either trial would be allowed. (IFJ, Free Expression Ghana)

HONDURAS

The Interior and Justice Ministry threatened to withdraw legal recognition for the children's rights organisation **Casa Alianza** on 9 October. In addition, the Ministry said it is revoking Casa Alianza's right to import goods tax-free because of the bad publicity that the organisation has generated for Honduras. Casa Alianza works on behalf of street children and those illegally detained. (World Organisation Against Torture)

HONG KONG

According to reports in Japan's *Sankei Shimbun* in early September, the local consulates of 13 countries that maintain diplomatic ties with Taiwan will be closed after Hong Kong reverts to China in July 1997. Countries will

NILOU MOBASSER

Identity parade

The television programme *Hoviyat* (Identity) should be made compulsory viewing for all those who believe that the Islamic Republic of Iran is of a piece. The programme's juxtaposition of words — a running commentary about 'West-toxicated Iranians who have lost or betrayed their cultural identity' — and images — a frightening mix of video clips of 'counter-revolutionary' Iranians living abroad, on the one hand, and of prominent Iranians living and working in Iran today on the other — can leave little doubt that this is a system in alarming ferment.

Many of the writers and thinkers portrayed as virtual fifth columnists for 'the West's cultural invasion' and for international Zionism and Freemasonry are contributors to and directors of journals published quite legally. Ezzatollah Sahabi, for example, who has come under repeated attack in *Hoviyat*, is the managing director of the journal *Iran-e Farda* (Iran Tomorrow), published in Tehran. In a letter to President Akbar Hashemi-Rafsanjani published in the Tehran daily *Salam* in July, he asked to be allowed to exercise his right to reply on the programme:

'The television programme *Hoviyat*, about 10 instalments of which have been shown so far on Iranian television, has repeatedly presented several journals as bases for the West's cultural invasion of Iran and has used contrived images and video gimmicks in conjunction with spiteful commentaries to portray *Iran-e Farda* — of which I am in charge — as the centre of this base. It may be the case that the government does not like my political, cultural or religious views and it may wish to respond to them. Nevertheless, in view of my 50-year record of social and cultural service, of which you [Rafsanjani] at least are aware, the claim that this journal is a central base for the West's cultural invasion is a blatant insult, calumny and slander.

'More importantly, in the two most recent instalments, which have focused specifically on me, the programme has not only misleadingly associated me with people with whom I have no links or familiarity but has broadcast, to an audience of millions, selective clips from video footage which was taken under severe psychological duress for the prison's internal archives while I was being interrogated during six months of illegal detention in 1369 [1990-91] and which lacks any religious, legal or social validity, thereby besmirching and tarnishing my social and political standing...'

Some of the people 'named' in recent instalments are Abbas Maroufi (*Index* 3/1996), Reza Baraheni, Esma'il Fassih (*Index* 3/1992) and, once again, Ezzatollah Sahabi. ❑

Nilou Mobasser is a specialist in Iranian affairs

only be allowed to retain their Hong Kong offices if they cut ties with Taipei. Problems also loom for semi-official Taiwanese organisations in Hong Kong, including the Taiwanese Kwang Hwa Information and Culture Centre, currently puzzling over what to do with 16,000 books inscribed with the potentially troublesome term 'Published in the Republic of China'. (*Far Eastern Economic Review, South China Morning Post*)

Access to an Internet enthusiast's homepage was barred on 24 September after his service provider received a complaint about the sexually suggestive content of the site. **Donald Tu,** whose page featured photos of himself topless and in briefs, has since removed the pictures from the site. (Newsbytes News Network)

HUNGARY

Budapest's Great Synagogue was reopened in early September. The 137-year-old synagogue was destroyed during World War II. The opening ceremony was attended by President Goncz and the former Israeli prime minister, Yitzhak Shamir, as well as concentration camp survivors. (*Times*)

INDONESIA

Three more people have been detained for alleged involvement with the outlawed People's Democratic Party (PRD). **Suwigno** was taken into custody in Jakarta on 3 September after he had visited the Indonesian Legal Aid Institute whilst **I Gusti Anom Astika** and **Wilson** were detained in Central Java. Meanwhile **Goenawan Mohamad** (*Index* 2/1996), founder and editor-in-chief of the banned magazine *Tempo*, was summoned in early September as a witness in the subversion case against PRD leader Budiman Sudjatmiko (*Index* 5/1996). (AI, Reuters)

A man, identified only as **KM**, went on trial in Jakarta on 20 September charged with blasphemy. KM stands accused of slandering the predominantly Christian community of South Sulawesi's Tana Torajan region when he spoke at a seminar on AIDS at the University of Indonesia and the Jakarta Islamic Hospital. In a statement published in the daily *Pelita* in April, he described most female school students in the area as having 'lost their virginity to tourists' and added 'those girls mostly are not Muslims.' (*Jakarta Post*)

At the opening of a 10-day course on the State Ideology Pancasila (Five Principles) President Soeharto called for accuracy in press reporting. The media, he said, must 'remain watchful and alert in presenting a news report or commentary by avoiding giving the impression that rioting or disorderliness is a legal means of protesting'. He also stressed the inspirational function of the press to 'brighten the people's thinking'. (*Antara*)

On 24 September, two weeks after opening new offices of the ousted faction of the Indonesian Democratic Party, **Megawati Soekarnoputri** and her secretary-general were given three days' notice to leave. According to the warrant issued by the governor of East Jakarta, Megawati's office violates zoning regulations. These regulations are regularly flouted by others. (Melbourne *Age*)

Recent publication: *East Timor — The Continuing Betrayal* (CIIR, September 1996, 43pp)

IRAN

A court sentenced 28 teenagers to punishment ranging from lashes to imprisonment for throwing a party and possessing illegal compact discs and video cassettes on 28 August. The daily *Kayhan* reported that the teenagers were arrested by anti-vice squad police who broke up the party in response to complaints by neighbours. *Kayhan* reported that, as well as illegal tapes and discs, 41 'vulgar' videotapes were found at the house. (Reuters)

Security forces entered the home of the German cultural attaché on 28 August, during a dinner at which several prominent Iranian writers were present, among them **Hushang Golshiri, Mohammadali Sepanloo, Reza Baraheni** and **Simin Behbahani.** The security men forced the guests to stay at the dinner table for a number of hours, during which time they were filmed. The cultural attaché was later offered an official apology but the film was not surrendered. It is thought that the film might be used as footage for the television programme

Hoviyat (Identity), which regularly features Iranian dissidents and links them with western governments. (PEN)

On 3 September an appeals court quashed a ruling that banned vice-president **Ataollah Mohajerani** from all press work for a year (*Index* 5/1996). Mohajerani was convicted in July of causing 'public confusion' in the weekly *Bahman*, which he edits. Mohajerani says he will soon resume publication of the magazine, which supports the centrist policies of President Rafsanjani. (Reuters)

On 8 September 12 writers who had gathered at the home of **Mansour Koshan**, editor of the banned literary magazine *Takapoo*, to draft a charter for the Iranian Writers' Association (IWA), which they are reviving, were detained by security officials. The writers, **Hossein Asghari, Mohammad Baharloo, Reza Baraheni, Roshanak Daryoush, Kaveh Goharin, Hushang Golshiri, Ghafar Hosseini, Kamran Jamali, Mohammad Mokhtari, Mohammad Mohammad-Ali, Faraj Sarkoohi** and **Farzaneh Taheri**, were blindfolded and taken to Evin Prison. Each was given a questionnaire to fill in and some were singled out for interrogation. Koshan's house was later searched by security forces and the draft charter confiscated. The writers were released several hours later and warned not to hold further meetings or publicise the IWA. (PEN)

The hardline conservative

Islamic daily *Jomhuri Eslami* vowed on 26 September that **Salman Rushdie** would be killed despite the government's assurances that it would not seek out the British author. It was referring to a recent Foreign Ministry statement which said that, although the *fatwa* is irrevocable, the Iranian government will 'not send any commandos' to kill Rushdie. (Reuters, *Times, Guardian*)

IRAQ

Around 30 journalists were prevented from entering Erbil in Iraqi Kurdistan on 15 September by officials from the Democratic Party of Kurdistan (PDK), which is supported by Iraq. The officials told the reporters: 'We have no instructions to let you through.' The journalists were accompanied throughout their trip to the region by officials from the Iraqi Information Ministry. (RSF)

IRELAND

The publicity poster for the film *Striptease* was rejected by the film censor Sheamus Smith a few days before it was due to open in Dublin on 20 September. Following an appeal by the film's Irish distributor, Abbey Films, to the Film Appeals Board a compromise decision ruled that the poster could be exhibited inside cinemas showing the film and in newspaper advertising, but not outside the cinemas or on bus shelters or outdoor poster sites. The censor is believed to have rejected the poster — which shows an undressed Demi Moore — in

the light of controversy over some recent outdoor ads which were regarded as offensive to women. (*Irish Times*)

ISRAEL

Mordechai Vanunu (*Index* 1/1987) remains in solitary confinement in Ashkelon prison, 10 years after his arrest on 30 September 1986. He was sentenced to 18 years' imprisonment for revealing top secret information about Israel's Dimona nuclear plant in the Negev desert. (Reuters)

Journalists have been banned by the army from entering Palestinian autonomous areas without prior authorisation. Army spokesman General Oded Ben Ami said the measure was imposed in the interests of journalists' safety and because the army did not want to risk involvement if an Israeli journalist was under threat in Palestinian areas. Radio journalists claim that the measure is intended to impede them in the performance of their professional duties. (RSF)

Several journalists were injured covering widespread clashes between Israelis and Palestinians in the West Bank and Gaza. On 25 September Palestinian Broadcast Corporation (PBC) cameramen **Abdel Karim Zeneid** and **Murad Siyyam**, and driver **Ali Shanaan**, were hit by rubber bullets when caught in crossfire in al-Birreh. On 26 September four PBC journalists — reporters **Muhammad Saadi** and **Ahmed Kaddoumi**, cameramen **Abdel Nasser** and **Khaled Abu Hattab** — and driver **Ghassan Kandah** were wounded, also by rubber bullets, while covering clashes in Ramallah. Several journalists remain in hospital after being shot by live ammunition while covering clashes on 26 September: CBS cameraman **Issa Freij** was shot in the chest in Ramallah; also in Ramallah AFP photographer **Manoocher Deghati** suffered fractures after being shot in the leg; Reuters cameraman **Shams Odeh** was shot in the leg in Gaza; WTN cameraman **Majdi al-Arabid** was shot by a sniper and wounded in the hands and leg near the Erez checkpoint in Gaza; freelance cameraman **Khalil Saada** was also wounded at Erez; and reporter **Yossi Eindor** and cameraman **Chaim Assias** from Israel's Second Channel were shot at and wounded — Assias seriously — by Palestinian police in Gaza, despite attempting to show their press ID. The police later claimed that they thought the group of journalists was an Israeli army patrol. (CPJ)

Recent publication: *Annual Report 1995* (Physicians for Human Rights, August 1996, 15pp)

JAPAN

Japanese patrol boats and helicopters prevented television crews and journalists from Hong Kong and Taiwan from coming within a three-mile radius of the disputed Diaoyu islands and threatened to detain reporters if they did not leave. One demonstrator, *South China Morning Post* photographer **David Chan**, drowned and another was injured during the protests. The disturbances continued throughout September. (*South China Morning Post, Straits Times*)

JORDAN

Usamah al-Rantisi of the daily *al-Ahali* was arrested on 22 August and held for 15 days. He is charged with 'inciting sedition' under the Press and Publications Law as a result of a 21 August article headlined 'These Events are not from Outside', which disputed government claims that August's bread riots were fomented by Iraq. If convicted he faces a prison sentence of between six months and three years. (CPJ)

The well-known writer **Ahmed Awaidi al-Abaddi** and **Jihad al-Mo'mani**, editor of the weekly *Shihan*, were charged with 'harming national unity' on 8 October. The charge arises from an interview which appeared in the paper in June, in which al-Abaddi said that Palestinian refugees in Jordan should be relocated to areas under the control of the Palestinian National Authority. Another *Shihan* journalist, **Nahed Hattar**, was also charged in early October with 'harming national unity', 'inciting the public' and 'insulting the king' in connection with articles he wrote arguing for unification between Jordan and Syria. (CPJ)

KAZAKHSTAN

Nina Sidorova, president of the Russian Centre in Kazakhstan, has been detained without charge since 20 August, apparently on suspicion of defamation and 'hooliganism'. Sidorova's supporters say the detention is linked to her attempts to gain legal recognition for a Cossack community organisation. (AI, OMRI)

On 9 September Almaty city authorities refused permission for the **Centre for Russian Culture of Almaty** to stage a demonstration in front of the US embassy. The demonstrators intended to protest at the US air raids on Iraq. (OMRI)

President Nazarbayev threatened to expel **Vladimir Ardayev**, the Kazakhstan correspondent for *Izvestia*, on 27 September and accused him of undermining friendly relations between the countries of the Commonwealth of Independent States (CIS). Nazarbayev's threats stem from recent reports in several media outlets, including *Izvestia*, about a letter sent by President Nazarbayev to President Karimov of Uzbekistan. In the letter Nazarbayev is alleged to have expressed scepticism about a customs agreement between Kazakhstan, Kyrgyzstan, Belarus and the Russian Federation. The National Committee for the Press and Mass Media wrote to *Izvestia*'s editor, Igor Golembiovski, saying that the administration was obliged to cut off all relations with Ardayev. (RSF)

KENYA

On 30 August police arrested **Mwangi Kianjuri**, an activist with the opposition party

Safina (*Index* 5/1995), at a seminar on political reform. Anti-riot police ordered the participants to disperse and occupied the premises for the remainder of the day. Safina has still not been granted a licence, despite efforts by the party to gain official recognition. (NDIMA)

On 31 August hundreds of Catholic youths, led by Cardinal Maurice Otunga, marched through the streets of Nairobi to protest against the introduction of sex education in Kenyan schools. The marchers ended up at Uhuru Park where the protest culminated in the burning of heaps of condoms and AIDS-awareness literature, including the short play *Life, Love and Aids* and the pamphlet *Peter and Anne Discuss Aids with Auntie Mary*. The demonstration came after a Synod meeting on 29 August at which the Kirinyaga Anglican Diocese in the Central Province of Kenya banned the active participation of bishops, priests and lay leaders in politics. (NDIMA)

Koigi wa Wamwere's lawyer, Mirugi Kariuki, wrote to chief magistrate William Tuiyot on 18 September complaining about the delay in hearing his client's appeal. It has now been a year since wa Wamwere and his co-accused were convicted, but their appeal has yet to be heard, apparently because the necessary documents have not been typed. On 4 September leading defence lawyer Paul Muite offered to provide the court with computers and typists, since the court's own computers had not been working for a long time. Earlier the same month, wa Wamwere wrote to the Kenyan Medical Association after medical staff at Kamiti prison had threatened forcibly to administer anti-depressant drugs. Tuiyot warned the Norwegian government to desist from commenting on the case on 9 October, after Norway's chargé d'affaires publicly criticised the conduct of wa Wamwere's trial. (NDIMA)

Four petrol bombs were thrown into the Nairobi compound of the weekly *People* shortly after midnight on 18 September. The bombs did not cause any major damage but later in the day anonymous callers made death threats to senior employees of the paper. Editor-in-chief **George Mbuggus** was warned to stop 'writing dirty things against the government'. Senior writer Irungu Ndirangu was later told: 'We are looking for you. Be careful about what you write for that paper.' (NDIMA)

KUWAIT

On 28 August Abdulla al-Hajri, an Islamist MP, called for government curbs on access to some Internet sites. He said he was concerned over 'sin-inducing' material being transmitted on the worldwide computer network. Kuwait maintains strict censorship on depictions of nudity in magazines and on television. (Reuters)

Further to an amnesty in April, three women held for 'collaborating' with the Iraqi occupying forces in 1990 through their work for the newspaper *al-Nida* have now been released. It is thought, however, that a further 16 journalists are still detained on similar charges. Shortly after the Iraqi invasion of Kuwait the Iraqis closed down the national newspaper *al-Qabas* and replaced it with *al-Nida*. It was the only newspaper allowed to publish and its staff allege that they were forced to work for the paper. (PEN)

LEBANON

Hundreds of people defied a ban on demonstrations to protest on 3 October against a government ban on the vast majority of private television and radio stations. All unlicensed stations must close by 30 November — a move that will put hundreds out of work. There are currently some 68 radio and 20 television stations operating, most catering to very specific sectarian groups, but the government has granted licences to just 15 of them. The four television stations that have received licences are: Future Television, part-owned by prime minister Rafiq al-Hariri; National Broadcasting Network (NBN), reportedly to be set up by Parliamentary speaker Nabih Birri: MTV, owned by the brother of deputy prime minister Michael al-Murr; and the Christian Phalangist Lebanese Broadcasting Corporation (LBC). Of the three radio stations allowed to broadcast news, two are owned by Hariri and Birri. Following the protests the government agreed to allow Hizbollah-run Manar Television and Radio

Light to carry news of resistance against Israeli forces but not to broadcast other political programming or news. Two new radio stations are to be set up as part of state-run Radio Lebanon to broadcast Islamic and Christian religious programmes. (SWB, Reuters, *Financial Times*)

Charges against singer **Marcel Khalife** of insulting Islam were dismissed on 20 September on the orders of prime minister Rafiq al-Hariri following protests by writers and journalists. Khalife, a Maronite Christian, had been charged two days earlier for allegedly using a verse from the Quran in a song titled 'Oh my father, I am Yusif'. The lyrics, 'Did I commit adultery when I said that I saw 11 planets and the sun and the moon kneeling in front of me', were said to resemble a Quranic verse in which Yusif addresses his father Jacob. The lyric was actually taken from poems by Palestinian poet Mahmoud Darwish. (Reuters)

Recent publication: *Accord — An International Review of Peace Initiatives* (Issue 1/1996: The Liberian Peace Process 1990-1996, 104pp, Conciliation Resources, 33 Islington High Street, London N1 9LH)

Raphael Pura, *Asian Wall Street Journal*'s Malaysia correspondent, is being sued for US$44 million in two defamation suits brought by business tycoon Tan Sri Vincent Tan and four Malaysian companies.

The plaintiffs accuse Pura of libel in an article entitled 'Malaysian Justice on Trial' published in the *International Commercial Litigation Magazine* in November 1995. (Institute for Studies on the Free Flow of Information)

On 26 September **Datuk Joseph Chong Chek Ah** was expelled from the Central Committee of the Gerakan, a multiracial party in the ruling National Front, for criticising leaders in public and 'tarnishing the party's image'. He and Penang chief minister **Tan Sri Dr Koh Tsu Koon** were later disqualified as candidates in the election for Gerakan national posts. (*Straits Times*)

The private television station **MetroVision** cancelled a scheduled broadcast of the Miss Malaysia contest on 4 October, after protests by Muslim youth groups and because the station had not gained Information Ministry approval for the broadcast, despite agreeing to omit the swimsuit event. (*Straits Times*)

Opposition parties denounced censorship measures imposed in the run-up to the elections of 11 October. Opposition candidates were given only three minutes' airtime on radio and television each to defend their policies, and any criticism of the government or discussion of issues such as slavery was censored. (SWB)

Hilario Mesino Acosta (*Index* 5/1996), leader of the

Southern Sierra Peasant Organisation (OCSS), remains in detention. He has reportedly been tortured to force him to confess to having links with the leftist rebel Popular Revolutionary Army (ERP). His family have also been threatened with death. (AI)

Razhy González Rodríguez, director of the Oaxaca-based magazine *Contrapunto*, was abducted by four armed men on 17 September. He was handcuffed, blindfolded and interrogated about the ERP. González is known for his reportage on the Zapatista insurgents in Chiapas and was among a group of journalists who interviewed ERP representatives in Oaxaca on 13 September. He was released on 19 September and said that although he had not been tortured, his kidnappers were experts at psychological torture and political interrogation and that threats had been made against him and members of his family. (AI, CPJ, RSF)

On 18 September the home of **Leticia Hernández Montoya**, director of the Guerrero state newspaper *Expresso* and correspondent for the national daily *Excelsior*, was visited by an official of the Attorney-General's Office. The official interrogated Hernández Montoya's family about her activities and her knowledge of the ERP. Hernández Montoya was among the journalists who interviewed ERP representatives on 13 September. The same day the Attorney-General's Office issued a public statement accusing the 14 journalists of

ADEWALE MAJA-PEARCE

Whatever happened to Ken?

What is Ken Saro-Wiwa's legacy, one year after he was hanged in Nigeria along with eight other minority rights activists on the orders of a military tribunal which had determined his guilt even before the start of what passed for a trial? Well, his murderer is still on the throne; and the West, which promised fire and brimstone in the immediate aftermath of what everyone agreed was a clear-cut case of judicial murder, is content these days to recommend the democratic imperative on the grounds that 'there is a growing body of evidence to show that the way in which a country is governed may affect its rate of development'. So says Dr Walter Carrington, the US Ambassador to Nigeria, citing the work of 'two American social scientists' (both unnamed) to buttress his thesis. But no mention of Ken Saro-Wiwa; no mention, either, of the Ogoni people in whose name he died and who, now, one year later, have been cowed into silence by an army of occupation whose ammunition is purchased from the proceeds of the very same oil that has brought them such grief.

Because to have talked about Ken would have meant talking about oil sanctions. This, after all, was what he demanded of the multinational companies — Shell, Chevron, Agip, Exxon, Total — that pay General Sani Abacha and his cronies millions of dollars every day as they maximise their profits on behalf of their shareholders, most of whom have never even visited Nigeria. Alas, no: 'There is not an appetite for that', the US Secretary of State, Warren Christopher, curtly declared on the first leg of his five-nation African tour in early October, even as he went on to profess himself 'troubled by the conduct of the government, by its violation of human rights and its degree of corruption', and then promised, in consequence, to mobilise international opinion in favour of a sports boycott.

It's a pity that the West — with the sole exception of Canada — has proved itself so feeble in its response to Ken's execution. The only beneficiary is General Abacha

collaborating with the ERP. A second communique, issued on 19 September, added a further 13 names to the list. (AI)

Silverio López Ramos, an activist with the People's Defence Committee (CDIP) and the Broad Front for the Construction of a National Liberation Movement (FAC-MLN), was arrested at his home on 4 September by members of the state police,

the army and the federal judicial police. Several members of these organisations have been targeted by the security forces in the recent clampdown on the ERP. In the early afternoon of 4 September **Evaristo Peralta**, a CDIP member in Miahuatlan, Oaxaca, was beaten and blindfolded before being carried away in a van to an unknown location. During his detention he was interrogated about the

ERP and threatened with death. He was released without charge the following day but the whereabouts of López Ramos remain unknown. (AI)

On 30 September President Zedillo introduced a Bill in Congress that would limit the length of time foreign journalists could stay in the country. The proposals call for the creation of a new category of 'correspondent' in the immi-

himself, a man who understands the meaning of patience, and who now, one year later, feels secure enough to keep Chief Moshood Abiola, the presumed winner of the annulled 1993 elections, in continued incarceration on a four-count charge of treason. This is to say nothing of Frank Ovie Kokori, the leader of the oil workers' union, who has been shut away for even longer, or the human rights activists and journalists — Dr Beko Ransome-Kuti, Chris Anyanwu, Kunle Ajibade, Ben Charles Obi and George Mbah — currently serving 15 years for plotting to overthrow the government, following a trial held in secret by a military tribunal. It seems that anybody can be a coup plotter in Nigeria these days.

Or you can be assassinated. The occasion of Dr Carrington's latest statement concerning his country's steadfast commitment to the democratic process in Nigeria was a public lecture in memory of Pa Alfred Rewane, an elder statesman who was shot dead in the bedroom of his house in October last year. The police have since dragged two different gangs of alleged armed robbers before the courts on two different occasions, but nobody is convinced. Pa Rewane was a fierce opponent of military rule in its latest incarnation and said so as loudly as possible at every opportunity. Besides, one can hardly be expected to believe the police in such a matter. As Pa Rewane himself understood only too well, military rule means just that; it means, in effect, that the person at the top is in charge and everybody else does what he says, period. The rest, as we like to say here, is just a lot of English grammar.

The list of Nigerian martyrs doesn't begin with Ken Saro-Wiwa, in other words, nor does it end with him. One morning last June, Alhaja Kudirat Abiola, the then 'senior' wife of the detained president (but this is Nigeria), was shot dead in her car at a busy junction in Lagos. The gunmen, who are yet to be caught (!), were not interested in snatching the vehicle, which is the other reason why motorists get killed. At the time of her death she was the most outspoken defender of her husband's mandate within the Abiola family. She had even pitted herself against some of the other family members who were apparently ready to reach a compromise with the military. The only question that remain now is, how many others must die before this country of ours is set free? But at least we now know that the matter of our salvation lies in our hands alone. This might be just as well in the long run. ❏

gration code which would allow foreign journalists to receive a one-year visa with a maximum of four annual extensions. It also calls for similar restrictions on visiting scientists, technical advisers, artists and religious workers. (RSF, Associated Press)

MONGOLIA

The Mongolian People's Revolutionary Party accused the ruling Democratic Union coalition of discriminating against 'nonconformism and party adherence' in mid-September. They claim that many people have lost their jobs or been demoted because of their political beliefs. (SWB)

NAMIBIA

Section 11 of the 1991 Racial Discrimination Act was ruled unconstitutional in the High Court on 27 August. The ruling was made in response to a challenge by **Hannes Smith**, former editor of the *Namibian*, and the paper's directors, **Esther Smith** and **Elizabeth Haase**, who had been charged under the Act in connection with an advertisement carried by the newspaper, commemorating the death of Rudolf Hess. The advertisement referred to Hess as a 'martyr of

---

peace' and the 'last representative of a better Germany' (*Index* 5/1995). (MISA)

Katutura Community Radio (KCR) has been told by the Namibian Communications Commission (NCC) that it must change frequencies or close down, following the launch of a new commercial station, Radio Energy, on a frequency very close to KCR's frequency. Radio Energy is owned by Radio 100; the majority shareholder of Radio 100 is Kalihari Holdings, a company owned by the ruling South West African People's Organisation. (MISA)

NEW ZEALAND

Telecom Xtra cut access to thousands of Internet users at the end of September after a complaint was made to the Internal Affairs Department's censorship compliance section about the availability of sexually explicit material. Telecom Xtra said: 'We were advised that we might be breaking the law...so it's fairly hard to dispute that.' The Internet Society, however, accused the company of overreacting by blocking access to a broad range of newsgroups, not all of them containing sexually explicit material. Telecom Xtra, which already provides users with filtering software, is currently seeking clarification of the legal situation from Internal Affairs. (*New Zealand Herald*)

NICARAGUA

On 25 September the Supreme Election Council (CSE) banned a television campaign ad attacking the former Sandinista government. The ad used footage taken during the period when the Sandinista Front for National Liberation (FSLN) ruled the country, between 1979 and 1990, to warn voters against supporting the party in the elections on 20 October. (Reuters)

NIGERIA

In Rivers State, radio producer **Okina Deesor** was arrested on 31 July after his station, Radio Rivers, broadcast the Ogoni national anthem. On 23 August, it was reported that he had been released, although no further details have been made available. (CCPJ)

Despite government claims that the six-month strike by university staff has been broken, many lecturers have still not returned to work. Lectures are reported to have restarted at a number of universities, however, including the University of Benin, Enugu State University of Science and Technology, and the Universitiy of Lagos. (*West Africa, Guardian* (Nigeria), *Post Express*)

In contrast to the report in *Index* 5/1996, the jailed opposition activist and lawyer **Gani Fawehinmi** remains in prison.

NORWAY

In late August the Norwegian branch of Save the Children established an international body to monitor child pornography on the Internet. Users discovering child pornography on the Net will be able to report to the group's site (children@risk.sn.no), and all information will be handed over to the police. Save the Children will work with Interpol to track down the sources of the material. (Reuters, Agence-France Presse)

PAKISTAN

Armed men attempted to kidnap the news editor of the *News*, **Aftab Syed**, from his Karachi home on 13 September. One of the men claimed to be a Sindh intelligence operative. Syed was threatened with death if he informed the police of the incident. (Pakistan Press Foundation)

Several journalists covering the murder of the prime minister's brother, Murtaza Bhutto, and six of his colleagues in Karachi on 20 September were beaten by police. Photojournalists had their cameras snatched and smashed. (Pakistan Press Foundation)

Khalid H Lodhi, former Islamabad and London bureau chief for the ruling Pakistan People's Party daily *Musawaat*, continues to receive anonymous threats in exile in London. His family in Pakistan also reports harassment and threats, believed to be connected with Lodhi's articles in the London-based *Daily Nation* and Urdu-language papers in Pakistan, alleging the involvement of prime minister Benazir Bhutto's husband, Asif Zardari, and other politicians and bureaucrats in corruption and drug trafficking.

Recent publication: *The Death Penalty* (AI, September 1996, 20pp)

PARAGUAY

On 15 September unknown individuals opened fire on the home of the parents of journalist **Vladimir Jara**. Jara, a court reporter for the daily *ABC Color*, has been the target of intimidation in the past few weeks: on two occasions unidentified individuals have entered his apartment; his wife has received death threats by telephone; and her parents' home has been vandalised. The incidents are thought to be linked to Jara's ongoing investigations into police misconduct. An investigation into the incidents has now been opened and the head of the National Police has assured Jara's safety. (FIP, RSF)

PERU

On 2 September unknown individuals threw a homemade petrol bomb at the home of radio journalist **Fernando Yenque Guevara** in Chulucanas, Piura region. Yenque, who reports for the news programme 1480 on Radio Supercontinental, had just left the house with the director of the Chulucanas branch of of the National Journalists' Association (ANP), **Carlos Vargas Castro**. They were going to interview the regional prefect, Pedro Garcia Saavedra, about an assault on Vargas at the end of August. Vargas had been covering the Santa Rosa de Lima marathon

when he was assaulted by the chief of the regional section of the National Police of Peru (PNP), Colonel Rodolfo Rodríguez García. (FIP)

The defence minister, General Tomas Castillo Meza, appeared before Congress on 13 September to deny that confidential intelligence reports, leaked by the television news programmes *La Revista Dominical* and *Contrapunto*, were genuine. Calling the leak 'a common crime', the General recommended that justice officials file charges 'against civilians involved in the development of the apocryphal document'. Falsifying news reports is an offence in Peru. (FIP)

On 1 October the government named the first prisoners to be freed on the recommendation of a new body created to speed the release of those wrongfully imprisoned on terrorism charges. A decree, published in the government daily *El Peruano*, granted pardons to three journalists: **Eduardo Sihue Cano, José Antonio Alvárez Pachas** and **Jesus Alfonso Castiglione Mendoza** (*Index* 6/1994, 5/1996). Sihue Cano and Alvárez Pachas both served six-year sentences, also related to terrorism charges. The special body has recommended pardons for 31 prisoners, so more releases are expected. Peru's so-called 'faceless' courts, which were responsible for many miscarriages of justice in terrorism trials, were due to stop operating on 15 October, but on 11 October Congress approved a Bill to extend the system for one

more year. (Reuters, Instituto Prensa y Sociedad)

The mayor of Lince ordered the confiscation of the popular dailies *Aja* and *El Chino* on 5 October. The papers are well known for printing pictures of international female celebrities on their front pages. The mayor said that the pictures were 'pornographic', a charge denied by the papers. (FIP)

PHILIPPINES

Two Tibetan and two Pakistani delegates were refused visas to attend an Amnesty International conference held in Manila in late August. Dharamsala-based **Gedun Rinchen** and **Tampa Tsering** were told that their participation in the conference, on human rights in China, was 'a sensitive matter'. (Reuters, *Straits Times*)

POLAND

Journalist **Jerzy Slavomir Mac** (*Index* 5/1996) who went missing on 27 August, was found on 2 September at a railway station in Warsaw. He says he was abducted on his way to meet a possible informant for a story about public television finances. He remembers little about his five days in captivity other than that he was held in a windowless room. (CPJ)

The Senate rejected a Bill liberalising the country's abortion law on 3 October. The Bill, passed by the Sejm at the end of August, would have allowed abortion up to the twelfth week of pregnancy. (OMRI)

ROMANIA

On 24 September the parliamentary Mediation Commission overruled a Chamber of Deputies decision of 10 September which criminalised homosexuality. The Commission recommended that only homosexual acts 'performed in public' or 'provoking a scandal' should be punishable. (OMRI, AI)

Ten journalists from various news organisations — **Mihai Antoci** and **Razvan Savaliuc** of *Ziua*; **Marius Ghilezan**, **Dan Preisz** and **Florin Esanu** of *Romania Libera*; **Oana Bratu** of Radio Contact; **Ovidiu Patrascanu** of *Evenimentul Zilei*; **Andreea Munteanu** of *Azi*; **Marius Hoc** of Tele 7 ABC; and **Mircea Marian** of the news agency Mediafax — entered offices where members of the ruling Party of Social Democracy (PDSR) were conducting telephone opinion polls on 30 September. The poll was allegedly heavily slanted against opponents of the PDSR and, it is alleged, was a deliberate attempt to mislead and influence voters in the run-up to the 3 November presidential election. The 10 journalists were later ordered by the PDSR to give up their notes and videotapes from the incident. Several of them were subsequently called in for questioning by the police, who also searched Oana Bratu's home on 3 October. (CPJ, Reuters)

RUSSIAN FEDERATION

Russia: In September the editor-in-chief of the daily *Pravda*, Alexander Ilyin, warned readers that a paper calling itself *Pravda-5* was not the real thing. *Pravda*, he said, had appeared only three times in August and September, owing to serious financial problems and a protracted dispute between editorial staff and the paper's Greek owners. (*Independent*, SWB)

On 19 September the commission responsible for declassifying documents of the Central Committee of the Communist Party of the Soviet Union permitted the release of information about the origin of the Strategic Missile Troops, political censorship in the USSR, and the history of the Communist International, among other things. (SWB)

The trial of Democratic Union of Russia leader **Valeriya Novodvorskaya** began in Moscow on 26 September. Novodvorskaya is charged with inciting interethnic discord and 'belittling the dignity of the Russian nation' in articles and broadcasts in which she talked, among other things, about the 'laziness, poverty and spinelessness of Russians'. (*Express-Chronicle*)

Alexander Nikitin (*Index* 3/1996) was formally charged with treason in the form of espionage on 27 September. The Federal Security Service (FSB) alleges that Nikitin, a former naval captain, used an out-of-date security pass to gain access to classified information about radioactive contamination in the Kola peninsula, which he then passed to the Norwegian environmental group Bellona. The charge against Nikitin carries the death penalty. (OMRI, AI)

The State Duma passed a non-binding resolution early in October calling for the renationalisation of **Russian Public Television (ORT)**. The resolution said that news coverage on ORT and state-owned **Russian TV** is biased and portrays Duma members as irresponsible. (OMRI)

Bashkortostan: **Eduard Khusnutdinov**, editor-in-chief of *Vecherny Neftekamsk*, has been threatened with five years in prison for libel by a local prosecutor for an article entitled 'No Smoke Without Fire' in which he is said to have alleged that the president of the autonomous Urals republic, Murtaza Rakhimov, took bribes in the run-up to the 3 July national elections. Khusnutdinov claims a typographical error is responsible and is seeking to have his case heard in Moscow. (CPJ)

Chechnya: Several journalists have gone missing in the region in recent weeks: on 27 September **Natalya Vasenina**, editor-in-chief of the Grozny paper *Nezavisimost* (Independence), was kidnapped from her home by two masked and armed people. Three television journalists from the Lita-M studio in Kharkov, Ukraine — **Vitlay Shevchenko**, **Andrei Bazvluk** and **Elena Petrova** — were reported missing in Grozny in September. And **Salman Betelgereyev** and **Bekhan Tepsayev**, journalists from a separatist television channel, were detained on 31 August by Russian federal border guards at the airport in Makhachkala in Dagestan upon arrival from Turkey. They were later exchanged for Russian Interior Ministry troops held captive by Chechen fighters on 22 September. (CPJ)

Recent publication: *Federal Security Service versus Prisoner of Conscience Aleksandr Nikitin* (AI, September 1996, 33pp)

SAUDI ARABIA

In mid-September the Ministry of Information warned commercial establishments (such as hotels, housing compounds and furnished apartments) against showing films which are not censored or approved by their authorised distributors. Permission is needed to show such films in accordance with international agreements on copyright, which are also mandated by Royal Decree. Violators of the decree, if found guilty, can either be fined up to US$2,600 or the establishments can be closed for 15 days, or both. Unauthorised users of the films will also be required to pay the appropriate damages to the copyright owners of the films. (*Saudi Gazette*)

SERBIA-MONTENEGRO

Kosovo: An agreement was reached in early September between President Milosevic and ethnic Albanians to end the boycott of schools which began in 1990. Albanian children had been attending underground schools as part of

a general boycott of official Serbian institutions. If the agreement is realised, Albanian education will move back into school buildings and operate in parallel to Serbian education. (*Financial Times*)

Serbia: In Stara Pazova, **Lazar Vladimir** is appealing against a two-year prison sentence imposed for refusing to perform military drill. Although conscientious objectors may legally refuse military service on religious or philosophical grounds, those who have performed military service and then refuse to do military drill are prosecuted. Jehovah's Witnesses, who frequently object to military service, have been labelled 'anti-Serbian' and 'Satanist' in the Serbian media. (RSF)

SIERRA LEONE

Ibrahim Seaga Shaw, publisher and editor-in-chief of *Expo Times* (*Index* 5/1996), was detained briefly on 28 August. Two other journalists arrested in the last two months, **Edison Yongai** and **Gibril Kroma** (*Index* 5/1996), have also been released. The day after Shaw's detention the information minister, George Banda Thomas, called a meeting of all the country's editors. The editors were warned against publishing 'sensitive' stories relating to the civil war. When it was pointed out that attempts to cross-check information by journalists were not dealt with effectively — if at all — by his department, Thomas assured the editors that he would try to be of assistance in such cases in the future. (CPJ)

On 6 September the Ministry of Information banned *Torchlight*, a new publication sponsored by the opposition United National People's Party (UNPP). The paper's launch was delayed because George Banda Thomas felt that it contained 'very uncomplimentary articles' about President Tejan Kabba. Later that day, however, Thomas revoked the ban, pending the Cabinet's review of recommendations for the new press law. These recommendations are expected to be forwarded to Parliament later this month. They are reported to include a requirement that newspapers hold insurance policies to cover possible libel costs. Journalists argue that this would lead to insurance companies demanding representation on editorial boards. (CPJ)

Recent publication: *Towards a Future Founded on Human Rights* (AI, September 1996, 37pp)

SINGAPORE

In late September **Lai Chee Chuan** was fined US$700 for each of 61 films he downloaded from the Internet and for possession of *Penthouse* magazine. Lai was caught following a tip-off from Interpol investigating a child pornography ring. Singapore authorities have stressed that, in spite of recent legislation (*Index* 5/1996), it is not policing the Internet. (Reuters)

SOUTH AFRICA

The controversial US film *Kids*, directed by Larry Clark, was banned by the Directorate of Publications on 6 September on the grounds that it 'promotes paedophilia and the sexual exploitation of children' and because it is 'immoral and undesirable'. Although the ban was imposed under the 1974 Publications Act, it closely followed strict new guidelines introduced under a parliamentary Bill in August, but which have yet to be approved by the Senate (*Index* 5/1996). If passed, child pornography would be banned outright and severe restrictions would be placed on material involving bestiality; sexual violence; extreme violence and 'degrading material'. (*Daily Variety*, Freedom of Expression Institute)

On 10 September **Nick Bezuildenhout**, journalist for the *Beeld* newspaper, announced that police had withdrawn their subpoena requiring him to disclose how he received secret documents. The subpoena was originally served on 21 August, after the newspaper published an article about Islamic militants. It was based on documents which police suspected were leaked from its offices in Mpumulanga in Johannesburg. (MISA)

SOUTH KOREA

Over 400 of the thousands of students detained after the Yonsei University riots of August (*Index* 5/1996) have been indicted on charges of violence and illegal demonstration. Between 30 and 40, including those accused of leading the protest, have also been charged under National Security Law for pro-North Korean activity. In addition, the apparent leaders have been charged with manslaughter for the death of a riot policeman during the week-long disturbances. (AI)

David Cronenberg's film *Crash* was shown in a censored form at the first Pusan Film Festival after the Public Performance Ethics Committee rejected the distributor's application for general exhibition. Thirteen minutes were cut from the sexually explicit film and some scenes were blurred. Meanwhile, the country's strict Movie Law was overturned by the Constitutional Court on 4 October because it contravenes the constitutional guarantees for freedom of expression. The Court was considering a case brought by **Kang Hon**, a filmmaker and member of the underground film group Changsankokmae, who was charged in 1993 in connection with his film *Opening the School Gate*, depicting union activity among school teachers. Teachers' unions are very active in South Korea despite being illegal. (*Daily Variety*)

SRI LANKA

Sanjeewa Niroshana, a photojournalist for *Lankadipa*, was assaulted by court employees in Colombo at the end of September. Niroshana was covering the trial of a prominent Buddhist monk. (Free Media Movement)

The government lifted censorship of news reports on the ongoing civil war on 8 October. A vetting system was imposed earlier this year, shortly before government forces launched an offensive against the Tamil Tiger stronghold in Jaffna. The government said the restrictions were needed to protect military secrecy, but critics charged that they were used to cover up corruption and incompetence. (Reuters)

SUDAN

Salah Omar, a photographer for Agence-France Presse (AFP) and the state-owned Sudanese News Agency (SUNA), was arrested by security forces in Khartoum on 2 September while taking pictures in the street. His current whereabouts are unknown. (RSF)

Babakr Othaman, Sudan correspondent for the Qatari newspaper *al-Watan*, was arrested at his home by security forces on 4 September. His colleagues believe his arrest is connected with articles he has written criticising the government. Othaman is being held incommunicado and it is feared that he may be tortured. (RSF, CPJ)

Television cameraman **Osama Ghandi** and technician **Hassan Saleh** are among 10 civilians currently being tried in camera by a military court for their part in an alleged coup attempt earlier this year. Ghandi, an employee of state-owned Sudanese Television, stated to the court on 18 September that he had been tortured by military intelligence agents to force him to confess. (CPJ)

TAJIKISTAN

Two men found guilty of killing the journalist **Zayniddin Muhiddinov** in February 1995, Abdunabi Baronov and Nurali Janjolov, were sentenced to death on 21 August by the Supreme Court. It is the first time since the government came to power in 1992 that someone has been convicted for killing a journalist. A total of 40 reporters have been murdered in that time. (OMRI)

TANZANIA

The information minister, Kingunge Ngombale-Mwira, announced on 6 September that state-owned media companies will not be privatised. The government has holdings in Tanzania Standard Newspapers, publishers of the English-language *Daily News* and the *Sunday News*. On a tour of the *Daily News* he said: 'The government has a role to educate the people, a role that cannot be fully left to the private media.' (Reuters)

THAILAND

In early September the Department of Foreign Affairs confirmed its refusal to allow the Asia Pacific Network to broadcast **Radio Free Asia**, due to go on air this autumn, from Thailand. Chinese, Vietnamese, and Laotian officials in the region support Thailand's decision to block pro-democracy programming. (*South China Morning Post*, SWB)

Some 80 reporters resigned from the *Siam Post* in early September in protest at the sacking of five news editors on 20 August and the new management's policy of covering Bangkok news only. (*Bangkok Post*)

At a meeting in mid-September the Confederation of Thai Journalists accused the government of intimidation and persecution of reporters from both state-owned and private organisations. Recent infringements on the press include the banning of reporter **Fongsanan Jamornchan** from covering the prime minister's trip to Osaka, the transfer of **Somjit Navakruasuntorn** from reporting on Government House, the closing down of a radio phone-in programme, the transfer of a political editor and a department chief from television's Channel 5, and the suggestion, made in mid-August, that television news should not report 'inessential' news from the opposition. On 9 September the deputy prime minister attacked the press as a 'tool of the opposition'. (*Bangkok Post*)

TIBET

Voice of Tibet radio station has reported further Chinese interference to its short-wave broadcasts. Chinese state radio, Radio China International, began the jamming on 30 August by broadcasting from Beijing on the same frequency. Oslo-based VOT has already been forced to change its frequency after China obliterated its broadcasts with white noise and same-frequency jamming in June and July (*Index* 5/1996). (Reuters)

TONGA

On 20 September **Kalafi Moala**, editor and publisher of the Auckland-based *Times of Tonga*, his Tongan-based deputy editor **Filokalafi 'Aka'uola** (*Index* 3/1996), and MP **Akilisi Pohiva** were jailed for contempt of Parliament for 30 days. Charges were brought against the three after the *Times* published the text of an impeachment writ against justice minister Tevita Tupou before it had been submitted to Parliament. International organisations which criticised the sentences were denounced by the government on 30 September as 'media terrorists'. (Pacific Island News Association, Asia-Pacific Network, IFJ)

TURKEY

Ayse Nur Zarakolu, director of the Belge publishing house, began a five-month prison sentence for 'disseminating propaganda for a terrorist organisation' on 29 August (*Index* 4/1995, 6/1995, 2/1996). She was sentenced in September 1995 for publishing the book *Birakuj* (Battle Between Brothers) by **Faysal Dagli**. The book concerns the civil war between Kurdish factions in Iraq and contains an interview with Abdullah Öcalan, leader of the Kurdistan Workers' Party (PKK). (*Info-Türk*, PEN)

The trial of 98 writers and intellectuals charged with being the joint editors of the book *Freedom of Thought* (see page 188) continued on 25 September (*Index* 4/1995, 1/1996). Another 86 defen-

SANAR YURDATAPAN

Before the law

'Name?' — 'Lale Mansur.'
'Profession?' — 'Actress and editor.'
'Name?' — 'Bülent Tanör.'
'Profession?' — 'Professor of constitutional law and editor.'
'Name?' — 'Ahmet Altan.'
'Profession?' — 'Journalist, author and editor.'
'Name?' — 'Ahmet Çavuşoglu.'
'Profession?' — 'Businessman and editor.'

At the end of September, when over 50 of the 98 intellectuals accused of violating Article 8 of Turkey's Anti-Terror Law and Article 312 of the Penal Code by co-publishing the book *Freedom of Thought* identified themselves to Istanbul's State Security Court in this way, nobody present — journalists, observers, or even the judges themselves — could conceal their amusement.

In this 'trial of the intellectuals', it is the accused who are pursuing the court, rather than the other way around. Faced with a total of 1,080 writers, thinkers, artists, actors, musicians, directors and producers who have added their names to the list of the book's collective publishers, the state prosecutor had a problem: he could either shut his eyes to this heinous crime; or he could go through the motions and demand the statutory 20-month minimum sentence for each offender. He chose the latter.

dants in the same case were in court on 30 September. All are charged with 'disseminating separatist propaganda' under Article 8 of the Anti-Terror Law. Actor **Mahir Günşiray** went on trial in Istanbul on 3 October, accused of 'insulting the bench' for reading out a passage from Franz Kafka's novel *The Trial* at an earlier hearing of the *Freedom of Thought* trial last May. The case has been adjourned until December. (PEN, Reuters)

Ihmur Cevik and **Hayri Birler**, editor and correspondent with the English-lan-guage *Turkish Daily News*, appeared in court on 8 October after the army's chief of staff sued them for publicly insulting the military. The offending article alleged that the army's general staff had commissioned a public opinion poll on how to solve a protracted government crisis and how to handle a stand-off with Greece over an Aegean islet. The chief of staff argues that the poll was commissioned by officers acting on their own initiative. (Reuters)

Recent publication: *No Security Without Human Rights* (AI, 1996, 128pp)

UNITED KINGDOM

A 'democratic audit' of political freedom in the UK (*The Three Pillars of Liberty: Political Rights and Freedom in the United Kingdom* by Francesca Klug, Keir Stormer and Stuart Weir, Routledge, £50hb, £14.99pb, September 1996), found 42 violations of international human rights standards, plus a further 22 examples of UK law or legal practice which come close to violating those standards. In five areas, including the use of lethal force in Northern Ireland, the report judged that actual practice subverts laws that do meet

If the defendants are found guilty and sent to prison
• at least 10 hugely popular television programmes will have to be cancelled
• five drama series will have to find new stars and change their storylines
• over 30 well-known journalists will disappear from view, and 15 very popular columns will go unwritten
• eight professors' chairs will be left empty and universities will have to find more than 30 new teaching staff
• theatre stages and film sets will need new artists, directors, musicians, and so on
• Turkish literature will gain a crop of over 20 new prison novels, if each writer produces one

It might not come to that. Our international support is strong, and includes 144 writers from 20 different countries. If each of them was to come to Istanbul to be questioned by the prosecutor at the State Security Court, there would be an international outcry which would help not only us, but also those intellectuals who are struggling for freedom of expression in other countries.

Franz Kafka has already lent us his support. When one of the accused, theatre artist Mahir Günşiray, read a paragraph from *The Trial* during his defence statement earlier this year, the prosecutor was furious and charged him with contempt of court. Günşiray's trial on the new charge began on 3 October. Needless to say, the rest have not abandoned him: having signed their names under the very paragraph that Günşiray read out, they presented it to the court. We are all happy and proud to add our names under Kafka's text and to stand together in the dock. And anyone who wants to is very welcome to come and join us. ❑

Şanar Yurdatapan runs the Initiative against the Criminalisation of Thought in Istanbul and has been involved in the case of the intellectuals since it began in June last year

international standards. (*Guardian*)

Following the lifting by the Independent Television Commission in April of the ban on religious advertising, an ad for the Church of Scientology was screened in mid-September on the satellite channels UK Gold and UK Living. The move drew criticism from the Cult Information Centre and other groups which accuse the church of using sophisticated sales techniques and psychological pressure to attract and keep new followers. (*Independent*)

On 16 September the Department of Health won a permanent High Court ban stopping the sale of the video *Everyday Operations* (*Index* 5/1996). The injunction extended a temporary ban made as it was about to go on sale in August, following concern that patients had not given consent for their operations to be filmed for this purpose. (*Guardian*)

Special Branch police officers with warrants issued under the Prevention of Terrorism Act raided the London office of the Kurdish-language satellite station **MED TV** (*Index*

5/1996) on 18 September. Computers, disks and files were seized, but no charges were brought. Simultaneous searches took place at the company's offices in Belgium (see above). (*Guardian*)

A photograph by **Robert Mapplethorpe** entitled 'Rosie', picturing a seated three-year-old girl wearing a dress but no underwear, was withdrawn from a major exhibition of his work at London's Hayward Gallery just a few days before it opened on 19 September. The decision was taken on the advice of the Metropolitan Police's Obscene

Publications Squad, which also advised against the photo 'Helmut and Brookes', which shows two men having sex. This picture was not withdrawn by the gallery. (*Independent, Daily Telegraph*)

On 26 September the government endorsed proposals for a public hotline for Internet users to report on the presence of obscene material on the network. The proposals, originated by the Safety-Net Foundation, have also been backed by the Internet Service Providers' Association and the Metropolitan Police. Reports received through the hotline will be investigated by the police, and if the material originated in the UK and is thought to be in breach of UK law, the relevant Internet Service Provider will be contacted and the person who put the information on the network asked to remove it. (*Computer Weekly, Financial Times, Independent*)

The film **It Happened Here**, depicting an imagined Nazi occupation of the UK, was released uncut for the first time on video on 1 October. The film was cut by its distributors in 1964, after protests about its documentary footage of British neo-Nazis. (*Sunday Times*)

The heritage secretary, Virginia Bottomley, signed an order banning the sale or promotion of decoder cards needed to receive the French hardcore satellite station Rendez-Vous on 10 October. The Paris-based station began transmission in September last year, mainly to France and the

UK. The legal situation, however, is unclear, in light of recent European Court rulings that a state may only legislate in respect of broadcasters established within its jurisdiction. Other hardcore satellite stations, such as Eurotica, can be received in the UK, even though they have no licence from the Independent Television Commission, because of a black market in decoders. (*Independent, Sunday Telegraph*)

Recent publications: *War and Words — The Northern Ireland Media Reader* edited by Bill Rolston and David Miller (Beyond the Pale Publications, September 1996, 500pp); *Lives Under Threat — A Study of Sikhs Coming to the UK from the Punjab* (Medical Foundation for the Care of the Victims of Torture, October 1996, 31pp)

USA

In early September the Wal-Mart retail chain blacklisted a pop album by **Sheryl Crow**, due for release later that month, because of the lyrics of the refrain in the song 'Love is a Good Thing': 'Watch out sister, watch out brother, watch our children as they kill each other with a gun they bought at the Wal-Mart discount store.' The Wal-Mart group has recently made efforts to tighten up on gun sales in the wake of public criticism and lawsuits. (*Financial Times*)

The Miami offices of the Spanish-language magazine *Viva Semanal* were attacked by unknown individuals on 2

September in what observers believe is retaliation for the magazine's recent criticism of corruption in the city, support for certain candidates running for public office and criticism of the strongly anti-Castro Cuban-American National Foundation. (IAPA)

On 20 September the Defense Department made public translated excerpts from seven Spanish-language US army intelligence manuals used to train Latin American military officers at the Army School of the Americas from 1982-1991. Also released was a summary of a secret 1992 Defense Department investigation into the material, according to which the material says that to recruit and control informants, counter-intelligence agents could use 'fear, payment of bounties for enemy dead, beatings, false imprisonment, executions and the use of truth serum'. The investigation concluded that the inclusion of the methods was the result of 'bureaucratic oversight'. The Army School of the Americas, situated in Panama until its move to Fort Benning, Georgia in 1984, has trained nearly 60,000 military and police officers from Latin America and the US since 1957. Some of the region's most notorious human rights abusers were trained there, including: Roberto D'Aubuisson (*Index* 4/1989), considered the mastermind behind El Salvador's death squads in the 1970s and 1980s; the 19 Salvadoran soldiers linked to the murders of six Jesuit priests in 1989 (*Index* 1/1990); Panama's Manuel Noriega; six Peruvian officers linked to the killings of students and a professor in the La Cantuta massacre (*Index* 8&9/1993); and Colonel Julio Roberto Alpírez, a Guatemalan army officer implicated in the murder of an American innkeeper in Guatemala and the killing of the guerrilla leader Efraín Bámaca Velásquez (*Index* 3/1995). (*International Herald Tribune*)

On 21 September it was reported that the wireless communications industry has decided to reject technology, backed by the government, which would make it possible for law enforcement agencies to keep closer tabs on cellular telephone users. The measures would enable the FBI to locate a cellular home caller within half a second, monitor cellular-phone voice-mail and conference calls. The Justice Department argues that it has the right to use new surveillance technology under a 1994 law to bring law-enforcement techniques into the modern era. (*International Herald Tribune*)

On 25 September the American Civil Liberties Union (ACLU), Electronic Frontiers Georgia and Georgia state representative Mitchell Kay filed a lawsuit seeking a preliminary injunction against a statute passed by the Georgia General Assembly restricting anonymous communication on the Internet. The law, which came into effect on 1 July, makes it a crime to use a name that 'falsely identifies' a speaker on the Internet, but fails to distinguish whether the person communicating had

any intent to deceive or defraud or simply wanted to keep his or her identity unknown. Under the law, those who knowingly 'transmit any data through a computer network...if such data uses any individual name...to falsely identify the person' face up to 12 months in jail and/or up to a US$1,000 fine (see also above, under Finland). The plaintiffs argue that the Commerce Clause of the Constitution bars state regulation of the Internet because it is an interstate medium. (Reuters, Interactive Daily)

Philadelphia's Court of Common Pleas heard arguments on 1 October from lawyers for **Mumia Abu-Jamal** (*Index* 2/1995, 5/1995) that the testimony of Veronica Jones be added to the appeal record. Jones says that the testimony she gave for the prosecution in Abu-Jamal's original trial in 1982 was untrue. Immediately after she recanted her testimony, Jones was arrested on a 1992 warrant for fraud. (Reuters)

On 3 October the Supreme Court of South Carolina began hearing a case in which an atheist claims that a clause in the state constitution — 'No person who denies the existence of a Supreme Being shall hold any office under this Constitution' — led to his application to become a notary public being refused. (Reuters)

The publishers of the magazine *Penthouse* brought a suit against the Defense Department in a New York District Court on 3 October.

They are challenging a law banning sexually explicit material from all military stores, naval ships and newsstands on Defense Department property. The Military Honor and Decency Act, signed into law on 23 September, bars the sale or rental of any video or magazine 'which depicts or describes nudity, including sexual or excretory activities or organs, in a lascivious way'. (Business Wire)

UZBEKISTAN

The Organization for Security and Cooperation in Europe (OSCE) was accused of undermining its own mandate at the start of October by sponsoring a forum on the media in Tashkent at which only government officials were invited to speak. The two-day round-table on Media Issues in the Transition to Democracy was meant to discuss the role of independent media in building democracy. Although censorship is explicitly forbidden under the constitution, newspapers, television and radio are nonetheless tightly controlled through the State Control Inspectorate, and police and security forces harass, intimidate and sometimes beat journalists for pursuing basic lines of inquiry. (HRW)

VIETNAM

Three democracy campaigners were found guilty of 'revealing state secrets' on 22 August. Former security official **Le Hong Ha** and scientist and writer **Ha Si Phu** (real name: **Nguyen Xuan Tu**) were jailed for two years and one year respectively, and former editor **Nguyen Kien Giang** received a 15-month suspended sentence. The state secret involved in the case was a letter written by prime minister Vo Van Kiet in August 1995 to the Politburo of the Communist Party. The contents of the letter had been widely leaked inside and outside the country by sources close to the government long before Ha Si Phu's arrest. (PEN, *International Herald Tribune, Financial Times*)

In an interview on 6 September Tran Hoan, minister of culture and information, said journalists must raise the standards of the media and assert the direction of the ruling Communist Party. Among the measures he listed was a plan to 'educate and re-educate journalists' on the Communist Party and government legislation. The media, he said, are an 'ideological instrument' to encourage the people to carry out government policies. Hoan also warned against the media's trend towards commercialisation and spoke of the need to 'adjust' so-called 'yellow journalism'. (Reuters)

A foreign news photographer was prevented from photographing a demonstration outside a market in central Hanoi on 9 September. The photographer was taken to a police station and his film was destroyed. Reports in the official *Ha Noi Moi* said that local journalists had been barred from reporting on a market traders' meeting on 7 September. (Reuters)

YEMEN

At least three people were injured during a demonstration on 25 September in the city of Mukallah. About 500 people had gathered to protest against water and power shortages. Security forces fired into the air and used tear gas to disperse the demonstrators. The protest is the latest in a series of clashes between demonstrators and security forces (*Index* 5/1996). (Reuters)

Police entered the Aden offices of the opposition paper *al-Ayyam* on 28 September in an attempt to arrest columnist **Abdel Rahman Khobara**. Khobara's colleagues refused to hand him over to the police because they had no warrant for the arrest. Khobara is well-known for being outspoken in his criticism of the government, most recently in his reports for Radio Kuwait on the Mukallah disturbances. (CPJ)

Writer and academic **Muhamma al-Saqqaf** was charged with 'publishing false information with malicious intent' on 30 September, in two articles for the weekly *al-Wahdawi* in which he criticised the High Elections Commission. (CPJ)

Salem al-Helali, a cartoonist for the weekly *al-Tagammu* (*Index* 5/1996) is currently under house arrest. His house has been under guard by the political police since 24 August, when security agents prevented an exhibition of al-Helali's cartoons in Aden from taking place. (RSF)

ZAIRE

The publisher of the opposition newspaper *Le Palmares*, **Michael Luya**, was arrested at his home on 17 September after an article appeared in the paper which suggested that President Mobutu was suffering from throat cancer. The information minister, Boguo Makeli, said the content of the article 'attacks the President of the Republic whose inviolability is constitutionally guaranteed...and aims to instil a collective psychosis of a nature to disturb the public order'. Luya has been charged with 'spreading false rumours' and *Le Palmares* has been suspended indefinitely. (RSF, Reuters)

Compiled by: Paul Currion, Anna Feldman, Kate Thal (Africa); Kate Cooper, Dagmar Schlüter (Americas); Nicholas McAulay, Mansoor Mirza, Sarah Smith (Asia); Ann Chambers, Robin Jones, Vera Rich (eastern Europe and CIS); Michaela Becker, Philippa Nugent (Middle East); Rose Bell (western Europe)

INDEX *online*
HTTP://WWW.ONEWORLD.ORG/INDEX_OC/